Deleuze and Ethics

Deleuze Connections

'It is not the elements or the sets which define the multiplicity. What defines it is the AND, as something which has its place between the elements or between the sets. AND, AND, AND – stammering.'

Gilles Deleuze and Claire Parnet, *Dialogues*

General Editor
Ian Buchanan

Editorial Advisory Board

Keith Ansell-Pearson

Rosi Braidotti

Claire Colebrook

Tom Conley

Gregg Lambert

Adrian Parr

Paul Patton

Patricia Pisters

Titles Available in the Series

Ian Buchanan and Claire Colebrook (eds), *Deleuze and Feminist Theory*

Ian Buchanan and John Marks (eds), *Deleuze and Literature*

Mark Bonta and John Protevi (eds), *Deleuze and Geophilosophy*

Ian Buchanan and Marcel Swiboda (eds), *Deleuze and Music*

Ian Buchanan and Gregg Lambert (eds), *Deleuze and Space*

Martin Fuglsang and Bent Meier Sørensen (eds), *Deleuze and the Social*

Ian Buchanan and Adrian Parr (eds), *Deleuze and the Contemporary World*

Constantin V. Boundas (ed.), *Deleuze and Philosophy*

Ian Buchanan and Nicholas Thoburn (eds), *Deleuze and Politics*

Chrysanthi Nigianni and Merl Storr (eds), *Deleuze and Queer Theory*

Jeffrey A. Bell and Claire Colebrook (eds), *Deleuze and History*

Laura Cull (ed.), *Deleuze and Performance*

Mark Poster and David Savat (eds), *Deleuze and New Technology*

Simone Bignall and Paul Patton (eds), *Deleuze and the Postcolonial*

Stephen Zepke and Simon O'Sullivan (eds), *Deleuze and Contemporary Art*

Laura Guillaume and Joe Hughes (eds), *Deleuze and the Body*

Nathan Jun and Daniel W. Smith (eds), *Deleuze and Ethics*

Frida Beckman (ed.), *Deleuze and Sex*

Forthcoming Titles in the Series

David Martin-Jones and William Brown (eds), *Deleuze and Film*

Inna Semetsky and Diana Masny (eds), *Deleuze and Education*

Visit the Deleuze Connections website at
www.euppublishing.com/series/delco

Deleuze and Ethics

Edited by Nathan Jun and
Daniel W. Smith

Edinburgh University Press

© editorial matter and organization Nathan Jun and Daniel W. Smith, 2011
© in the individual contributions is retained by the authors

Edinburgh University Press Ltd
22 George Square, Edinburgh

www.euppublishing.com

Typeset in 10.5/13 Adobe Sabon
by Servis Filmsetting Ltd, Stockport, Cheshire,
and printed and bound in Great Britain by
CPI Antony Rowe, Chippenham and Eastbourne

A CIP record for this book is available from the British Library

ISBN 978 0 7486 4117 8 (hardback)
ISBN 978 0 7486 4116 1 (paperback)

The right of the contributors
to be identified as author of this work
has been asserted in accordance with
the Copyright, Designs and Patents Act 1988.

Contents

Acknowledgments

We would like to thank Ian Buchanan, editor of the "Deleuze Connections" series, for agreeing to take on this project; and Carol Macdonald of Edinburgh University Press for her patience and encouragement.

Introduction

Nathan Jun

It is customary to introduce a book of this sort by offering a brief overview of its essays and articles. I hope the reader will forgive me for straying from this convention – conventions being, after all, somewhat beside the point in a book about Deleuze. (A quick glance at each chapter's opening will prove sufficient to glean its gist and will hopefully serve to pique your interest as well.) Instead, I want to provide an introduction which is, one might say, apologetic rather than synoptic. Specifically, I want to stumble in the general direction of explaining why I think this volume is relevant, timely, and at least marginally important. Why Deleuze? Why ethics? Why now, and why ought we to care?

Ten years into the Deleuzian century, and fifteen since *la mort de la même*, few would disagree that the world as we know it is sinking into an economic, political, social, and ethical abyss of previously unimaginable depths. Back in the halcyon days when that world was still in its infancy, Deleuze was widely heralded as a visionary who would help us demystify the web of global technological and financial networks which was, at that time, just starting to be spun. Since then, the prophecies have largely come to pass; everyone from Žižek to Badiou is fond of saying that the conceptual and methodological tools with which we make sense of this age are Deleuzian tools. But make sense *in what sense*? Even a cursory glance at the literature reveals that Deleuze has long been and continues to be viewed chiefly as a metaphysician and a historian of philosophy – that is, as an analyst, rather than a critic, of the systems by and through which we organize and are organized in turn. For many, therefore, the Deleuzian tool is a lens, not a hammer.

That lens is sharp, to be sure, and no one doubts that Deleuze (and Guattari) have made profound contributions as analysts. But some would argue that this is *all* they have done, or that this is *all* they ever aspired to do, or that this is *all* they were ever capable of doing – in other words, that the Deleuzian-Guattarian project is not, or never was, or never could be, *critical*, let alone *ethico-normative*, in nature. Our view, as evidenced by the very existence of this volume, is different. We contend that there *is* a deeply ethico-normative dimension to Deleuzian-Guattarian philosophy but that it has tended to be ignored, overlooked, downplayed, and misunderstood in the literature. This book makes a preliminary contribution to the task of uncovering and elucidating that dimension, not only for the sake of enriching Deleuze-Guattari scholarship, but also in the hope of promoting a more engaged philosophical practice based in, and responding to, Deleuzian-Guattarian ethics.

In the aftermath of the notorious "Battle of Seattle" ten years ago, when "anti-globalization" was a new and meaningful addition to our vocabulary and phrases such as "Resistance is Global" and "Other Worlds Are Possible!" became the rallying cries of a nascent global justice movement, many looked to Deleuze (and Guattari) again – this time to make sense of what Girard might call globalization's "monstrous double." To many, Deleuze and Guattari were (and are) not only the theoretical voice of this movement, but its conscience as well. In defiant response to the TINA ("There is No Alternative") doctrine of neoliberalism, Deleuze and Guattari offer a moral and political vision in which possibilities – multiplicities, differences, in short, *alternatives* – are infinitely augmented and expanded. Deleuzian-Guattarian philosophy promised to be an anarchism for postmodernity.

Perhaps the global justice movement has not altogether failed, but it certainly has not come anywhere close to succeeding. Indeed, it is now buried so deeply underground that we are hard-pressed to recognize its contemporary relevance. The same is true, or so it is said, of Deleuze and Guattari with respect to moral and political concerns. Witness, again, the many critics who claim that Deleuzian-Guattarian philosophy aspires, at best, to describe systems as they are and to enumerate the conditions of possibility for their transformation; or, at worst, adopts quietist or even collaborationist views towards the systems it exposes and, in all events, fails to take any firm position on how they "ought to be." This is essentially the critique levelled by Boltanski and Chiapello, who argue that Deleuzian-Guattarian philosophy is simply the most recent iteration of what they term "the spirit of capitalism," the ideology which justifies and reinforces capitalist domination. (See Jeffrey Bell's response on pp. 8–13.) Žižek, too, identifies a reactionary element in Deleuzian-Guattarian philosophy while simultaneously acknowledging its important contributions to anti-capitalist resistance movements.

This bespeaks a troubled and conflicted philosophy which ultimately produces troubled and conflicted ideas.

At the same time, does it really come as a surprise that revolutionary Deleuzian-Guattarian philosophy contains a lurking micro-fascism? After all, didn't Deleuze and Guattari warn that every avant-garde thought contains such a germinal possibility within itself? If so, Deleuzian-Guattarian philosophy is no worse off than any of its peers and competitors. One might even argue that this is precisely what happened, in whole or in part, to the global justice movement itself – i.e., that a sizeable portion of it was captured by external reactionary forces and ultimately transformed and incorporated into said forces. The worry is that perhaps a similar fate has befallen Deleuzian-Guattarian philosophy. That with its arcane terminology and dense, complicated texts, it has become, at best, a harmless fetish of effete academics who use it to buttress their pseudo-radical posturing; at worst, a vanguardist discourse *par excellence* embodying the worst excesses of Marxist-Leninist technocracy. Twenty or thirty years ago, a kind of generic Derridean "deconstructo-speak" was the *lingua franca* of humanities departments throughout North America. This is slowly but surely being replaced (some would say already *has been* replaced) by a vulgar Deleuzian argot that is every bit as trite and pretentious as its predecessor. The crucial and tragic difference is that Derrida has never been championed as an intellectual hero of the radical Left to the same degree as Deleuze. The latter's thoughts have always tended to be seen, rightly or wrongly, as aligned with truly revolutionary possibilities and actions. For those who continue to share this vision, therefore, the academic domestication and fetishization of Deleuze (or, worse still, the accusation of Deleuzian-Guattarian vanguardism) is a cause of legitimate anxiety.

Fortunately Deleuze and Guattari themselves provide the critical apparatus necessary to carefully reflect on these issues, if not to altogether resolve them. Deleuze and Guattari, academics, intellectuals – all conceptual personae! They – *we* – play a role in the generation, operation, and transformation of other assemblages, other machines. The task, which is ultimately ethical in nature, is not to understand these things as they are but as they might be: the conditions of possibility for thinking, doing, and being otherwise. This, in turn, requires the radical pursuit of difference and the destabilization of identity. For every teacher, becoming-student! For every scholar, becoming-dilettante! For every beautiful soul, becoming-philistine! For every intellectual, becoming-dullard! And if you meet Deleuze and Guattari on the road, kill them! And though Deleuze and Guattari do not offer a "conventional" moral critique of capitalism, patriarchy, racism, and other forms of oppression, this scarcely entails uncritical endorsement of or complicity with oppression. On the contrary, it is precisely by articulating ethics in terms of "lines of flight" – which are, *inter alia*, the conditions of possibility for revolutionary political, social, and economic transformation – that Deleuze and Guattari provide the grounds for a critique of capitalism that is arguably much more effective than anything on offer from traditional moral philosophy.

Perhaps the most tragic and frightening aspect of contemporary life is its systemic lack of imagination – the hopeless acquiescence of the powerless to those in power, coupled with the latter's insistence that everything is the way it is because, in some sense, it could not be otherwise. For Deleuze and Guattari, the ethical question isn't "What ought we to do?" but "What might we do?" or "What could we do?" The reason that we are living in decidedly evil times isn't just that people aren't asking the ethical question, but that they are routinely denied the ability to ask it or, worse, are placed in situations where the desire to ask it never emerges on its own. I think this volume will show that Deleuze and Guattari have much to say on the issue of ethics, and will have much to say in the future if given adequate opportunity. In order for their words to be even slightly helpful, however, we need to avoid relegating Deleuze and Guattari to the academic ghetto and reducing them to the playthings of professional wordsmiths. We must not ask, "What do Deleuze and Guattari say?" or even "What ought Deleuze and Guattari say?" but "What *could* Deleuze and Guattari say?"

Chapter 1

Whistle While You Work: Deleuze and the Spirit of Capitalism

Jeffrey Bell

In his *Economic and Philosophic Manuscripts of 1844* Marx pointedly argues that within the capitalist system "the worker is related to the product of his labor as to an alien object" (Marx 1984: 71). As Marx contends, and as is well known, it is precisely the power of labor that has become "congealed in an object," that is, in a commodity (or service) that exists independently and "becomes a power on its own confronting him." In short, the life which the power of labor has conferred on "the object confronts him as something hostile and alien" (Marx 1984: 72). Our work has become a foe, a test and trial we must endure before we can begin to do what we really want to do. Work or play, as Deleuze and Guattari note, has become one of the great molar segments that divides us, an exclusive disjunction that pervades daily life. There is the melancholy of the Monday morning blues; there is the hope that emerges as Wednesday, hump day, draws to a close and there is less of the drudgery of work before us than behind us; and finally how many times have we heard our colleagues at work express joy at the fact that it is Friday. We can even spend our hard-earned cash at T.G.I. Friday's, for now it is time to play.

Despite the alienation Marx speaks of, we nonetheless continue to show up for work. The reason we do so is simple: necessity. As Marx puts it, labor has become "merely a means to satisfy needs external to it" – namely, it allows us to put food on the table. It was for this reason that Marx argues that the worker "no longer feels himself to be freely active in any but his animal functions," (Marx 1984: 74) for as this point is clarified a few pages later, animals such as bees, beavers, and ants produce "only under the dominion of immediate physical need, while *man produces even when he is free from physical need and only truly produces in freedom therefrom*" (Marx 1984: 77). It is this latter point that will be a primary focus of the following paper. What does it mean to produce in freedom from physical need? Max Weber has provided us with one answer to this question. One's labor is freed from physical need when it is in response to a Divine calling, a calling the fulfillment of which assures our personal salvation. One is thus no longer responding to worldly necessity but rather to a Divine mandate, to one's moral calling. It is this sense of fulfilling one's calling, or what Weber will call the spirit of capitalism, that, far from undermining the alienation of workers from the products of their labor, actually provides the impetus to initiate and maintain the very process of capitalist exploitation. Acting in a manner that promotes our own alienation is thus not simply a consequence of necessity but has become, according to Weber (following Marx) our moral duty. Marx states the point as follows:

> Its [political economy's] moral ideal is the worker who takes part of his wages to the savings-bank, and it has even found ready-made an abject *art* in which to clothe this its pet idea: they have presented it, bathed in sentimentality, on the stage. Thus political economy – despite its worldly and wanton appearance – is a true moral science, the most moral of all the sciences. Self-denial, the denial of life and of all human needs, is its cardinal doctrine. The less you eat, drink and read books; the less you go to the theater, the dance hall, the public-house; the less you think, love, theorize, sing, paint, fence, etc., the more you *save* – the *greater* becomes your treasure which neither moths nor dust will devour – your *capital* . . . the less you express your own life, the greater is your *alienated* life. (Marx 1984: 118–19)

In their book *The New Spirit of Capitalism*, Luc Boltanski and Eve Chiapello set out to update Weber's account of the spirit of capitalism, an update they argue is necessary in order to reflect post-'68 political and economic realities. With Marx's analysis of the alienation of labor taken as a given, Boltanski and Chiapello argue that it becomes necessary to provide an account of the spirit of capitalism, for, as they put it,

> capitalism is an absurd system: in it, wage-earners have lost ownership of the fruits of their labor and the possibility of pursuing a working life free of subordination. As for capitalists, they find themselves yoked to an interminable, insatiable process, which is utterly abstract and dissociated from the satisfaction of consumption needs, even of a luxury kind. For two such protagonists, integration into the capitalist process is singularly lacking in justifications. (Boltanski and Chiapello 2007: 7)

It is the spirit of capitalism that provides for the justification that is lacking: "We call *the ideology that justifies the engagement in capitalism* 'spirit of capitalism'" (Boltanski and Chiapello 2007: 8). And the spirit of capitalism, as Boltanski and Chiapello define it, "is precisely the set of beliefs associated with the capitalist order that helps to justify this order and, by legitimating them to sustain the forms of action and predispositions compatible with it" (Boltanski and Chiapello 2007: 10). In particular, the spirit of capitalism infuses the worker with the willingness to work, and with a sense of doing the right thing (in Marx's moral sense of the term). For Boltanski and Chiapello, the beliefs that sustain this willingness to work underwent a profound transformation beginning in the late 1960s. In response to the critique of transcendent power with its hierarchical structure and its stultifying, standardized forms of production, there emerged in its place an emphasis on the power of immanence, the power of a network of encounters that are unplanned, decentralized, non-hierarchical, and yet which allows through processes of self-organization and self-regulation for a more authentic and individuated creativity. In their book Boltanski and Chiapello single out Deleuze as among the vanguard whose critique of transcendent power and affirmation of immanence exemplifies the new spirit of capitalism, and thus Deleuze's philosophy, on their view, is simply the most recent ideology that has, as they put it, "opened up an opportunity for capitalism to base itself on new forms of control and commodify new, more individuated and 'authentic' goods" (Boltanski and Chiapello 2007: 467).

In what follows we will examine Boltanski and Chiapello's critique of Deleuze. To do this we will first detail how Deleuze (and Deleuze and Guattari) can be used to rethink Marx's theory of alienation. This will allow us to show that central to Marx's understanding of alienation, and to Boltanski and Chiapello's subsequent understanding of the role ideology plays, is the separation of a productive process – namely, labor – from that which is the product of this process. More to the point, labor is alienated from the value it produces, and it is this value that confronts the worker as a hostile and alien force when it is in the hands of the capitalist. In the reading offered here, however, it will be seen that Deleuze fundamentally rethinks this traditional labor theory of value. Where this rethinking of Marxism most markedly diverges from a more traditional reading is in their interpretation of the relationship between labor-power and labor. As traditionally understood, labor-power is what creates value – hence the labor theory of value – and surplus-value emerges when the capitalist pays less for one's labor than the value created by one's labor-power. For Deleuze and Guattari, by contrast, labor-power is thought of as desiring-production, and although desiring-production can indeed be captured by the transcendent power of the capitalist in the form of wage labor, desiring-production is at the same time inseparable from and yet irreducible to wage labor and moreover allows for the possibility of a value creation that cannot be captured by the nets of the capitalist. Yet is this not simply the new spirit of capitalism Boltanski and Chiapello decry Deleuze for justifying? It is to answer this question that we now turn.

I.

To see precisely how Deleuze's thought is taken to be exemplary in legitimizing the new spirit of capitalism, let us look again at what this spirit entails for Boltanski and Chiapello. First, and most importantly, the new spirit of capitalism is a consequence of the rejection of the spirit of capitalism that preceded it. In particular, it results from the condemnation of the capitalism that, as Boltanski and Chiapello put it, was characterized by "closed, fixed, ossified worlds, whether by attachment to tradition (the family), legalism and bureaucracy (the State), or calculation and planning (the firm)"; and in its place what is encouraged is "mobility, fluidity and 'nomads' able to circulate, at the cost of many metamorphoses, in open networks" (Boltanski and Chiapello 2007: 145). Rather than envisioning a professional life where one's entire career is spent climbing the hierarchy of one and the same organization, what is encouraged is "a proliferation of encounters and temporary, but reactivatable connections with various groups" (Boltanski and Chiapello 2007: 104). The occasion that reactivates these connections, albeit only temporarily, is the project. What is prized in this setting, and as is repeated again and again in the management literature Boltanski and Chiapello analyze, is the ability to move fluidly and easily from one project to another, and to be capable of reactivating diverse and heterogeneous connections suited to the project at hand. The successful capitalist and entrepreneur, or the "great man" from the perspective of the new spirit, "renounces having a single project that lasts a lifetime (a vocation, a profession, a marriage, etc.). He is mobile. Nothing must hamper his movements. He is a 'nomad'" (Boltanski and Chiapello 2007: 122).

With this call for mobility and nomadism, however, comes a tension between "the requirement of flexibility" on the one hand and "the need to be someone," on the other, the need to have a reputation or to "possess a self endowed with specificity (a 'personality') and a certain permanency in time" (Boltanski and Chiapello 2007: 461). In short, there is a tension between the need to deploy an ever-changing array of skills throughout a series of heterogeneous projects *and* the need to establish the unchanging reputation as the "go to guy." A consequence of this tension is that the personal qualities of the worker become more important than what they might currently be doing. As Boltanski and Chiapello argue, "The reference-point is no longer the division of labor objectified in a structure of posts, but the qualities of the person: 'what can he do?' replaces 'what does he do?'" (Boltanski and Chiapello 2007: 465). And the ideal answer to the former question – the moral ideal in fact – is that they can do about anything; they are mobile, flexible. They are, in short, good nomads, good Deleuzians. For was not Deleuze himself exemplary in his capacity to take on diverse projects, to write on Hume, Spinoza, Leibniz, and Nietzsche, among others in the philosophical tradition, but also equally comfortable grappling with such diverse topics as D. H. Lawrence, Proust, Riemann, or cinema, among many others (as a short perusal of *A Thousand Plateaus* will show)? It is for this reason, finally, that Boltanski and Chiapello argue that those intellectuals and philosophers such as Deleuze and Guattari who where "in the vanguard" of the critique of capitalism "in the 1970s often emerged [if unwittingly] as promoters of the transformation" to the new spirit of capitalism and its attendant moral ideal.

To begin to show that Boltanski and Chiapello's critique of Deleuze is off target we can turn briefly to the chapter from Deleuze's *Expressionism in Philosophy: Spinoza*, titled "What can a body do?" Among the many issues discussed in this chapter, the most relevant for our present purposes concerns the contrast Deleuze notes between Spinoza and Leibniz concerning the dynamism of the body. On Deleuze's reading, Spinoza's conception of dynamism is "opposed to" Leibniz's in that "Spinoza's dynamism and 'essentialism' deliberately excludes all finality," whereas Lebiniz's does not (Deleuze 1990: 233). For Leibniz what a body can do has been predetermined by the pre-established harmony of the universe, while for Spinoza the power of the body is a modal expression of God's absolutely indeterminate power, by which is meant that God's power cannot be reduced to, or thought in terms of, any determinate, identifiable cause or condition.[1] It is for this reason that Deleuze argues that Spinoza stresses the "physics of intensive quantity corresponding to modal essences," again in contrast to Leibniz who stresses the "physics of extensive quantity, that is, a mechanism through which modes themselves come into existence" (Deleuze 1990: 233). From the mechanistic perspective the dynamism of a mechanism is closed and predetermined by an already established and identified function. A physics of intensive quantity, by contrast, cannot be reduced to any identifiable function and/or end. Intensive quantities are the condition for the identification of extensive properties and functions, but rather than anticipate through resemblance the extensive properties that actualize the intensive properties, the intensive assures the transformation and metamorphosis of the extensive and identifiable.

We can now begin to see how Deleuze is doing something quite different than what Boltanski and Chiapello attribute to him. When Boltanski and Chiapello argue that what is important is fluidity, mobility, and a nomadic capacity to engage in and navigate diverse transformations and metamorphoses, this capacity is subordinate to the identity of the project, and to the projects that follow upon this one, and so on and so forth. To be successful entails establishing a reputation for taking on new and different projects, for doing what counts, *and often*, and yet this is precisely in line with an extensive, mechanistic understanding of capitalism and social interaction. In fact, recent work in social network analysis has sought to show how success in everything from getting a job to becoming a famous philosopher occurs when one accumulates a greater *quantity* of diverse contacts (Granovetter 1995; Collins 1995). Similarly, Jorge Hirsh, a physicist at UC San Diego, has argued that a better gauge in determining how good a scientist one is can be had not by knowing how many articles they have published and in what journals, but rather how many times their articles are cited by other published articles. Referred to as the h-index, it has become a tool that has not surprisingly been adopted by university administrators to help them in making their tenure and promotion decisions. What is key to each of these approaches is that a particular dynamic and process – getting a job, becoming an important philosopher, becoming a good scientist, etc. – is analyzed by way of measurable, identifiable characteristics. The point for Deleuze, by contrast, is *not* to increase extensive quantities, to capture market share. This would be, to use Deleuzian phrasing, to emphasize the becoming-perceptible nature of work, where work is the actualization of the intensive. This does indeed happen, but again for Deleuze the point of work as desiring-production is not the product, the end result; it is, rather, the becoming-imperceptible, the becoming-intensive nature of work, that Deleuze will stress. This is not a technique or ploy to enable us to foster greater creative powers, powers that are to be evidenced by the appearance of new works. Although such works may be a consequence of affirming multiplicity, to prioritize them as the primary instances of a non-capitalist work would be to reintroduce a hierarchical judgment, and in doing so would play into the hands of a capitalist reading of Deleuze (à la Boltanski). To have done with the judgment of God, as Deleuze and Guattari would have us do (echoing

Artaud), is to affirm the immanence and univocal nature of work. Consequently, from a Deleuzian perspective, one is not becoming-intensive and imperceptible in one's work solely when one brings novelties to the world; one may, as Zen master Shunryu Suzuki once said, attain enlightenment wherever one is, even while going to the bathroom (Suzuki 200: 42).

Turning now to Deleuze's understanding of intensive quantity, it is indeed what comes to be actualized within the mechanism of extensive quantities. Intensive quantities themselves, however, are processes without a goal or end. In *Anti-Oedipus* this is discussed as desiring-production, and it is here that the significance of Deleuze and Guattari's understanding of labor emerges. In particular, Deleuze and Guattari do not interpret labor mechanistically, whereby a determinate input is taken up by labor and a determinate output is the end product. It is this product, as we saw, that is taken up by the capitalist and confronts the laborer as an alien, hostile object. Nor is labor an organic, natural process that is indistinguishable from its product, the product being simply the natural extension of one's labor. In this view nothing new can be produced by labor for the new would simply be a fold or extension of what one already is or possesses. This, in essence, is one of Badiou's central criticisms of Deleuze. He reads Deleuze as one who does reduce the new to being a fold or extension of what already is, and hence as not really being new.[2] For Badiou, Deleuze makes the same mistake Heidegger does by reducing the event to the historical and the natural, thereby ignoring the fact that (for Badiou) the new is an event that is a rupture with the historical – it is an ahistorical Truth that then comes to be naturalized and historicized. Haydn's music, to take one of Badiou's examples, can be seen to be a natural extension and historical evolution of the Baroque, but interpreting it this way ignores the fact that Haydn's music, as an event, was a rupture and void that could not be placed within the Baroque context.[3]

With reference to the Haydn example, there is an important extent to which Deleuze and Guattari agree with Badiou. In discussing style and literature, though this could be extended to music and hence Haydn's "classical" style, Deleuze and Guattari claim that what is important is not the style itself as an identifiable pattern, unity, etc., but rather

> the absence of style – aysntactic, agrammatical, the moment when language is no longer defined by what it says, even less by what makes it a signifying thing, but by what causes it to move, to flow, and to explode – desire. For literature is like schizophrenia: a process and not a goal, a production and not an expression. (Deleuze and Guattari 1983: 133)

In other words, Haydn's efforts that came to be identified as the classical style of music cannot be reduced to a set of identifiable characteristics, including pre-existing historical precedents. On this point, Deleuze and Guattari would agree with Badiou. At the same time, however, they would not reduce Haydn's efforts to a rupturing void, to an absence or null set that cannot be placed within any determinate, identifiable context. For Deleuze and Guattari it is desire – or desiring-production – that accounts for the emergence of a style that is an absence of style, a novelty that cannot be reduced to that which preceded it. Desiring-production, however, is not a void or null set; to the contrary, "desiring-production is pure multiplicity, that is to say, an affirmation that is irreducible to any sort of unity" (Deleuze and Guattari 1983: 42). Put in other terms, desiring-production as pure multiplicity and affirmation is an affirmation of difference without identity, an affirmation of difference as difference. In discussing the schizophrenic, Deleuze and Guattari argue that "He does not reduce contraries to an identity of the same, he affirms their distance as that which relates the two as different" (Deleuze and Guattari 1983: 77). The pure multiplicity is this distance; or, as this is discussed in Deleuze's *Difference and Repetition*, this distance and multiplicity is the intensive quantity that becomes actualized as extensive, identifiable differences – namely, as differences in kind or as differences in degree (Deleuze 1994: 239).

We can see at this point why Boltanski and Chiapello refer to the critique of capitalism set forth by Deleuze and Guattari, among others, as the artistic critique, for in this critique the artist emerges as a prime example of one who affirms multiplicity. This is certainly true in *Anti-Oedipus*. Whereas the schizophrenic is an example of desiring-production in its "raw state," as Ian Buchanan puts it (Buchanan 2008: 35), a state lacking in coherence and order, "the great artist," Deleuze and Guattari argue, "is indeed the one who scales the schizophrenic wall and reaches the land of the unknown, where he no longer belongs to any time, any milieu, any school" (Deleuze and Guattari 1983: 69). The great artist is one who affirms multiplicity and intensive quantities that cannot be reduced to "any time, any milieu, any school"; in the case of an artist such as J. M. W. Turner, for Deleuze and Guattari his work is an example of "art as a *process* without goal, but that attains completion as such" (Deleuze and Guattari 1983: 370). We could take Kafka as yet another example. On the night of September 22, 1912, Kafka wrote the story "The Judgment" in a single sitting. As Reiner Stach describes the event in his biography of Kafka, "Suddenly – without guide or precedent, it seemed – the Kafka cosmos was at hand, fully equipped with the 'Kafkaesque' inventory that gives his work its distinctive character ..." (Stach 2005: 115). As Kafka experienced that night, however, it was not of a rupturing, unnamable void that, on a Badiouian reading, he then maintained fidelity to in his remaining writings; to the contrary, rather than an unnamable void, Kafka experienced it as an excess that is unnamable not because it is a void but because it exceeds all that can be said. As Kafka put it in his diary the day after he wrote the story: "How everything can be said, how for everything, for the strangest fancies, there waits a great fire in which they perish and rise up again" (Kafka 1982: 232). In affirming pure multiplicity without succumbing to the raw state of desiring-production, the "great artist" is able to forge a style that belongs to no time, place, or school. Moreover, this affirmation need not seek uncharted territories to assert itself but rather the artist (or the Zen master as discussed above) can and precisely does affirm multiplicity right where they are. When David Sudnow, for instance, struggled to learn how to play improvisational jazz, he came to realize he did not need to prefigure the paths his hands would take across the keyboard. As Sudnow put it, "I began to see and then find use for further work in the observation that note choices could be made anywhere, that there was no need to lunge, that usable notes for any chord lay just at hand, that there was no need to find a path, image one up ahead to get ready in advance ..." (Sudnow 1993: 94). When Deleuze and Deleuze and Guattari thus come to conceptualize work and labor as desiring-production, a preferred example is the work of the artist. We will now turn to discuss Deleuze's analysis of Francis Bacon to show that, contrary to Boltanski and Chiapello's claims, the artistic critique does not legitimize the new spirit of capitalism but rather sets forth an understanding of work as becoming-imperceptible, a work that problematizes capitalism and extends well beyond the work of the "great artist."

II.

A central concern of *Anti-Oedipus* is to lay out the tasks of schizoanalysis, and these tasks, as Deleuze and Guattari envision them, are intended to range over a wide array of issues other than the artistic. First and most obviously, as the title *Anti-Oedipus* itself reveals, Deleuze and Guattari contrast the task of schizoanalysis with psychoanalysis. As they put it, in contrast to psychoanalysis, "schizoanalysis attains a nonfigurative and nonsymbolic unconscious, a pure abstract figural dimension ... flow-schizzes or real-desire, apprehended below the minimum conditions of identity" (Deleuze and Guattari 1983: 351). Rather than reveal already identified elements within the unconscious that have been repressed and refused entrance into the realm of consciousness, schizoanalysis taps into "a nonfigurative" and "pure abstract figural dimension" that is the very condition for the production of identifiable elements. It is precisely here that Deleuze and Guattari's work explodes well beyond the work of the artist and opens onto countless processes of the production of identity, or countless forms of work. To see how this unfolds we will begin with Deleuze's work on Francis Bacon, for it is here where Deleuze lays out in most detail his understanding of the figural in contrast to the figurative, and also examines the techniques and practices associated with the work of creating the figural.

For Deleuze the contrast between the figurative and the figural is quite straightforward: "the figurative (representation)," Deleuze argues, "implies the relationship of an image to an object that it is supposed to illustrate . . .," while the figural, "through extraction or isolation" attains an autonomy that cannot be reduced to a represented object (Deleuze 2002: 6). Key to how Bacon painted the figural are the "'involuntary free marks' lining the canvas, asignifying traits that are devoid of any illustrative or narrative function" (Deleuze 2002: 8). These marks, Deleuze adds, "belong to an original system which is neither that of the landscape, nor that of the formless, or the ground (although, by virtue of their autonomy, they are apt to 'make' a landscape or to 'make' a ground, or even to 'make' darkness)" (Deleuze 2002: 8). Throughout his book on Bacon, Deleuze charts the course, or logic of sensation, he sees Bacon following in his construction of the figural, but for our purposes we shall focus on the role played by these asignifying traits or "involuntary free marks." These elements are crucial, for they are what Deleuze will refer to in other places as the pre-individual singularities, "apprehended below the minimum conditions of identity." And how they come to "make" an identity, a landscape, ground, figure, etc., is through a process of what Bacon calls "coagulation."[4]

How a multiplicity of asignifying traits as an "original system" can "make" an identity through "coagulation" was already a concern of Deleuze's in his first book on Hume. As I have argued elsewhere, a number of the problems that have arisen among Hume's commentators can be resolved, and Hume's social and political thought further clarified, if his impressions are not taken to be the *pre-existent identities* upon which the rest of his system is built. Hume himself admits that the idea of identity and "continu'd existence" is critical but he likewise admits that this idea cannot arise from the perception of "one single object," for this "conveys the idea of unity, not that of identity." It conveys, in other words, the idea of the unity of an object but not the idea of the "continu'd existence" and identity of this object in time; and yet if the impressions maintain their identity so as to assure that ideas are faithful copies of them, or that memories successfully recall the earlier impressions, then this understanding of impressions presupposes their continued existence and identity in time. At the same time a multiplicity of distinct impressions does not give rise to the idea of identity in time, for here we have separable and distinct existences and not the continued self-identity of one and the same existence. "To remove this difficulty," Hume proposes that we

> have recourse to the idea of time or duration. I have already observ'd, that time, in a strict sense, implies succession, and that when we apply its idea to any unchangeable object [i.e., to a unity], 'tis only by a fiction of the imagination, by which the unchangeable object is suppos'd to participate of the changes of other co-existent objects ... This fiction of the imagination almost universally takes place; and 'tis by means of it, that a single object, plac'd before us, and survey'd for any time without discovering in it any interruption or variation, is able to give us a notion of identity. (Hume 1978: 200–1)

Identity, in short, is the result of an artifice, a fiction, a generative, systematizing process that "coagulates" and accumulates pre-individual, asyntactic and agrammatical traits – a multiplicity – and identity, whether of a sensation, Figure, impression, or self is the result of this process.

This process, however, does not begin *ex nihilo*. The fictioning of identities always begins in the midst of identity – *in media res* – or thinking, as Peirce said, always begins where one is.[5] The same is true for Bacon. Bacon does not begin with nothing, with a blank canvas; to the contrary, as Deleuze argues, and as Bacon admits in an interview, "He [Bacon] does not paint in order to reproduce on the canvas an object functioning as a model; he paints on images that are already there, in order to produce a canvas whose functioning will reverse the relations between model and copy." A painter, Deleuze claims, "has many things in his head, or around him, or in his studio" (Deleuze 2002: 71). Bacon in particular frequently drew from photographs, newspaper stories, and other images from film and elsewhere that functioned as the givens from which he worked. These givens are taken up in a "prepictorial figuration," or as what "is on the canvas and in the painter's head, in what the painter wants to do, before the painter begins." These givens are indeed a "first figuration," as Deleuze puts it, a starting point or intention of what the painter wants to do or represent. They begin, in

short, as models, as the figurative that "cannot be completely elimi-
nated; something of it is always conserved" (Deleuze 2002: 79). Despite
beginning with the figurative, with clichés, Bacon disrupts the relationship between these givens as a model to be represented in his work as a
painter by interjecting a diagram. The "diagram," Deleuze claims, "is
indeed chaos, a catastrophe, but it is also a germ of order or rhythm.
It is a violent chaos in relation to the figurative givens, but it is a germ
of rhythm in relation to the new order of the painting" (Deleuze 2002:
83). The painter must be careful, however, for one can easily slip into
cliché, into figurative painting or into a modern form of abstraction (à
la Mondrian) which reduces "the abyss or chaos ... to a minimum";
on the other hand there is the risk of deploying, in the style of Jackson
Pollock, the abyss or chaos to the maximum (Deleuze 2002: 84–5). On
Deleuze's reading, what sets Bacon's works apart is that he does not
allow the diagram, the infusion of chaos, "to eat away at the entire
painting." The "violent methods" of Bacon, and of nonfigurative artists
in general, "must not be given free rein, and the necessary catastrophe
must not submerge the whole" (Deleuze 2002: 89). The diagrammatical
work of an artist, therefore, is work at the edge of chaos, and as such it
infuses the figurative givens with an irreducible chaos, with involuntary
marks and asignifying traces which allow – if the diagram is not reduced
to a minimum, to an equilibrium state, or if it does not swallow the
entire painting – for the emergence of a "new order of the painting."
Diagrammatical work, therefore, as Deleuze summarizes it, comes down
to this: "The essential point about the diagram is that it is made in order
for something to emerge from it, and if nothing emerges from it, it fails.
And what emerges from the diagram, the Figure, emerges both gradually
and all at once . . ." (Deleuze 2002: 128).[6]

In his discussion of Deleuze and Guattari's arguments in A Thousand
Plateaus regarding the state axiomatic, William Connolly offers a
helpful way to understand the sense in which what emerges from the
diagram does so "both gradually and all at once." By the state axiomatic, Connolly means, agreeing with Weber, "a set of heretofore
floating elements [that] became knotted together by hook and by crook"
(Connolly 2008: 13). In particular, the state axiomatic is the set of institutions and elements – namely, money, national banks, state taxation,
free labor, among others – that are crucial in instilling "confidence in
promises about the future that it promotes." This axiomatic, Deleuze
and Guattari argue, emerged in "a single stroke."[7] Connolly asks the
obvious question: "How could such a complex axiomatic emerge in 'a
single stroke'?" (Connolly 2008: 23). For Connolly "a single stroke"

may indeed be gradual – "It may last a minute, a month, or a few decades" – but this "duration counts as 'a single stroke,'" Connolly argues, "because during it the markers by which we recognize relatively durable things are under suspension" (Connolly 2008: 24). Connolly refers to such a state of suspension as a state at the edge of chaos. What is crucial to understand is that the elements themselves that are within the edge-of-chaos state are perfectly identifiable, but they enter into relationships that are far from equilibrium and hence are not yet the systematic identity that emerges from this chaos, an identity that will be irreducible to the elements themselves. This is the becoming-imperceptible of the identifiable elements. For Francis Bacon as well, while he may begin with photographs, news clippings, etc., that are already on the canvas before he begins to paint, these will become imperceptible through the work of painting itself, through Bacon's diagrammatics, which instills chaos into these models such that the copy subverts the identity of the model in a way that allows for the emergence of a Figure that is not the copy of a model.

Revisiting our earlier examples we can see that although the "Kafkaesque" world emerged in a single stroke on the night of September 12, 1912, the elements that would come to form this world had been gradually developed, worked, and reworked. Kafka would not have had that night if it had not been for this work. Similarly for David Sudnow's efforts to learn improvisational jazz, although it is true that his successful performances could not be reduced to the time spent memorizing scales, jazz-sounding phrasings, scalar devices, etc., he also would not have been able to play improvisational jazz had it not been for this work. Turning to a quite different example, we could say that Louis Pasteur discovered, in a single stroke, microorganisms; and yet, as Bruno Latour has argued, it was only as the results of Pasteur's researches became increasingly connected to other areas of research and life (e.g., antibiotics, pasteurization, etc.) that these microorganisms became increasingly real and autonomous, thereby becoming the entities the textbooks credit Pasteur for discovering in a single stroke (Latour 1988). The textbook fact is taken to be irreducible to the various processes associated with establishing their increased connections to other researchers and to life, and to the work involved in making these connections – the work of scientists as Latour understands it – and yet these textbook facts, or this ready-made science as Latour calls it, would not have been possible without this work. And finally, to return to Connolly, his goal is to challenge what he refers to as the "evangelical-capitalist resonance machine," namely the neoliberal orthodoxy that largely equates "capitalist innovation and divine providence," but which in the end merely provides cover for the increasing economic inequalities of society and the destruction of our natural habitats and resources. What is needed for Connolly is the effort and work of publicizing and participating "in microeconomic experiments that reduce inequality, enact sustainable modes of consumption, and return a larger portion of surplus to localities and workers" (Connolly 2008: 145). If a non-capitalist resonance machine emerges it will be irreducible to the varied efforts and experiments that will have been attempted, and yet it would not have been possible without this work and effort.

We can now see that work is not by its nature, for Deleuze, alienating drudgery. From the perspective of a physics of extensive quantity, work is indeed measured by that which is produced, and the product, as Marx argued, can indeed become appropriated by capitalists and used in a way that reduces the value of the labor that produced it. For those who by Wednesday are glad to be over the hump of the workweek and eagerly await Friday, here again work is viewed relative to an end or purpose external to it. Work is merely a means to another end or goal. Now such work cannot be avoided for we are always situated within an extensive physics, within a world of ends and goals. But Deleuze, as we have been arguing, recognizes a work that is irreducible to the work of extensive quantities – or, we might say, following Marx, that this is a work free from the extensive physics of physical necessity. From this perspective, work becomes desiring-production, or it is the becoming-imperceptible of the work of ends and goals. And if one whistles while one works it will not be in order to distract oneself from the drudgery of the work itself, but rather because work has become a process without goal, and yet a process inseparable from the work of ends and goals. As Nietzsche reminds us: "Not every end is the goal. The end of a melody is not its goal, and yet if a melody has not reached its end, it has not reached its goal. A parable" (Nietzsche 1967: 183).

References

Badiou, A. (1994), "Gilles Deleuze: *The Fold: Leibniz and the Baroque*," in C. Boundas (ed.), *Gilles Deleuze and the Theater of Philosophy*, New York: Routledge, 51–69.
Badiou, A. (2001), *Ethics: An Essay on the Understanding of Evil*, trans. P. Hallward, London: Verso.
Badiou, A. (2005), *Being and Event*, trans. O. Feltham, London: Verso.
Bell, J. (2006), *Philosophy at the Edge of Chaos*, Toronto: University of Toronto Press.

Bell, J. (2009), *Deleuze's Hume: Philosophy, Culture and the Scottish Enlightenment*, Edinburgh: Edinburgh University Press.

Boltanski, L. and E. Chiapello (2007), *The New Spirit of Capitalism*, trans. G. Elliott, New York: Verso.

Buchanan, I. (2008), *Deleuze and Guattari's* Anti-Oedipus: *A Reader's Guide*, Continuum: London.

Collins, R. (1999), *Sociology of Philosophies*, Cambridge, MA: Harvard University Press.

Connolly, W. (2008), *Capitalism and Christianity, American Style*, Durham: Duke University Press.

Deleuze, G. (1990), *Expressionism in Philosophy: Spinoza*, trans. M. Joughin, New York: Zone Books.

Deleuze, G. (1994), *Difference and Repetition*, trans. P. Patton, New York: Columbia University Press.

Deleuze, G. (2002), *Francis Bacon: The Logic of Sensation*, trans. D. W. Smith, Minneapolis: University of Minnesota Press.

Deleuze, G. and F. Guattari (1983), *Anti-Oedipus: Capitalism and Schizophrenia*, trans. R. Hurley, M. Seem and H. R. Lane, Minneapolis: University of Minnesota Press.

Deleuze, G. and F. Guattari (1987), *A Thousand Plateaus: Capitalism and Schizophrenia*, trans. B. Massumi, Minneapolis: University of Minnesota Press.

Granovetter, M. (1995), *Getting a Job*, Chicago: University of Chicago Press.

Hume, D. (1978), *A Treatise of Human Nature*, ed. L. A. Selby-Bigge, Oxford: Clarendon Press.

Kafka, F. (1982), *The Diaries of Franz Kafka*, ed. Max Brod, New York: Penguin.

Latour, B. (1988), *The Pasteurization of France*, Cambridge, MA: Harvard University Press.

Marx, K. (1984), *Economic and Philosophic Manuscripts of 1844*, Amherst: Prometheus Books.

Nietzsche, F. (1967), *On the Genealogy of Morals/Ecce Home*, trans. W. Kaufmann, New York: Penguin Books.

Peirce, C. S. (1955), "The Essentials of Pragmatism," in J. Buchler (ed.), *Philosophical Writings of Peirce*, New York: Dover Publications.

Stach, R. (2005), *Kafka: The Decisive Years*, trans. S. Frisch, New York: Harcourt.

Sudnow, D. *Ways of the Hand* (1993), Cambridge, MA: Harvard University Press.

Suzuki, S. (2003), *Not Always So*, New York: HarperOne.

Notes

1. For more on this see Bell 2006, Chapter 2.
2. See Badiou's essay, "Gilles Deleuze: *The Fold: Leibniz and the Baroque*." In this essay Badiou argues that Deleuze's position in his Leibniz book, whereby he understands the world as a relentless folding, unfolding, and refolding of events, is ultimately left unable to account for the new that would be beyond the given, beyond the "presentifying" (Badiou 1994: 68) descriptions of immanence.
3. For Badiou's discussion of Haydn's music as an event see Badiou 2001: 68; for his critique of Heidegger, see Badiou 2005: 124–9; and for more extended discussion on these themes see Bell 2009.
4. Deleuze 2002: 33. As Deleuze elaborates upon Bacon's claim, he states that for Bacon "Every sensation, and every Figure, is already an 'accumulated' or 'coagulated' sensation . . ." (33).
5. See Peirce 1955: 256: "But in truth, there is but one state of mind from which you

can 'set out,' namely, the very state of mind in which you actually find yourself at the time you do 'set out'."

6. Deleuze follows "all at once" with "as in Painting," referring to Bacon's 1946 painting entitled *Painting*.

7. Connolly 2008: 23. Connolly is quoting from *A Thousand Plateaus*, plateau 13: "We are always brought back to the idea of a State that comes into the world fully formed and rises up in a single stroke" (Deleuze and Guattari 1987: 472); see also: "The question now becomes: Once the State has appeared, formed in a single stroke, how will it evolve?" (Deleuze and Guattari 1987: 495).

Chapter 2

The Ethics of the Event: Deleuze and Ethics without Aρχή

Levi R. Bryant

Sex, Politics, Viruses, and Vaccines

In 2007 Governor Rick Perry of Texas issued an executive order (it was not the result of the legislative process) requiring all girls in the sixth grade (between the ages of 11 and 12) to be vaccinated against the human papillomavirus (HPV). The rationale behind this executive order was that Gardisal and Cervarix, the vaccines produced by the pharmaceutical companies Merck and Glaxo respectively, significantly reduce the chances of HPV developing into a variety of different cancers, most prominent among them being cervical cancer, as well as genital warts. Given the high likelihood of women contracting some form of HPV throughout their life, with estimates of 12,000 women contracting cervical cancer every year and 4,000 dying from it,[1] these vaccines would go a long way towards preventing needless deaths and protecting the health of women.

However, no sooner than the new vaccines were announced did controversies begin to swirl. Conservative religious groups such as Focus on the Family and the Family Research Council protested that these vaccinations would encourage premarital sex and promiscuity.[2] Health insurance companies protested the exorbitant cost of the vaccine – $122 per shot, with three treatments required – wondering how they would cover the vaccinations.[3] Parents belonging to the anti-vaccine movement worried about potentially dire unintended side-effects of the vaccine. Others saw the issue as one of parental rights, objecting to children being *mandated* to receive the vaccine. Parents could, however, have their children opt out of the treatments. Feminists saw Perry's order as an ironic victory for women's rights and health, coming as it did from an arch-conservative. Meanwhile, questions were raised about Governor Perry's motives, noting that he discussed the vaccine on the very day he received a $5,000 campaign contribution from the pharmaceutical corporation Merck.[4]

My aim here is not to take a position on the HPV vaccine, though I do support it, but to use this little vignette from Texas politics both as a launching point for a criticism of how we currently discuss ethics and to underline some salient features of ethical "phenomenology." It is my position that the dominant traditions of ethical thought are almost entirely useless with respect to genuine ethical problems, and that fundamentally they approach the question and problem of ethics from the wrong side, focusing as they do on *rule-based* models of ethical deliberation. The HPV vaccine controversy is a sort of parable for the impotence of this sort of ethical thought – dominated by utilitarian and Kantian deontological models of ethical deliberation – fit only for classroom exercises where students are made to apply abstract rules and principles that have little bearing on the sort of *situations* that evoke ethical *controversy*. In place of these transcendent rule-based models of ethical deliberation where everything is known in *advance*, I propose a *problem-based* model of ethical *composition* without pre-existing αρχή or foundation, where the ethical is not understood as the *application* of pre-existent moral principles to particular situations, but is conceived as the emergence of a *problem* and the re-composition of a collective undertaken in response to this problem. With such a "model" of ethical thought perhaps "the problems of ethics" – a dear pedagogical tool used by philosophy professors to torment undergraduates by requiring them to jump through hoops by applying various ethical theories to particular situations – can attain a higher dignity, denoting not the subsumption of a content to a particular ethical scheme, but rather the *inventiveness* proper to the domain of the ethical. Working towards this end I will draw heavily on the ethical thought developed by Deleuze in *The Logic of Sense* and *Difference and Repetition*.

Practical Philosophy and its Discontents

When confronted by the HPV vaccine controversy, how is the utilitarian or the Kantian deontologist to respond? In his *Groundwork of the Metaphysics of Morals*, Kant advises us "never to act except in such a way that I could also will that my maxim should become a universal law" (Kant 1996: 57). To apply Kant's categorical imperative we are to identify the verb or proposed action we wish to evaluate, universalize it, and determine whether the action becomes contradictory or impossible when universalized. All of this is to be done with the important caveat that we ignore any *inclinations* we might have regarding the issue, as well as the *circumstances* or context pertaining to the decision to be made (Kant 1996: 55). To consider the circumstances, which are always specific and singular, would be to ruin the universality to which Kant's practical philosophy aspires.

For Kant, the paradigmatic example of ethical deliberation is to be found in contractual agreements and questions of whether or not we ought to tell the truth. Here it is notable that Kant's ethical theory closely mirrors the requirements of liberal and neoliberal ethical theory as required by the structure of capitalism. Thus, suppose I wish to determine whether or not it is moral to tell a lie in a particular situation for ethical gain. The verb in this action is that of lying. I now ask myself whether I can *consistently* formulate a law or maxim that would bind *all* people to lie when given the opportunity to do so. When I universalize this action as a law – and here law should be thought in terms of laws of *nature* that operate *ineluctably* – I discover straight away that my proposed action becomes *impossible* when universalized in this way. The conditions under which it is possible to *successfully* tell a lie require the person to whom I am lying to believe that I am telling a truth. Paradoxically, he who would lie is parasitically dependent on the moral law, for lies can only be successful where the other works on the premise that we *ought* to tell the truth. However, in a universe where lying is a universal law, it becomes *impossible* to lie by virtue of the fact that everyone would work on the premise that every statement pertaining to truth is a fabrication. Thus, lying is immoral.

So far, so good. Yet how does Kant's moral philosophy fair when applied to situations like the Texas HPV vaccination controversy? The verb or proposed action here seems to turn on administering the vaccine to young girls. Remember, we are not to consider any of the circumstances in which the action is to be undertaken, including contextual features like what the drug does. For Kant, to consider potential benefits of the drug would be to fall into the domain of *hypothetical imperatives*, where we are speaking of *probable* outcomes, not the universal. Thus, for example, we are to ignore the possibility that these girls might someday contract HPV, despite strong statistical evidence that this will occur for many women. When we universalize administering the vaccine, we seem to encounter no contradiction rendering the action impossible. Therefore we might initially suppose that the action is moral. However, here we should apply Kant's moral law *twice*, once for the proposed action, and once for its *contrary*. What do we discover when we universalize the rule that would *not* administer the vaccine to all girls? Here again we find that no contradiction is encountered, that no impossibility is engendered, and that not administering the vaccine is every bit as permissible within the framework of Kantian moral theory as administering it would be.

In short, in this case, Kant's practical philosophy provides us with no decision criteria for determining whether or not the action is morally permissible. At this juncture we could, perhaps, adopt the moderate strategy of suggesting that *both* administering the vaccine *and* not administering it are moral actions, but if we take this route we have effectively concluded that the question of the vaccine is *outside* ethical concerns. Given all the controversies that swirl around Governor Perry's executive order, this seems like a strange conclusion indeed. Yet deontological ethics seem to provide us with no resources for deciding the issue.

Faced with situations such as the foregoing, utilitarian moral thought appears to fair a bit better, yet here too we run into problems. In *Utilitarianism*, Mill proposes the Greatest Happiness Principle as the technology by which we determine whether or not actions are right or wrong. As Mill puts it:

> The creed which accepts as the foundation of morals, Utility, or the Greatest Happiness Principle, holds that actions are right in proportion as they tend to promote happiness, wrong as they tend to produce the reverse of happiness. By happiness is intended pleasure, and the absence of pain; by unhappiness, pain, and the privation of pleasure. (Mill 2001: 7)

Consequently, to determine whether an action is right or wrong we need to calculate the happiness or pleasure the action promotes among all parties involved. Administering the vaccine will be right if it promotes the greatest amount of happiness for the greatest number of people, and wrong if it diminishes that overall happiness. Unlike the Kantian practical philosophy that presupposes a universal subject identical in all situations and that divorces ethical deliberation from any meditation on circumstances, Mill allows us to take into account both the different parties involved and the probable outcomes of a proposed course of action.

Nonetheless, daunting difficulties still haunt Mill's ethical philosophy. First, what, precisely, counts as pleasure, or as pain? In deciding that, are we to count the ire of the religious fundamentalists who see the vaccination proposal as contributing to sexual promiscuity even if this ire is founded on the improbable? Why, or why not? What about the financial concerns of the insurance companies? Are we to take into account only the health of the women involved and public health in general? Yet how are we to measure this outcome against *other possible worlds* where the vaccine wasn't administered? And what of all those women who would not have contracted HPV anyway? And what, again, of the unintended consequences of the vaccination that cannot presently be foreseen? How do we factor these consequences into our deliberations? In short, there are severe difficulties in determining just how general happiness is to be calculated and what is to be considered and what is to be ignored.

Of greater concern are the essentialist presuppositions regarding subjects that seem to underpin utilitarian ethical theories. While the utilitarian emphasis on *affect* is to be commended, nonetheless our capacity to be affected pleasurably or painfully here seems to be assumed as a brute and unchanging given. In other words, for the sort of calculation proposed by Mill and like-minded utilitarians to get off the ground, it seems that we must assume that our capacity to be affected is more or less fixed. If this is so vital to the core premise of utilitarian thought, then it is because utilitarianism is a *consequentialist* ethical philosophy. If the rightness of an action is to rise or fall with its consequences, or its ability to produce pleasure as an *outcome*, then it must be possible to *track* the relation between an action and its consequences. But this requires the homogeneity of our capacity to be affected. Yet what are we to do if *action itself* transforms our capacity to be affected by generating *new* capacities to be affected? Here it is no longer possible to track the relation between action and affect in the way proposed by utilitarianism, and the more we understand about neuronal plasticity and development, the more it appears that affect is not fixed in this way.[5]

Actors and Crisis: Ethical "Phenomenology"

As I suggested earlier, traditional ethical philosophy suffers from approaching ethics the wrong way round. The maneuver seems to be as follows: The ethicist begins with well-determined situations that have *already occurred* and then proceeds to search for a rule that would allow him or her to evaluate whether the action is right or wrong. In ethical philosophy and theorization everything seems to proceed as if the action were *already* accomplished and *then* the action gets evaluated. However, this reversal becomes *unconscious* in the mind of the theorist, such that the rule allowing for the evaluation of the action is treated as *preceding* the event to be evaluated. Part of the problem here lies in the ethical theorist *implicitly* asking the *wrong* sort of question. And by asking the wrong sort of question, the ethical theorist situates himself in the wrong ethical "phenomenology." Rather than rushing to answer the question of *what* ethics is, or *how* we distinguish right from wrong, we should first ask the *strange* question of *when* ethical problematics arise. In this connection, Deleuze was right to denounce the question "what is x?" As Deleuze writes:

> Rationalism wanted to tie the fate of [problems] to abstract and dead essence; and to the extent that the problem form of [problems were] recognized, it even wanted that form tied to the question of essences – in other words, to the "What is X?". How many misunderstandings are contained in this will! . . . Once it is a question of determining the problem or the Idea as such, once it is a question of setting the dialectic in motion, the question "What is X?" gives way to other questions, otherwise powerful and efficacious, otherwise imperative: "How much, how and in what cases?" (Deleuze 1994: 188)

The question of the "when" of ethical problematics would at least possess the virtue of suspending a number of our assumptions pertaining to what ethics is *about*, and setting us on the track of a more accurate ethical phenomenology.

The problem with the traditional ethical philosophies I discussed earlier is that they know everything in advance. Here it is simply a question of applying a rule or a scheme to a particular *case*. Yet when we look at actual ethical situations such as the one depicted at the beginning of this chapter, we notice that they are above all characterized by *uncertainty*. Somehow, within the framework of traditional ethical theories it is this moment of uncertainty, of crisis, that utterly disappears and is erased. To be sure, traditional ethical theory attenuates the question of what is to be done, but almost always within the framework of clearly delineated possibilities and alternatives. What is missing is precisely this moment of the uncertain that gives the ethical, whether at the level of an individual life or in relations amongst elements or actors in a collective, its particular flavor. If the moment of the ethical is characterized by anything – and note I've shifted from a substantialist language to a *temporal* language – it is characterized by precisely that moment where an organized and stable situation has become *unsettled* and it is no longer clear as to how that stability is to be maintained or whether a new organization entirely should emerge. If this approach to ethics is so egregious it is because it restricts the ethical to the moment of reduction and normalization, to subsumption under a category or rule, failing to recognize the inventiveness and creativity that ethics embodies. Indeed, the invention and creation that lies at the heart of the ethical, constituting its very being.

Phenomenologically, the moment of the ethical is precisely the moment of *crisis*. And it is this that recourse to αρχή, foundations, or principles so thoroughly obscures, for it is exactly where principles fail that we encounter the *problem* of the ethical. The question of the ethical is *not* the question of how crisis can be ameliorated by recourse to pre-existing principles for the simple reason that the ethical is encountered at just that moment where "principles" governing a composition no longer hold. Rather, the question of the ethical is that of how situations must be re-composed in response to this moment of crisis. And in this respect, the fetishistic obsession of traditional ethical theory with whether or not lying is moral or whether or not it is just to kill another person completely trivializes the proper theme of ethics and confuses ethics with questions of customs organizing a flourishing collective. Did anyone ever really doubt whether we should, by and large, keep our contracts, be honest, or not murder our fellows? It is astonishing that such trite issues could justify the destruction of so many trees.

Let us return to the example of the HPV vaccine and try to imagine the situation not as we see it in retrospect or from a dis-involved perspective floating up above, but rather from the perspective of the *event* as it unfolds. The first thing we notice is that this situation is composed of all sorts of heterogeneous actors: young girls, parents, insurance corporations, pharmaceutical companies, schools, fundamentalist religious groups, governors, gods, religious texts, legislators, *but also* scientists, doctors, laboratories, viruses, cancers, genital warts, sexual activities, outcomes of research indicating that a statistically significant number of women will contract the HPV virus at some point of their lives, and vaccines.

It will be objected that viruses, vaccines, diseases, and laboratories are not *actors*, but mere *objects*, functioning as nothing more than *means*. Objects, it will be said, display *behavior* but not *action*, and therefore fall outside the purview of ethics which is concerned with goal-directed *intentional* action alone. However, following Bruno Latour, it has become increasingly difficult to discern how nonhuman objects are not themselves genuine actors. Thus, for example, nonhuman objects act in the laboratory all the time, betraying and surprising the intentions of the scientist with their responses, and completely modifying the coordinates of the situation.[6] To argue that nonhuman actors should be excluded from ethical thought or treated as mere *means* to an end is to fall prey to a fallacy similar to that which Marx denounced under the title of "commodity fetishism." Just as commodity fetishism prevents us from seeing the complex networks of labor involving workers, technologies, materials, etc., ethical fetishism prevents us from seeing the complex networks of nonhuman actors that play such a significant role in perturbing collectives, bringing about the moment of the ethical.

Moreover, given the manner in which humans always employ other objects and are employed by other objects in their actions, the idea of humans acting *alone* without the intermediary of other objects at work in their action is itself a fiction (Latour 2005: 43–86). For Latour, an actor is just any entity that modifies "a state of affairs by making a difference" (Latour 2005: 71). In and of itself this would not be enough to call the distinction between action (of humans) and behavior (of objects) into question, were there not an issue of *who* and *what* is acting in the case of humans. In this connection Latour gives the marvelous example of television and the remote control to illustrate his point. Would I have become a couch potato, switching endlessly from channel to channel, he asks, if I did not have a remote? (Latour 2005: 77). The point here is not that the remote *determines* me to become a couch potato, but rather the far more disturbing consequence that we cannot firmly draw the distinction between actors (humans) and mere behaviors (objects).[7] "Our" action is a *network* composed of human and nonhuman actors, rather than two ontologically heterogeneous domains composed of humans and action on one side, and objects functioning as mere means and possessing only behaviors on the other. For this reason, I include nonhuman entities among the list of actors in collectives or situations. Ethical theory has suffered tremendously as a result of treating ethics exclusively as the domain of the human divorced from all relations to the nonhuman.[8]

Returning to the discussion of the HPV vaccine, *prior to* the research linking the HPV virus to cervical cancer, genital warts, and other cancers, and prior to the invention of the HPV vaccine, we had a more or less smoothly running collective. Parents sent their kids to school. These kids grew up and had sex. Some of them got cervical cancer or genital warts, others didn't. No one had ever heard of HPV. Doctors treated these diseases. Sometimes insurance companies covered the treatments, sometimes they didn't. Some lived, some died.

If the *question* of the ethical came to *befall* this collective composed of parents, children, doctors, diseases, and so on, then this was the result of the *surprising* appearance of *new* objects or actors within the collective: the appearance of the HPV virus, its correlation to various cancers and sexually transmitted diseases, and the HPV vaccine. One might object that the HPV virus and its link to these diseases had been there all along. This would be true. The point however is that it hadn't been *registered* or *counted* by the collective as a *member* of the collective. It is with the appearance of these new actors that the prior collective becomes beset with *uncertainty*, and enters a state of *crisis*. With the appearance of these new actors within the collective, relations among the existing members of the collective are transformed and the question emerges as to how these new actors are to be *integrated*. Here, then, the relation between women and their bodies is transformed, the question arises of whether or not the children should take the vaccine, relations between insurance companies and their clients are modified, government is faced with questions of whether or not it should mandate vaccination, fundamentalist religious groups encounter the issue of whether these vaccines conflict with established religious norms, anti-vaccination groups face the question of whether or not there will be dire unintended side-effects to these vaccines, and so on.

It is here that the *work* of ethics begins. And here the question of the *work* of ethics concerns not the application of a pre-existing rule to an existing situation, but rather how a collective is to be assembled or composed in light of the appearance of these strange new actors, these strangers, or how a *new* collective is to be formed. In this regard, rather than thinking ethics on the model of judgment, it would be more accurate to think the ethical as a sort of construction or building. The question of ethics then becomes: "given this event, how is our collective to be built?" Alternatively, it is the question of whether the new actor knocking at the door of the collective should be inducted into the collective at all. In this respect, it does not seem that wide of the mark to draw a connection between the Greek ἦθος from whence we derive the term "ethics," and οἶκος which is the root of terms such as "ecology" or "economy." ἦθος originally signified "accustomed place" (i.e., habitat), whereas οἶκος refers to home or dwelling. Whether or not an etymological connection actually exists between these two terms, what is at stake here are questions of collective composition involving humans and nonhumans, such that the ethics is essentially a question of ethical ecology or the composition of collectives in response to events that buffet collectives.

Deleuze and the Ethics of the Event

Deleuze is not ordinarily the first to come to mind when one considers continental philosophers who have made significant contributions to ethical thought. Although Deleuze has much to say in criticism of rule-based moral philosophies such as that of Kant, he appears to offer little in the way of a robust ethical philosophy of his own. To be sure, we find that he has much to say about ethics and affect in texts such as *Spinoza: Practical Philosophy* and about the production of new values in *Nietzsche and Philosophy*, yet it is difficult to see just how these ethical claims can do the work of other competing moral theories. Moreover, the explicit claims Deleuze makes about ethics and moral philosophy in *The Logic of Sense*, a work written in his own proper name rather than as a commentary on another philosopher, are so cryptic that it is difficult to determine just what to do with them. Nonetheless, despite the maddening difficulty of trying to extract a coherent ethical philosophy from Deleuze's thought, it is impossible, after reading him from start to finish, to escape the impression that some sort of ethics winds its way through his thought like a thin red line. Like Lewis Carroll's mythical Snark, Deleuze's ethical theory always appears just within grasp, only to elusively disappear a moment later.

But perhaps Deleuze's cryptic and fleeting remarks about ethics, especially as they appear in *The Logic of Sense* with respect to the ethics of the event, take on a different light when ethics is taken the other way around. In other words, where ethics is no longer concerned with the formulation of norms or principles *preceding* situations that would allow us to *judge* those situations, but rather becomes the moment of thinking uncertainty when new actors emerge within a collective, perhaps Deleuze's obscure remarks about the relationship between events and ethics takes on a new resonance, providing surprisingly valuable resources for thinking ethics. Here my aim will not be to provide a commentary on Deleuze's ethics of the event that would render clear all he has to say (a task I believe well nigh impossible given the brevity and allusiveness of his remarks), but rather to get at the sense of what Deleuze was trying to bring to light with respect to the relationship between events and ethics.

Deleuze's rejection of rule-based ethical philosophy follows directly from constraints arising from his own ontology regarding both transcendent forms and the status of the subject or of persons. In *Difference and Repetition*, Deleuze had carried out a careful critique of transcendent forms or essences, proposing instead an immanent account of the *genesis* of individuals. Summing up this trajectory of thought, Deleuze would later remark that

> I have always felt that I am an empiricist, that is, a pluralist. But what does this equivalence between empiricism and pluralism mean? It derives from the two characteristics by which Whitehead defined empiricism: the abstract does not explain, but must itself be explained; and the aim is not to rediscover

the eternal or the universal, but to find the conditions under which something new is produced (*creativeness*). (Deleuze and Parnet 1987: vii)

When Deleuze here characterizes his position as empiricist, he is not referring to *epistemological* issues pertaining to how we *know*, but rather to an *ontology* that rejects pre-existent and transcendent forms or essences and that emphasizes the pluralism of being.[9] For this reason, when it comes to issues of ethics Deleuze cannot appeal to a transcendent moral law, even one given by reason to reason as in the case of Kant, because his ontology forbids him from appealing to pre-existent forms or laws. At most, within the framework of differential ontology, abstract and formal laws are the *outcome* or *product* of genetic processes of actualization, not the *ground* of ethical deliberation. Likewise, where traditional ethics places emphasis on the autonomy and ontological priority of the agent or subject making choices, emphasizing the duties, responsibility, and obligations of this agent, Deleuze treats both subjects and objects as the result of a development or genetic process of actualization, not as something given at the outset of a process. As a consequence, Deleuze's ontology, if correct, requires significant revision as to how we think about ethics.

In *The Logic of Sense* Deleuze tells us that "ethics is concerned with the event; it consists of willing the event as such, that is, of willing that which occurs insofar as it does occur" (Deleuze 2009: 163). This prescription requires more commentary, for certainly if ethics were nothing more than willing things exactly as they happen it would be useless indeed. For the moment what is important to note is that ethics pertains to the specificity or singularity of *events*, which are, in their turn, always specific to situations and which are irreplaceable.

In this connection we should think of Deleuze's incessant return to the metaphor of throwing dice as characteristic of the conditions under which thought takes place. As Deleuze will write in one instance (though examples can be found throughout his work):

It is rather a question of a throw of the dice, of the whole sky as open space and of throwing as the only rule. The singular points are on the die; the questions are the dice themselves; the imperative is to throw. [Problems] are the . . . combinations which result from throws. The throw of the dice is in no way suggested as an abolitition of chance (the sky-chance) . . . The most difficult thing is to make chance an object of *affirmation*, but it is the sense of the imperative and the question that it launches. [Problems] emanate from it just as singularities emanate from that aleatory point which every time condenses the whole of chance into one time. (Deleuze 1994: 198)

A throw of the dice beautifully encapsulates what is at stake in the notion of an event. An event is squarely situated in the singularities that characterize a situation or that turn up in a situation. Rather than beginning with a pre-established rule or set of actors, we instead find ourselves enmeshed in the aleatory appearance of actors we never could have expected or anticipated. The question is how to respond. If there is a shortcoming to Deleuze's metaphor here it lies in the fact that reference to a dice-throw suggests someone throwing the dice, when in fact events do not issue from subjects, but rather subjects find themselves in events. The question is then how to affirm what comes up on the dice. And here we might think of the procedure of the jazz musician who doesn't begin with a set score or routine, but rather responds to the "moves" of the other musicians generating a musical event that could not have been anticipated and that had, in principle, many possible paths as it unfolded.

A bit later in *The Logic of Sense*, Deleuze goes on to clarify what he has in mind by willing the event, remarking that:

> Either ethics makes no sense at all, or this is what it means and has nothing else to say: not to be unworthy of what happens to us. To grasp whatever happens as unjust and unwarranted (it is always someone else's fault) is, on the contrary, what renders our sores repugnant – veritable *ressentiment*, resentment of the event. There is no other ill will. What is really immoral is the use of moral notions like just or unjust, merit or fault. What does it mean then to will the event? Is it to accept war, wounds, and death when they occur? It is highly probable that resignation is only one more figure of *ressentiment*, since *ressentiment* has many figures. If willing the event is, primarily, to release its eternal truth, like the fire on which it is fed, this will would reach the point at which war is waged against war, the wound would be the living trace and the scar of all wounds, and death turned on itself would be willed against all deaths. (Deleuze 2009: 169–70)

With respect to willing the event, everything hinges on determining what it means to be worthy of the event, and of determining just what Deleuze has in mind when he refers to events. Already, in the passage just cited, we see Deleuze moving to remove ethics from the domain of *judgment*, focused as it is on assigning debt and blame.[10] Yet willing the event is not a *passive acceptance* of what happens.

For this reason Deleuze will distinguish between morality on the one hand and ethics on the other. As he will write elsewhere:

> Ethics, which is to say, a typology of immanent modes of existence, replaces Morality, which always refers existence to transcendent values. Morality is

the judgment of God, the *system of Judgment*. But Ethics overthrows the system of judgment. The opposition of values (Good–Evil) is supplanted by the qualitative difference of modes of existence (good–bad). (Deleuze 1988: 23)

Where morality is concerned with judgment or assigning praise and blame, responsibility and obligation, ethics is concerned with affective relations among bodies in a composite or collective, and those assemblages that fit together in such a way so as to enhance the power of acting among the elements of the collective and those that are unable to fit together.

If we are to understand what it is to will and be worthy of the event, we must first of all determine just what Deleuze means by the event. Here, due to constraints of space, I cannot discuss all the intricacies of Deleuze's theory of the event, and so must restrict myself to the salient features of the theory relevant to the issue at hand.[11] For Deleuze, the event is a *bifurcated* structure, divided between its spatio-temporal localization in a state of affairs and an ideal structure in excess of any of the entities that embody the event. As Deleuze will put it:

> Events are ideal. Novalis sometimes says that there are two courses of events, one of them ideal, the other real and imperfect – for example, ideal Protestantism and real Lutheranism. The distinction however is not between two sorts of events; rather, it is between the event, which is ideal by nature, and its spatio-temporal realization in a state of affairs. The distinction is between *event* and *accident*. (Deleuze 2009: 64)

Events, indeed, happen to things, but they are not identical to the things to which they happen. In this connection, Deleuze will often describe events as "floating" or "hovering" above the bodies that they express: "Comparing the event to a mist rising over the prairie, we could say that this mist rises precisely at the frontier, at the juncture of things and propositions" (Deleuze 2009: 30). And later, "If the battle is not an example of an event among others, but rather the Event in its essence, it is no doubt because it is actualized in diverse manners at once, and because each participant may grasp it at a different level of actualization within its variable present" (Deleuze 2009: 116). The point here is that no matter how deeply we look into the bodies of the actors involved in the battle, we never find the battle itself. Rather, the battle is somehow everywhere in these bodies and independent of these bodies. It is what gathers these bodies together.

Here we encounter two of the most important features of Deleuze's concept of the event. First, in treating the event as something that "hovers over" the bodies that it expresses, Deleuze's ethics pertains not so much to the judgment of the actions of *individual agents,* as in traditional moral thought, but rather is something that individual actors find themselves *within,* or that *gathers* actors together in a collective. The question then is that of how to respond to this event.

Second, Deleuze will perpetually emphasize the manner in which the event is *indifferent* to determinations such as the universal and the particular.

> From the point of view of quantity, [the event] is neither particular nor general, neither universal nor personal. From the point of view of quality, it is entirely independent of both affirmation and negation. From the point of view of modality, it is neither assertoric nor apodeictic, nor even interrogative (the mode of subjective uncertainty or objective possibility). From the point of view of relation, it is not confused within the proposition which expresses it, either with denotation, or with manifestation, or with signification. Finally, from the point of view of the type, it is not confused with any of the individuations or any of the "positions" of consciousness that we could empirically determine thanks to the play of the preceding propositional traits: intuitions or positions of empirical perception, imagination, memory, understanding, volition, etc. (Deleuze 2009: 117)

The key point, then, is that insofar as the event is *indifferent* to all of these categorical determinations drawn from the transcendental analytic of Kant's *Critique of Pure Reason,* it is able to move fluidly among these determinations in drawing together actors or elements in a collective. For example, the event is *simultaneously* general *and* particular, personal *and* collective. As Deleuze will write a little later:

> The splendor of the "they" is the splendor of the event itself or of the fourth person. This is why there are no private or collective events, no more than there are individuals and universals, particularities and generalities. Everything is singular, and thus both collective and private, particular and general, neither individual nor universal. Which war, for example, is not a private affair? Conversely, which wound is not inflicted by war and derived from society as a whole? Which private event does not have all its coordinates, that is, all its impersonal social singularities? (Deleuze 2009: 173)

Like the battle that involves soldiers, horses, various weapons, the lay of the land, civilians, supply lines, generals, governments, nations, weather, trees, rivers, etc., the event is simultaneously a collective that gathers together all these actors *and* something that is intensely private, grasped from a different point of view by all involved. Events are thus something that actors in a collective find themselves *in,* not something that is *in* the actors. Or rather, events are like a Möbius strip, simultaneously issuing from these assemblages of bodies *and* organizing these assemblages of bodies.

Yet it is crucial here to recall that the event is not to be confused with its spatio-temporal actualization in states of affairs or bodies. When Deleuze speaks of a universality and eternity specific to the event, he is referring to its curious capacity to exceed and overflow all limits of the situation in which it occurs, detaching itself from the specific circumstances in which it takes place. In this connection, a connection that recalls Benjamin's recovery and revitalization of lost fragments of history, Deleuze will occasionally speak of our relation to the event as similar to that of the *mime* or the actor on stage (Deleuze 2009: 167). The mime is one who liberates the pure essence of an event from its specific spatio-temporal actualization in the world or specific circumstances, capturing the *sense* of that event independent of any context or circumstances. For example, the mime simulates trying to control one's umbrella while being buffeted by the wind in a rainstorm despite the fact that no umbrella, wind, or rainstorm is present. In short, the mime is able to *preserve* the event independent of its spatio-temporal actualization in a state of affairs.

Much later, with Guattari, Deleuze will articulate a similar thesis with respect to art, discussing the manner in which art both preserves affects and percepts, and generates percepts that are independent of a particular subject or experience (Deleuze and Guattari 1994: 163–4). If this point is so crucial for Deleuze's ethics, this is because it shows how the event itself becomes an *actor* within the collective, living beyond its spatio-temporal actualization in a state of affairs and taking on a life of its own. Not only is the event something that takes place, but it is as if being registers and records the event, such that the event becomes an actor in subsequent states of the collective. This marking or registering of the event is a necessary condition for the spatio-temporal actualization of the event. Returning to the example of the battle, the individual participants are unable to engage in battle without the battle as such being one of the actors in this situation. However, the battle itself persists after the event has ceased, as when it is subsequently evoked by actants as something that must be responded to.

In this connection, Deleuze will speak of the counter-actualization of events as a sort of release of this pure essence of the event from its spatio-temporal actualization in a state of affairs (Deleuze 2009: 172) *and* of the necessity of re-actualizing events in a state of affairs (Deleuze 2009: 166). The first moment refers to the manner in which the event is purified and transformed into an actor in its own right, while the latter movement from counter-actualization to actualization refers to the life this new actor subsequently enjoys within the collective. Thus, from actualization to counter-actualization to re-actualization what we get is an *inventiveness* proper to the event, for in counter-actualizing the event the event is transformed in the action of the "mime" and in transforming the collective in relation to the counter-actualized event the situation is transformed. Something *new* is created both in response to the event and *through* the event.

Problems and Events

Speaking of the event, Deleuze remarks that there is something about it "that implies something excessive in relation to its actualization, something that overthrows worlds, individuals, and persons, and leaves them to the depth of the ground which works and dissolves them" (Deleuze 2009: 191). Here Deleuze's ethics of the event converges with the thesis that ethics is not the application of a rule to a specific situation in order to *judge* that situation, but rather something that *erupts* within a collective, calling for its transformation. Consequently Deleuze will remark that "[t]he mode of the event is the problematic. One must not say that there are problematic events, but that events bear exclusively upon problems and define their conditions" (Deleuze 2009: 65). If we are to understand what it means to affirm or be worthy of the event, it is thus necessary for us to understand Deleuze's account of problems.

In many respects Deleuze's account of problems is the single most important feature of his ontology and is crucial to understanding his conception of ethics. Here, again, I can touch only on the salient features of Deleuze's concept of problems and problematics.[12] The first key point not to be missed is that for Deleuze, problems are not a *psychological* or *epistemological* category, but rather an *ontological* category.

> It is an error to see *problems* as indicative of a provisional and subjective state, through which knowledge must pass by virtue of its empirical limitations . . . The "problematic" is a state of the world, a dimension of the system, and even its horizon or its home: it designates precisely the objectivity of Ideas, the reality of the virtual. Problems are not in the *mind*, but rather belong to the world. (Deleuze 1994: 280)

Consequently, if there were no sentient beings, there would still be problems. While it is true that Deleuze will use the terms "problem" and "Idea" synonymously in *Difference and Repetition* ("Idea" being a term that Deleuze will, to my knowledge, never again use in this sense), his use of the term "Ideas" should be understood as closer to Plato than Locke. Here the accent is not on Ideas as *universals* or forms, but as genuine real beings that exist in their own right. For Plato the Ideas would be there regardless of whether any minds existed to grasp them. They are not psychological entities as they are for Locke. Likewise in the case of Deleuze. While problems will be closely bound up with questions of knowledge and learning, it is crucial to understand that they are real dimensions of being. And, in this respect, it is worthwhile to recall that events gather together a multiplicity of actants, such that the same can also be said of problems.

Closely related to this point, it is also important to recall that, for Deleuze, problems do not *disappear* with their solutions. "A problem does not exist, apart from its solutions. Far from disappearing in this overlay, however, it insists and persists in these solutions" (Deleuze 1994: 164). Consequently, problems aren't to be thought as a negativity or lack that disappears as soon as a solution is found; rather, problems themselves preside over the production of solutions and persist with the coming-to-be of the solution.

What, then, does Deleuze have in mind by problems? Later in *Difference and Repetition*, Deleuze remarks that "[p]roblems have an objective value, while Ideas in some sense have an object. 'Problematic' does not mean only a particularly important species of subjective acts, but a dimension of objectivity as such which is occupied by these acts" (Deleuze 1994: 169). And what is this real dimension of objectivity to which Deleuze refers? Deleuze will go on to claim that "[t]he problematic or dialectical Idea is a system of connections between differential elements, a system of differential relations between *genetic* elements" (Deleuze 1994: 181, emphasis added). Deleuze defines this *part* of the object as "[t]he reality of the virtual consist[ing] of the differential elements and relations along with the singular points which correspond to them" (Deleuze 1994: 209). The problem or problematic is not the object itself, the object in its actuality, but is rather the virtual field presiding over the *genesis* of the object. These singularities, in their turn, can be thought as *inequalities* the object resolves as it actualizes itself, determining the final form the object or state of affairs will embody. As Deleuze will claim further on, "[i]ntensity is the uncancellable in difference of quantity, but this difference of quantity is cancelled by extension, extension being precisely the process by which intensive difference is turned inside out and distributed in such a way as to be dispelled, compensated, equalized and suppressed in the extensity which it creates" (Deleuze 1994: 233). The extensity is the actualized object or state of affairs, while the differential relations among singularities and intensities are the genetic factors that preside over the actualization of this state of affairs.

All of this is rather abstract, so let's see if we can flesh it out a bit with a concrete example. One of Deleuze's favorite analogies is the comparison of the world to an egg. Drawing on this comparison, Deleuze writes:

> A living being is not only defined genetically, by the dynamisms which determine its internal milieu, but also ecologically, by the external movements which preside over its distribution within an extensity. A kinetics of population adjoins, without resembling, the kinetics of the egg; a geographic process of isolation may be no less formative of species than internal genetic variations, and sometimes precedes the latter. Everything is even more complicated when we consider that the internal space is itself made up of multiple spaces which must be locally integrated and connected, and that this connection, which may be achieved in many ways, pushes the object or living being to its own limits, all in contact with the exterior; and that this relation with the exterior, and with other things and living beings, implies in turn connections and global integrations which differ in kind from the preceding. Everywhere a staging at several levels. (Deleuze 1994: 217)

Setting aside the important role that population plays in biological speciation,[13] Deleuze is here discussing the process by which a living organism comes to be actualized and take on the form it has. Far from incarnating a predefined *form*, whether in the sense of an Aristotelian species or a genetic code, far from merely *instantiating* a universal, the organism is instead the progressive resolution of a *problem*.

Here we get a clearer sense of just what Deleuze has in mind by insisting upon the ontological status of problems and the absence of any negativity within problems. The problem posed for the organism lies in a differential field composed of internal and external milieus or ecologies and a time proper to actualization. The external milieu is composed of the relations the egg or seed entertains to other entities in its environment. The internal milieu is composed of the genetics of the seed, but also relations between all the substances in the seed and the organs in the seed. Suppose we take a grape seed. As the seed develops it must contend with its environment, vying with other plants in the region, the nutrients or lack of nutrients in the soil, rain, sunlight, insects, birds, rodents, and so on. The seed integrates these elements as it develops. Moreover, as the seed develops into a grapevine, it is simultaneously undergoing internal cell division. The rates at which different substances in the plant reach one another, at which they divide, and so on, play a crucial role in what the final product will be. The problematic just is this field, while the process of actualization is the integration of the field. And here it is above all important to note that no two grapevines are identical and that a single grapevine never produces fruit with the same qualities from year to year. It is for this reason that the year of a wine label is every bit as important as the producer, for each year the grapes from which the wine is produced are *new*. In short, in the process of actualization being is *inventive*.

We now have a better sense of just how events are problematics and of what it might mean to will or affirm the event. When Deleuze speaks of events overthrowing worlds, individuals, and persons, when he speaks of the ground literally dissolving us, the point is that we find ourselves thrown into a problematic field, a genetic field, that calls for new actualizations and developments – not only of ourselves, as in the case of learning, but also of our relations to other entities in the world around us. Being worthy of the event and willing the event consist in affirming this labor or work of actualization, this inventiveness proper to the ethical, and undertaking this genesis that the event calls for.

On the Evaluation of Problems

Nonetheless, there is a significant difficulty in drawing an analogy between the manner in which a plant organizes itself in its response to a problematic field and the way in which we respond to ethical problems. The plant actualizes itself of its own accord and with a certain degree of inevitability, regardless of whether or not the outcome is *positive*, despite the inventiveness and novelty of this process in each instance. For example, if there is little rain in a season or the summer months are exceedingly cold, the basil will be sickly. Clearly this will not do as an analogy when thinking about problems of an ethical and political nature, for the whole point here lies in determining what to *do*, and there is no doing here, only execution. It is also true that when discussing problems of a social and political nature, Deleuze is deeply ambiguous on this point.

The source of the difficulty can be found in a central claim that haunts Deleuze's account of the relationship between problems and solutions. Sometimes Deleuze will say that "[w]e always have as much truth as we deserve in accordance with the sense of what we say" (Deleuze 1994: 154). At other times he will remark that "the solution necessarily follows from the complete conditions under which the problem is determined as a problem" or that "[a] solution always has the truth it deserves according to the problem to which it is a response, and the problem always has the solution it deserves in proportion to *its own* truth or falsity" (Deleuze 1994: 159). Deleuze's thesis is that solutions come into being of their own accord with the tracing of a problem. The developed basil just *is* the solution to the problematic field posed by its own internal and external ecology.

Yet if this is the case, then disturbing consequences follow for political and ethical ecology, for given that subjects are actualizations of problematic fields, given that they are *solutions* to problematic fields, it seems that we are stuck with whatever solutions might come to be, regardless of how ugly, cruel, or terrifying they are. As Deleuze will write with reference to Marx:

> The famous phrase of the *Contribution to the Critique of Political Economy*, "mankind always sets itself only such tasks as it can solve", does not mean that the problems are only apparent or that they are already solved, but, on the contrary, that the economic conditions of a problem determine or give rise to the manner in which it finds a solution within the framework of the real relations of society. Not that the observer can draw the least optimism from this, for these "solutions" may involve stupidity or cruelty, the horror of war or "the solution of the Jewish problem". More precisely, the solution is always that which a society deserves or gives rise to as a consequence of the manner in which, given its real relations, it is able to pose the problems set within it and to it by means of the differential relations it incarnates. (Deleuze 1994: 186)

Is Deleuze condemning us to simply endure, like the basil plant, whatever "solutions" happen to actualize themselves within our lives and the social field as a function of the problems or events within which we find ourselves enmeshed? Certainly a reading that emphasized Deleuze's stoicism in a particular way would suggest this; however, as we've already seen, Deleuze sees passive resignation as one more figure of resentment.

A key point not to be missed in this passage is Deleuze's reference to the *posing* of problems. While it is indeed true that we get the solutions we deserve based on the problems we have posed for ourselves, Deleuze nonetheless retains some freedom in the posing of problems. In this connection, he argues that the test of the true and the false (and likewise of the right and the wrong) should be applied to *problems* themselves, not solutions. As Deleuze will say, "[f]ar from being concerned with solutions, truth and falsehood primarily affect problems" (Deleuze 1994: 159). It is here, finally, that we come to understand what Deleuze is proposing when he speaks of affirming the event or being equal to the event. To be worthy of the event, to affirm the event, to be equal to the event, is to engage in the work of tracing the true problems. This consists in tracing the differential relations, intensities, and singularities that haunt a collective in a moment of perplexity proper to a situation and assisting in the birth of new solutions. The evaluation of true and false problems will be the ethical work that, in Deleuze, replaces the logic of judgment in our decision-making process.

Closely connected to this labor of posing problems there will also be the diagnosis of *false* problems. On the one hand, there will be those instances where problems are posed that fail to properly distinguish between ordinary and singular points. As Deleuze writes:

> Teachers already know that errors or falsehoods are rarely found in home-work (except in those exercises where a fixed result must be produced, or propositions must be translated one by one). Rather, what is more frequently found – and worse –are nonsensical sentences, remarks without interest or importance, banalities mistaken for profundities, ordinary "points" confused with singular points, badly posed or distorted problems – all heavy with dangers, yet the fate of us all. (Deleuze 1994: 159)

If there is an ethical duty in Deleuze it lies in a pedagogy of problems, in an exploration of milieus to discover their singularities, their significant points, their ecological factors so as to progressively trace solutions or actualizations in the formation of new forms of thought, ways of life, and new collectives. Rather than judging *acts*, the question will be one of exploring the generative field in which acts are produced. And this is a painstaking and laborious task that requires constant engagement with the milieu. It is a question of *learning*. In this connection Deleuze's favorite example is learning how to swim. One learns how to swim by conjugating the singularities of one's body with the singularities of the water. Yet this conjugation is not something that happens automatically, but is an exploration that progressively unfolds, generating body-water solutions that can be grotesque or beautiful.

The diagnosis of false problems, however, does not simply consist in learning to distinguish significant points from ordinary points. There are also problems that haunt thought and action, generating terrifying solutions. As Deleuze remarks:

> There are few who did not feel the need to enrich the concept of error by means of determinations of a quite different kind. (To cite some exam-ples: the notion of superstition as this is elaborated by Lucretius, Spinoza, and the eighteenth-century *philosophes*, in particular Fontanelle. It is clear that the "absurdity" of a superstition cannot be reduced to its kernel of error. Similarly, Plato's ignorance or forgetting are distinguished from

error as much as from innateness and reminiscence itself. The Stoic notion of *stultitia* involves at once both madness and stupidity. The Kantian idea of inner illusion, internal to reason, is radically different from the extrinsic mechanism of error. The Hegelian idea of alienation supposes a profound restructuring of the true–false relation. The Schopenhauerian notions of vulgarity and stupidity imply a complete reversal of the will–understanding relation.) (Deleuze 1994: 150)

And a little further on Deleuze will say that "[c]owardice, cruelty, baseness and stupidity are not simply corporeal capacities or traits of character or society; they are structures of thought as such" (Deleuze 1994: 151). In all of these instances what we have are structures of thought that pose false problems or prevent us from the work of tracing problems. The ethical is both the tracing of problems and the inventiveness that it engenders and that form of philosophical therapy – recall that the term "clinical" figures heavily in the title of one of Deleuze's books – which diagnoses and frees us from false problems.

References

Bennett, J. (2010), *Vibrant Matter: A Political Ecology of Things*, Durham: Duke University Press.

Bryant, L. R. (2008), *Difference and Givenness: Deleuze's Transcendental Empiricism and the Ontology of Immanence*, Evanston: Northwestern University Press.

DeLanda, M. (2002), *Intensive Science and Virtual Philosophy*, New York: Continuum.

Deleuze, G. (1988), *Spinoza: Practical Philosophy*, trans. R. Hurley, San Francisco: City Lights Books.

Deleuze, G. (1994), *Difference and Repetition*, trans. P. Patton, New York: Columbia University Press.

Deleuze, G. (1997), "To Have Done with Judgment," in G. Deleuze, *Essays Critical and Clinical*, trans. D. W. Smith and M. A. Greco, Minneapolis: University of Minnesota Press, 126–35.

Deleuze, G. (2009), *The Logic of Sense*, trans. M. Lester and C. Stivale, ed. C. Boundas, New York: Continuum.

Deleuze, G. and C. Parnet (1987), *Dialogues*, trans. H. Tomlinson and B. Habberjam, New York: Columbia University Press.

Deleuze, G. and F. Guattari (1994), *What is Philosophy?*, trans. H. Tomlinson and G. Burchell, New York: Columbia University Press.

Harman, G. (2009), *Prince of Networks: Bruno Latour and Metaphysics*, Melbourne: Re-Press.

Hughes, J. (2008), *Deleuze and the Genesis of Representation*, New York: Continuum.

Kant, I. (1996), *Practical Philosophy*, trans. M. J. Gregor, Cambridge: Cambridge University Press.

Latour, B. (1993), *We Have Never Been Modern*, Cambridge, MA: Harvard University Press.

Latour, B. (2005), *Reassembling the Social: An Introduction to Actor-Network-Theory*, Oxford: Oxford University Press.

Malabou, C. (2008), *What Should We Do With Our Brains?*, trans. S. Rand, New York: Fordham University Press.

Mill, J. S. (2001), *Utilitarianism*, Indianapolis: Hackett Publishing Company.

Protevi, J. (2009), *Political Affect*, Minneapolis: University of Minnesota Press.

Williams, J. (2009), *Gilles Deleuze's Logic of Sense: A Critical Introduction and Guide*, Edinburgh: Edinburgh University Press.

Notes

1. Centers for Disease Control and Prevention, http://www.cdc.GovStd/hpv/STDFact-HPV-vaccine-young-women.htm#why
2. Brendan Coyne, "Cervical Cancer Vaccine Raises 'Promiscuity' Controversy," *New Standard*, November 2nd, 2005, http://newstandardnews.net/Content/index.cfm/ items/2552
3. Sandra G. Boodman, "Who Gets Stuck? Doctors, Patients Want Insurers to Pay More for Vaccine," *Washington Post*, May 1st, 2007, http://cancer.about.com/ gi/o.htm?zi=1/XJ&zTi=1&sdn=cancer&cdn=health&tm=8&f=10&su=p284.9.336.ip_p736.8.336.ip_&tt=2&bt=0&bts=1&zu=http%3A//www.washingtonpost.com/wp-dyn/content/article/2007/ 04/27/AR2007042702631.html
4. Liz Austin Peterson, "Perry's Staff Discussed Vaccine on Day Merck Contributed to Campaign," *Associated Press*, February 22nd, 2007, http://www.statesman.com/ news/content/ region/legislature/stories/02/22/22perry.html
5. For the intriguing implications of neural plasticity cf. Malabou 2008. For the developmental plasticity of affect, cf. Protevi 2009.
6. On this point, cf. especially sections 2.2–2.5 in Latour 1993.
7. For an excellent discussion of Latour's object-oriented ontology, cf. Harman 2009.
8. For an excellent discussion of the need to treat nonhuman actors as full-fledged actors in ethical and political thought, cf. Bennett 2010.
9. For a discussion of Deleuze's ontological empiricism cf. Chapter 1 of Bryant 2008. For an excellent discussion of the genesis of individuals within the framework of Deleuze's ontology, cf. DeLanda 2002.
10. Towards the end of his life Deleuze will call for having done with judgment. Cf. "To Have Done with Judgment" in Deleuze 1997: 126–35.
11. For two excellent discussions of Deleuze's theory of the event, as developed in *The Logic of Sense*, cf. Chapter 2 of Hughes 2008, and Williams 2009.
12. For a detailed discussion of Deleuze's account of problems, cf. Chapters 6 and 8 of Bryant 2008.
13. For an excellent discussion of population thinking in Deleuze, cf. Chapter 2 of DeLanda 2002.

Chapter 3

While Remaining on the Shore: Ethics in Deleuze's Encounter with Antonin Artaud

Laura Cull

This chapter seeks to address the question of ethics in Deleuze and Guattari's thought by way of an analysis of their engagement with Antonin Artaud.[1] Deleuze and Guattari "use" Artaud in a variety of different ways: as an exemplary artist credited with discovering the "body without organs" (BwO); as both pioneer and model of a "thought without image"; and as a figure operating on the plane of immanence who refuses the transcendent judgment of God over the earth. But above all, perhaps, Deleuze and Guattari employ Artaud's writing in order to argue that "schizophrenia is not only a human fact but also a possibility for thought" (Deleuze 1994: 148). Intensive, schizophrenic experience has philosophical implications that must be brought to bear on how we conceive thought, language, and the encounter with difference, they argue. And it is here, in part, that ethical issues arise and indeed are raised by Deleuze and Guattari themselves. Is the academic use of Artaud opportunistic in the same way as was Lewis Carroll's use of nonsense, as Artaud himself once claimed? Do Deleuze and Guattari exploit Artaud's suffering by co-opting the concepts that arguably emerged from it – such as "cruelty" and the BwO – given that they did not undergo such suffering themselves? Is it unethical, as Artaud's friend Paule Thevenin once claimed, to brand Artaud "schizophrenic" in the first place? Or, finally and more broadly, to what extent does Deleuze and Guattari's affirmation of immanence and tempered advocacy of risk and experiment – where failure, including dangerous failure, is always an option – help us to practice an ethical but also sustainable relation to "madness"?

This chapter will explore these different ethical dimensions of the encounter between Deleuze and Guattari and Artaud. It is divided into two parts. The first undertakes the necessary exposition of the basic ideas generated through Deleuze's engagement with Artaud, in particular the ethics of immanence found in his theatrical work. The second half operates at a meta-theoretical level by looking at the ethics of this engagement and questioning the efficacy and value of a philosophy *of* the schizophrenic (as opposed to a schizophrenic philosophy). In the first part, I provide a brief outline of "To Have Done with Judgment" – Deleuze's late essay on Artaud, in which he critiques transcendent judgment for suppressing the production of novelty. In this text – as in Artaud's censored 1947 radio play *To have done with the judgment of god*, from which Deleuze's essay borrows much of its vocabulary – "God" is the enemy of an ethics of creation – whether He takes the form of the imposition of bodily organization, the invocation of a transcendent realm to be infinitely awaited, or the measure of plenitude in relation to which life's differential presence will always be found wanting. Here, I also argue that Deleuze's essay is of note insofar as it locates the theater as a key venue for ethical thought. In the following section, I move on to a consideration of the BwO as an exemplary ethical figure given Deleuze's definition of ethics as a typology of immanent modes of existence. We see how Artaud discovered, but then went on to actively perform the BwO and, in particular, its destratified voice, which howls and cries against the morality of articulation. The second part of the chapter then considers the ethics of Deleuze's treatment of Artaud as part of a broader consideration of the ethics of academia in relation to mental health, extreme experience and suffering. As Susan Sontag has proposed, there are few other writers who have provided "as tireless and detailed a record of the microstructure of mental pain" as Artaud (Sontag 1976: xxi). It is this record that exposes the complexity of Artaud's relationship to his "own" suffering as both the profound revelation and the torturous effect of the immanence of mind and matter, the simultaneously essential and alienating experience that authenticates but also eludes his thought and writing. The causes of this suffering are similarly resistant to identification given Artaud's deliberate organization of encounters with peyote (as well as opium) in addition to his subjection to electro-shock therapy at the hands of the French psychiatric profession.

Shoreline Reflections

What is the ethical (rather than exploitative or condescending or romanticizing) way for "abstract speakers" like Deleuze – and indeed, all Artaud scholars – to relate to those who belong to suffering minorities? We are concerned here, in part, with the question of whether there is a "microethics" of mental health to be extracted from Deleuze's thought with respect to his engagement with Artaud. In *The Logic of Sense*, for instance, Deleuze discusses Fitzgerald's alcoholism alongside Artaud's madness and questions the "ridiculousness" of the academic who positions herself outside of these dangerous experiments:

> Each one risked something and went as far as possible in taking this risk; each one drew from it an irrepressible right. What is left for the abstract speaker once she has given advice of wisdom and distinction? Well then, are we to speak always about . . . Fitzgerald and Lowry's alcoholism, Nietzsche and Artaud's madness, while remaining on the shore? Are we to become the professionals who give talks on these topics? (Deleuze 1990: 157)

Likewise, in *A Thousand Plateaus*, Deleuze and Guattari ask: "Is it cowardice or exploitation to wait until others have taken the risks," to wait until others – whether they are drug users, artists or schizophrenics (or all three, like Artaud) – have reached the plane of immanence, before constructing one's own experiment (Deleuze and Guattari 1988: 286)? By this stage of his writing, though, Deleuze (with Guattari) feels more confident to answer "no" to his own question and, in addition, to affirm the possibility of getting drunk just on water – emphasizing process over content, the line of flight over any one model. Thanks to the starting points mapped out by Artaud, we too can join in the undertaking to construct a plane of immanence "in the middle."

As such, Deleuze's work involves a changing attitude towards writing a philosophy built from experiences of extreme intensity, or what Deleuze calls "pure lived experience" (Deleuze 2004: 238). The question remains, however (at least for us), whether we also owe it to such trailblazers not to repeat the mistakes involved in their chosen means. Might there be less dangerous, but no less effective ways of becoming-mad or making oneself a philosopher without organs as alternative, immanent methods of academic research in contrast to the opportunistic, transcendent implications of "remaining on the shore"? The aim here is not to "judge" Deleuze by measuring his academic conduct in relation to some general principles of academic ethics – the very transcendent, predetermined nature of which his own conception of ethics rejects. Rather, I want to consider how Deleuze's "ethological ethics" (Ansell-Pearson 1999: 11) might pertain to academia itself, particularly in the encounter with "Artaud" – not as a scholarly object, but as a performative body which challenges us to explore the unknown aspects of our own powers of thinking and acting, potentially disorganizing the identities of philosopher and theater practitioner alike. Given Deleuze's own equation of ethics and immanence, how might we think in connection *with* Artaud rather than merely speaking *about* his madness?

To Have Done With Judgment: The System of Cruelty and Theater as a Site of Ethical Thinking

A short excursus on Deleuze's 1993 essay "To Have Done with Judgment" is necessary here, both for its value in providing a rare extended discussion of Artaud, as well as for being a key text in the articulation of Deleuze's ethics of creativity. The focus of Deleuze's essay is the concept of judgment, from which we must desist – above all – because judgment brings only pre-existing criteria to bear upon that with which it is concerned and, as such, oppresses creativity and the production of the new. Judgment, Deleuze argues, can "neither apprehend what is new in an existing being, nor even sense the creation of a mode of existence . . . Judgment prevents the emergence of any new mode of existence" (Deleuze 1998: 135). As Philip Goodchild notes, "an ethics that lacks judgment would *appear* to mark the death of ethics" (Goodchild 1996: 206, emphasis added). However, as Goodchild goes on to say, what Deleuze wants to do away with are *moralizing* codes of conduct in favor of an *ethics* able to affirm the experimental nature of real encounters between particular bodies. In this sense, judgment participates in what Deleuze, in his work on Spinoza, calls "Morality" as distinct from "Ethics." Whereas the former "always refers existence to transcendent values," the latter constitutes "a typology of immanent modes of existence" (Deleuze 1988: 23), including, as we will see, the BwO.

Moreover, alongside Nietzsche, D. H. Lawrence and Kafka – each of whom had also "personally, singularly suffered from judgment"[2] – Artaud is credited by Deleuze as having developed a "system of cruelty" as a new basis for ethics against this "doctrine of judgment" (Deleuze 1998: 126). Indeed, Deleuze's essay strongly resonates with Nietzsche's *On the Genealogy of Morals* (1887), which diagnoses contemporary culture as suffering from the dominion of a "slave morality" initiated and sustained by priests and philosophers whose belief in a transcendental realm leads them to promote asceticism and the negation of life. Likewise, for Deleuze and for Artaud, judgment involves any use of transcendent principles to measure the value of life, whether in the context of religion or elsewhere. For instance, we will find echoes of Nietzsche's hatred of society's agents of transcendent values (albeit a hatred tinged with admiration) in Artaud's argument that "Existence itself is one idea too many and little by little, softly and brutally, philosophers, savants, doctors and priests are making this life false for us. Really, things are without profundity, *there is no beyond or hereafter* and no other abyss than this one into which one is put" (Artaud, cited in Dale 2001: 127, emphasis added). But "To Have Done with Judgment" is also notable for the attention it pays to the theater as a site of ethical thinking. In fact, Deleuze opens the essay by linking the ethical impact of "Greek tragedy and modern philosophy," arguing that we can see the doctrine of judgment at work in the tragedies of Sophocles. For Deleuze, this doctrine seems to involve the prescription of destiny, insofar as he argues that "a doctrine of judgment presumes that the gods give *lots* to men, and then men, depending on their lots, are fit for some particular *form*, for some particular organic *end*" (Deleuze 1998: 128).[3] With the arrival of Christianity, or what Deleuze calls "the second movement of the doctrine of judgment," we no longer act out our debt to the gods by conforming to the forms or ends we are assigned; rather, we "have become in our entire being the infinite debtors of a single God" (Deleuze 1998: 129). In turn, theater demonstrates this system at work in modern tragedies such as *Don Juan*.

In contrast to the doctrine of judgment, Deleuze claims, one can hear the echoes of the system of cruelty in the tragedies of the Greek playwright, Aeschylus – and by implication, in Artaud's "theater without organs." Yet, whereas for Deleuze theater seems to perform its ethical work via characters and plot, for Artaud theater opposes judgment by allowing cruelty to penetrate its every aspect, particularly the nature of its relationship to its audience. According to Artaud, "cruelty" – by which he meant a force "closely related to destruction, without which nothing can be created" – was *the* ontological principle "fundamental to all reality" (Artaud in Schumacher 1989: 73). As such, it was by embracing cruelty that theater could reconnect with the ontological realm. Making yourself a theater of cruelty, then, is not about "wielding a butcher's knife on stage at every possible opportunity" in order to represent cruelty, Artaud explained; rather, it means creating "a real transformation" in your audience by acting "deeply and directly" on their sensibilities (Artaud in Schumacher 1989: 96, 67, 103). For Artaud, we might argue, theater enacts the ethics of the system of cruelty insofar as it is "unafraid of exploring the limits of our nervous sensibility," when it questions what the body of the audience can do (Artaud in Schumacher 1989: 110).

The BwO and the Ethics of Disorganization

Before returning to this notion of an ethical theater, I want to look at the other key concept that Deleuze takes from Artaud: the BwO – the paradigm case of "the good life" as immanent experimentation. The image of a "body without organs" first appears in the conclusion of Artaud's censored 1947 radio play *To have done with the judgment of god*, in which, like Spinoza and Nietzsche before him, Artaud suggests that our mode of construction or existence determines what we are able to think and do. We must remake the sickly anatomy of Man the organism, including the organ of the mind, if we want to think and act alongside and within life, rather than continuing to operate as the living dead, performing "automatic reactions" scripted by god and, now, by his medical colleagues (Artaud in Sontag 1976: 571).[4]

In turn, it is via the BwO that Deleuze is able to emphasize the extent to which judgment is an oppressive and stultifying force operating "at the level of the body" or matter, as much as at the level of the social – via Church, State and sometimes, as we've seen, theater (Deleuze 1998: 130). Already in *A Thousand Plateaus*, Deleuze and Guattari had argued that the judgment of God "is precisely the operation of He who makes ... an organization of the organs called the organism, because He cannot bear the BwO ... The organism is already that, the judgment of God, from which medical doctors benefit and on which they base their power" (Deleuze and Guattari 1988: 159). Alluding again here to the complicity of the medical profession with the doctrine of judgment, Deleuze and Guattari suggest that the judgment of God is all the strata, or phenomena of stratification, that operate on the intense matter of the BwO *put together*: "For many a strata, and not only an organism, is necessary to make the judgment of God" (Deleuze and Guattari 1988: 159). "To Have Done with Judgment" then elaborates upon this idea of judgment as "a veritable organization of the bodies through which it acts: organs are both judges and judged, and the judgment of God is nothing other than the power to organize to infinity ... The way to escape judgment is to make yourself a body without organs, to find your body without organs" (Deleuze 1998: 131). And this is exactly what Artaud does; in the broadcast itself, particularly focusing on disorganizing the voice and its use of language in a manner which we might now come to see as an ethical act. This emphasis on the linguistic manifestation of the BwO is also notable in *The Logic of Sense* (1969), in which the concept of the BwO first appears in Deleuze's work. Here, Deleuze proposes that the BwO corresponds to Artaud's triumphant composition of a novel usage of language. As a "new dimension of the schizophrenic body," Deleuze argues that the BwO does not achieve self-identical expression with its cries, but rather feels the problem of language through its suffering; "namely, the schizophrenic problem of suffering, of death, and of life" (Deleuze 2004: 101). Deleuze suggests that the specifically schizophrenic experience of an absence of distinction between "things" and "propositions" draws attention to an ontological capacity of language to *act on* bodies rather than merely represent them (Deleuze 2004: 100). For the schizophrenic, language is not a separate kind or level of being that transcends bodies. In his discovery of the BwO as, in part, a relation to language, Artaud breaks free from passively suffering the wounds that "words without sense" inflict upon the schizophrenic body. Having made himself a BwO, the schizophrenic is not sheltered from language but actively uses it as "words without articulation," as words that become "illegible and even unpronounceable, as it transforms them into so many active howls in one continuous breath" (Deleuze 2004: 102).

At first, this may seem to be no more than a simple redirection of the force of language, shifting from occupying the position of one to whom things are done with words, to the one who uses language to act. But for Artaud, this is a relation that must be performed and enacted, just as he did, firstly through writing and poetry, and then latterly in performed lectures and his foray into radio, which constitutes a prime example of this new use of language. And here we arrive at Artaud's ür-text for the BwO. Recorded a year after Artaud finally returned to Paris having been in psychiatric institutions for the previous nine years, *To have done with the judgment of god* was never publicly broadcast before his death in 1948 (at least not in the way that Artaud had hoped; see Schumacher 1989: 188).[5] Wladimir Porché, the director general of the radio station who functioned as the God-form on this occasion, judged Artaud's text to be "studded with violent words" and "terrible language" that were certain to scandalize the French public; the broadcast was duly cancelled at the last minute, much to Artaud's frustration (Artaud in Sontag 1976: 579).

With such aborted projects in mind, it has become commonplace to argue that Artaud failed to achieve in practice what he set out to do in theory. In contrast, one could argue that *To have done with the judgment of god* exemplifies a "theater without organs" which performs its ethical work in its construction of a "destratified voice."[6] In the case of the voice, destratification involves putting elements like intonation, diction, pitch, and meaning into variation. For example, in *Anti-Oedipus*, Deleuze and Guattari argue that the BwO resists the "torture" of organization partly by way of a particular relation to the phonological aspect of language: "In order to resist using words composed of articulated phonetic units, it utters only gasps and cries that are sheer unarticulated blocks of sound" (Deleuze and Guattari 1984: 9). In this respect, the phoneme is like an "organ" of language that the destratified voice would rather be without. But aside from such explanatory accounts by philosophers, we might see Artaud's vocal performance as a kind of philosophy in itself. Indeed, we know that for Artaud, the world is not merely "like" theater and performance – as in the case of the old *theatrum mundi* metaphor; rather, theater actually performs metaphysics or ontology. Artaud insisted that theater can put us in contact with "metaphysics in action"; that it "reconciles us with Becoming; or, in one of his last letters, that "Theater is in reality the *genesis* of creation: It will come about" (Artaud in Schumacher 1989: 77, 113, 200). In turn, one could consider Artaud's chanting, glossolalia, and speaking in tongues *as* thinking, albeit in a different way from what is traditionally recognized as philosophical activity.

Artaud as Example: Exploitation and Responsibility in Deleuze's Affirmation of Immanence

I want to move on to consider more directly the ethics of philosophical practice and the relationship between extreme experience and what such experience, seemingly, makes it possible to think. To begin with, a cynical characterization of experimenting with extremes would see philosophy function as the opportunistic outside, watching the activities of artists and "madmen" from the sidelines, and gathering up the debris of their experiments which, it is claimed, must be explained by others in order for their full value to be appreciated. From this perspective, Artaud, being too caught up in the experience of suffering itself, needs Deleuze to step in and explain what he really meant by judgment and the BwO. Deleuze's own figuration of the "abstract speaker" still haunts. The question that arises in contrast to this position, therefore, is whether there might be another, less exploitative way to relate to Artaud's madness than to give talks about it as a topic. For his own part, Artaud tried to turn his own lectures – such as the one he delivered at the Sorbonne in 1933 – into performances, though not without resistance. According to Anaïs Nin's diaries, the audience greeted Artaud's Sorbonne lecture with laughter and many of them walked out. After the lecture, Artaud complained to Nin about the audience's attitude: "They always want to hear *about*; they want to hear an objective conference on 'The Theater and the Plague,' and I want to give them the experience itself, so they will be terrified, and awaken" (Artaud in Schumacher 1989: 118). So, we ask, can theater (and madness) terrify and awaken philosophy with its experiences, or is the role of philosophy always to lecture theater (and madness) on what it means but cannot say?

In *What is Philosophy?*, Deleuze and Guattari attempt to bridge the gap between Artaud's "madness" and their own experience, chiming in with the observation that there is nothing "more distressing than a thought that escapes itself, than ideas that fly off, that disappear hardly formed, already eroded by forgetfulness or precipitated into others that we no longer master" (Deleuze and Guattari 1994: 201). Goodchild has already questioned the elevation to an absolute of the relatively "mundane" nature of the philosophers' experience of suffering. Could Deleuze have developed the concept of the "thought without image," without Artaud, without Nietzsche, without the "lessons" of madness, which, we might argue, Deleuze himself experienced in a thoroughly diluted form? We know that Artaud's ideas, unlike Deleuze's, emerged in the context of profound suffering: the trauma of his experience of schizophrenia and its inexact treatment by means of electro-shock therapy (amongst other things).[7] In turn, this distinction is thematized in Artaud's critique of the artificiality of Carroll's *Jabberwocky*, a poem whose style echoed but did not truly emerge from the experience of bodily suffering to which Artaud assigns an authenticating value. Indeed, Artaud goes as far as to contend that "'Jabberwocky' is the work of an opportunist who wanted to feed intellectually on someone else's pain" (Artaud in Sontag 1976: 449). Just as Artaud rejects the instrumentalization of theater for political (rather than metaphysical) ends elsewhere, he also criticizes the outside observers' appropriation of experiences of suffering for intellectual purposes.

As such, might we not level a similar critique of opportunism at Deleuze? In the first instance, as Gregg Lambert (among others) has discussed, moral objections have already been raised, particularly as regards *Anti-Oedipus*, to Deleuze and Guattari's use of the term "schizophrenia," which many critics saw as "romanticizing the real suffering of the clinical schizophrenic and using it for a purely cultural vehicle of free-wheeling expression" (Lambert 2006: 3). Lambert goes on to argue that where these kinds of critical interpretations go wrong is not in the objections themselves (which he acknowledges are often "right on the money"), but in the way that interpretation per se mistakes the nature of Deleuze and Guattari's project. *Anti-Oedipus* is not a book, Lambert reminds us: it is one response amongst others to flows of desire not currently being channelled by dominant discourse. And within the field of Artaud Studies this certainly remains the case: we read *The Logic of Sense* and *Capitalism and Schizophrenia* because they address our desire to escape the deadening, deconstructive accounts of the "impossibility" of the Theater of Cruelty or the frustrating reductions of Artaud to Gnosticism. Works such as *Difference and Repetition* also open a window within Artaud Studies insofar as they break with the dominant tendency to view Artaud's symptoms in terms of lack and to pity his suffering.

Alternatively, Deleuze could be seen to repay Artaud through a reading that rehabilitates him, not only from Jacques Rivière's famous misunderstandings (in the correspondence between Artaud and Rivière, the editor of the *Nouvelle Revue Française* to whom Artaud submitted his poetry in 1923), but, arguably, from Artaud's misunderstandings of himself (at least from a Deleuzian perspective). That is, for all that Deleuze assigns to Artaud the triumph of having discovered both the body without organs and a correlative thought without image, there are clear examples within Artaud's writing of an aspiration to a self-identical presence of thought, and demonstrations of an unwillingness to embrace the foreignness of language. In turn, Deleuze suggests that what Artaud experiences as a powerlessness or impotence in relation to the articulation of thought, *is* the very power of thought. Artaud ought not to have been asking Rivière for forgiveness for failing to express himself clearly. Rather, Deleuze implies, Rivière ought to have asked Artaud to forgive him for failing to encourage Artaud to embrace the creative and metaphysical value of this experience of the impossibility of expression.

That said, it is important to contextualize Deleuze and Guattari's arguably romantic characterization of artistic "madness" with reference to scholarship in other fields, such as Graham Ley and Jane Milling's work in Theater Studies. Ley and Milling note, for instance, the extent to which "madness" is given a "positive charge" and corresponds to the "possibility of vision or revelation" in the writings of Rimbaud, particularly in an 1871 manifesto (composed in letter form) "in which he claims that the 'I' of the poet must be a 'visionary,' a 'seer,' and a voyant: 'I say one must be a visionary, make oneself a "visionary".'" To do so, Rimbaud insists, the poet must practice

> a long, gigantic and rational *derangement* of *all the senses*. All forms of love, of suffering, of madness . . . he searches himself, he exhausts in himself all the poisons, to keep only the quintessences. Unspeakable torture in which he needs all his faith, all his superhuman strength, in which he becomes . . . the great accursed – and the supreme man of learning! – Because he reaches the *unknown*! (Rimbaud in Ley and Milling 2001: 91)

Indeed, as Ley and Milling relate, this association of the "mad" with the visionary has a long cultural history from Erasmus' *Praise of Folly* to the 1960's endorsement of drug-induced euphoria or hallucination as insight (Ley and Milling 2001: 90). Correlatively, we might note that Artaud himself indulged in a comparable romanticization of Van Gogh, describing him as "one of those natures whose superior lucidity enables them in all circumstances to see farther, infinitely and *dangerously farther*, than the immediate and apparent reality of facts. I mean that he saw farther in his consciousness than consciousness usually contains" (Artaud in Sontag 1976: 494, emphasis added).

But even if we appreciate the fresh air that Deleuze and Guattari's text releases into Artaud Studies, there are still questions concerning how we might evaluate Artaud's achievements as an artist, vis-à-vis Deleuze's own contention that what Artaud achieved was a "wonderful breakthrough" that was, ultimately, "worth" all his suffering. How do we reconcile this validation of suffering with Deleuze's argument in *Spinoza: Practical Philosophy* that "only joy is worthwhile . . . The sad passions always amount to impotence" (Deleuze 1988: 28)? This is a complex question, not least because we might suggest that it is not suffering itself that counts as a sad passion, only a particular set of responses to suffering, including "sadness itself . . . fear, despair . . . anger, vengeance" (Deleuze 1988: 26). Artaud's suffering was worthwhile, then, not in his hours of despair, but in his moments of triumph: in his discovery of the BwO and the language of howl-words and breath-words that emerges from it; a discovery that Deleuze (at times) implies was not only worth the suffering Artaud's experiments entailed, but *could only* be discovered through that suffering – recalling the determining relation between our thought and our mode of existence we have already noted with respect to the BwO. It is precisely because Lewis Carroll did not suffer the problem of language as Artaud did that Deleuze rejects his creation of portmanteau words as superficial plays with nonsense, rather than authentic cries from the depths in which the distinction between words and things has been thoroughly dissolved. Deleuze concludes the thirteenth series of *The Logic of Sense* with the claim that he "would not give a page of Artaud for all of Carroll" and argues that "Artaud is alone in having been an absolute depth in literature, and in having discovered *the vital body and the prodigious language of this body*" (Deleuze 2004: 105).

Add this affirmation of the aesthetic value of suffering to Deleuze and Guattari's preference for Van Gogh, Fitzgerald, Pollock over "happier" artists and it is hard not to begin to sympathize with those who criticize the philosophers for their perpetuation of a romantic stereotype of the struggling, tortured artist. In contrast, Umberto Artioli questions Deleuze's description of Artaud as having achieved a "wonderful breakthrough" and suggests instead that "Artaud's revolt, far from attaining the miracle of the breakthrough, resonates with the devastating cry of setback" (Artioli in Scheer 2004: 147). Likewise, despite the occasional caveats of *A Thousand Plateaus*, we might argue that extreme experiences (including ones of suffering) hold an unnecessarily privileged place in Deleuze and Guattari's account of living immanently, and therefore, ethically. What about the more seemingly banal encounters with difference such as the experience of waiting for sugar to dissolve that we find in Bergson (Bergson 1911: 10)?

A further matter that arises here is the question of Artaud's relation to the categories of intention and necessity, of artistic practice and the practice of mental health patients. With his concepts of *intonation*, *vibration*, and *incantation* (to which we will return below), Artaud seems to be *actively* pursuing a new usage of language in performance; contrary, perhaps, to Deleuze's emphasis on the *passively* schizophrenic origins of his approach (with regards to authorial intent). Indeed, *The Logic of Sense* caused something of a controversy when it was published, insofar as Deleuze was seen by some to be annexing "Artaud's writing to the realm of the schizophrenic" (Morfee 2005: 108) and thus *denying him artistic control* or credit for his work. For example, Paule Thévenin – Artaud's friend and collaborator – railed against Deleuze's reading of Artaud in his article "Entendre/Voir/Lire." Here, as Jeffrey Atteberry reports, Thévenin objects to Deleuze's use of existing clinical terminology to categorize Artaud's work, which she suggests makes him complicit with the violence done to Artaud by the medical profession. "Straight away," Thévenin argues, "Deleuze falls into the major trap of identifying Artaud as a schizophrenic" (Thévenin in Atteberry 2000: 716).[8] In response, Attebury adds that "[w]hether or not Deleuze here uses the term schizophrenia in a manner that is in strict accordance with clinical practice, he clearly has recourse to the language of psychoanalysis as a means of explicating Artaud's texts, a strategy that would appear to make Artaud's writing into a case study." And in this way, Atteberry suggests, Deleuze "finds himself in a vulnerable position and open to charges of partaking in the crimes against Artaud" (Atteberry 2000: 716). In contrast, Deleuze himself defended the ethical basis of his medical categorization when he argued that:

It is meaningless to say that Artaud was not schizophrenic – worse, it's shameful and stupid. Artaud was clearly schizophrenic. He achieved a "wonderful breakthrough," he knocked down the wall [of the signifier], but at what price? The price of a collapse that must be qualified as schizophrenic . . . It would be irresponsible to turn a blind eye to the danger of collapse in such endeavors. But they're worth it. (Deleuze in Scheer 2004: 240)

But is Thévenin's criticism entirely fair to Deleuze? Given her subsequent tempering of her position, we might conclude that she herself would now think not.[9] For instance, we know that in subsequent work, such as *Anti-Oedipus*, Deleuze and Guattari do not merely appropriate the terms "schizophrenic" and "schizophrenia," but reinvent them (as the "schizo") in the light of the artistic practices and extreme experiences of those who attempted to document their encounters with the unbearable and overwhelming nature of Life at its most intense and vital. At the same time, this reinvention of terms interrogates the failure of psychoanalysis to encounter the creativity and becomings within the experiences it pathologizes.

Nevertheless, Catherine Dale has questioned whether Deleuze and Guattari might be seen to "limit" or domesticate Artaud's values and chaotic energy by means of the caution they exhibit in later works such as *A Thousand Plateaus* and *What is Philosophy?* (Dale 2002: 95). That is, whilst *Anti-Oedipus* has been criticized by some for failing to make a "clear case against" a reading of it as a thoroughly un- or anti-ethical call for "limitless liberated desire" (Bourg 2007: 120),[10] the later texts have been correspondingly critiqued for a lamentable degree of compromise. As Dale accepts: "Perhaps Deleuze's caution is a way of assembling life so that it can support the most extreme intensities, so that it can risk anything at all?" However, she goes on to argue that "Deleuze's desire for Artaud's craziness is still dangerous, in staying so stratified he risks repeating the banality of the destruction of a transvaluation of both their forces of life" (Dale 2002: 95). Likewise, in *The Logic of Sense*, Deleuze repeatedly returns to the problem of how to stay at the surface of the crack, at the incorporeal event without actualizing oneself in the quicksand and clamor of its body (Deleuze 1990: 154–61). Here, Dale suggests that Deleuze is "striving for a kind of balance between surface and depth. . . . He wills the crack and its perils and yet warns us to stay at its edges like the paradox of the intrepid tourist" (Dale 2002: 94). In these discussions, Deleuze himself draws the distinction between the safety of the shore and the instability of the surface. If we locate ourselves on the former, we become ridiculous abstract speakers who merely give talks on Artaud's madness (as, arguably, we are doing here). But if we risk positioning ourselves on the latter, we attempt to see "the crack" for ourselves by becoming "a little crazy" in a "precious juggling act" (Dale 2002: 95). "The shore," in this case, is one side of the struggle faced by anyone who takes up Deleuze's ethics. It is on the side of death, which, as Goodchild has discussed, "is the completion of living, the grasping of which shelters us from access to vital forces – perhaps an opinion, a cliché, a product, a feeling, a perception." Walking towards the sea, we then confront the other side of the struggle: "against a too-vital life that overwhelms, scattering singularities and unbearable intensities all around" (Goodchild 1996: 206).

"Madness" By Other Means

While this chapter cannot hope to do complete justice to these issues,[11] it remains important to return, in conclusion, to the value that both Deleuze and Artaud place on the theater in the fight against the oppression of Life by judgment. For his part, Artaud gave much careful consideration to how one might *consciously* effect an *unconscious* vibration, or create an encounter, in one's audience (or in oneself), developing theatrical but also ethical concepts such as "incantation" and "vibration," alongside those of cruelty and the BwO upon which Deleuze chooses to focus. For example, Artaud argues that incantation involves using language in a way that gives it "its full, physical shock potential," restoring to language its metaphysical or performative power to manifest something new rather than merely represent the already existing (Artaud in Schumacher 1989: 97). This experience is both "shocking" and "shattering," rather than "harmonious" for the audience because they are forced to encounter the novelty of that which has been incanted, *physically*. And yet it would be a mistake to overemphasize the importance of "shock" to Artaud as a mode of relation to his audience. As is well known, Artaud's broadcast *To have done with the judgment of god* was banned precisely for fear that it would *shock* the French public. Indeed, Adrian Morfee notes that it is typical to find in Artaud's late writing "the infantile delight in naming lower bodily fluids and processes" (Morfee 2005: 126), a delight which, Morfee argues, tends to undermine rather than aid Artaud's thought. However, for all the talk of "caca," farts and sperm in the radio play, one might argue that Artaud places a greater value on the concept of "vibration" – a more subtle mode of audience response which in fact needs to be protected from being overwhelmed by the shocking or the scandalous in order to function. The concept of vibration appears several times in Artaud's oeuvre. In a 1948 letter to Wladimir Porché, the director of the radio station that banned Artaud's radio work, he writes:

> I wanted a fresh work, one that would make contact with certain / organic points of life, / a work in which one's whole nervous system / illuminated as if by a miner's cap-lamp / with vibrations, / consonances / which invite / man / TO EMERGE / WITH / his body / to follow in the sky this new, unusual, and radiant Epiphany. / But the glory of the body is possible / only if / nothing / in the spoken text / happens to shock / happens to damage / this sort of desire for glory. (Artaud in Sontag 1976: 579)

Here Artaud expresses his ambition to create a work that will cause the audience's nervous systems to vibrate, leading them to a renewed understanding of their bodies. However, he also makes it clear that any conscious, "shocked" response to the text will get in the way of this more intuitive reaction. Equally, although Artaud is often accused of positing a mind/body distinction, the concept of vibration seems more concerned to contrast habitual responses ("shock") with the emergence of the new ("Epiphany"). In this respect, we might conclude by arguing that, for both Deleuze and Artaud, language, and here specifically Artaud's radio play, can act as less risky but no less potentially successful agents of immanence than can madness, alcoholism or drug-taking. As Deleuze and Guattari emphasize in *A Thousand Plateaus*, the latter provide no guarantee that we will be able to leap from the plane of organization to that of immanence or consistency. Why not try to encounter difference by *listening* to Artaud or experimenting with our own incantations; generating our own becomings-mad in contact with "lunatics" rather than becoming "professional lecturers on Artaud" (Deleuze 1995: 11)?[12] In his "Letter to a Harsh Critic," Deleuze argues that:

> What's interesting isn't whether I'm capitalizing on anything, but whether there are people doing something or other in their little corner, and me in mine, and whether there might be any points of contact, chance encounters and coincidences rather than alignments and rallying-points . . . The question's nothing to do with the character of this or that exclusive group, it's to do with the transversal relations that ensure that any effects produced in some particular way (through homosexuality, drugs, and so on) *can always be produced by other means.* (Deleuze 1995: 11)

Likewise, having emerged from Rodez, Artaud himself alluded to the possibilities for theatrical acting of attending to "the compulsive and impulsive behavior patterns of the mentally ill" (Artaud in Schumacher 1989: 185). In the late text entitled "Deranging the Actor" (1948), for instance, Artaud envisaged the development of a "methodically trau-matized actor" who did not imitate the movements of the "mad" but created his own "hot-tempered and petulant gravitations," undergoing the psychophysical experiments necessary to perform "a feverish activity of the limbs" (Artaud in Schumacher 1989: 185). To pursue these other means is neither a matter of remaining on the shore, nor of wildly des-tratifying, but of searching for the effects of "madness" through careful experimentation and the development of contagious modes of perform-ance (with their own kinds of philosophizing) and embodied modes of philosophy (with their own kinds of performance). This is not a call for compromise, but for a situation in which every body lives on the edges, at the limit of its own powers of transformation and becoming.

References

Ansell-Pearson, K. (1999), *Germinal Life: The Difference and Repetition of Deleuze*, London and New York: Routledge.

Artaud, A. (1996) *To Have Done With God's Judgment* (audio CD), Sub Rosa, AISIN: B000008RHQ.

Atteberry, J. (2000), "Reading Forgiveness and Forgiving Reading: Antonin Artaud's Correspondance avec Jacques Rivière," *MLN*, 115:4, 714–40.

Bergson, H. (1911), *Creative Evolution*, trans. A. Mitchell, New York: Henry Holt and Co.

Bourg, J. (2007), *From Revolution to Ethics: May 1968 and Contemporary French Thought*, Montreal: McGill-Queens University Press.

Cull, L. (2009), "How Do You Make Yourself a Theater without Organs?: Artaud, Deleuze and Differential Presence," *Theater Research International*, 34:3, 243–55.

Dale, C. (2001), "Knowing One's Enemy: Deleuze, Artaud, and the Problem of Judgment," in M. Bryden (ed.), *Deleuze and Religion*, London: Routledge, 126–37.

Dale, C. (2002), "Cruel: Antonin Artaud and Gilles Deleuze," in B. Massumi (ed.), *A Shock to Thought: Expression after Deleuze and Guattari*, Minneapolis: University of Minnesota Press, 85–100.

Deleuze, G. (1988), *Spinoza: Practical Philosophy*, trans. R. Hurley, San Francisco: City Lights Books.

Deleuze, G. (1990), *The Logic of Sense*, trans. M. Lester and C. Stivale, ed. C. Boundas, New York: Columbia University Press.

Deleuze, G. (1994), *Difference and Repetition*, trans. P. Patton, London: Athlone.

Deleuze, G. (1995), *Negotiations 1972–1990*, New York: Columbia University Press.

Deleuze, G. (1998), *Essays Critical and Clinical*, trans. D. W. Smith and M. A. Greco, London: Verso.

Deleuze, G. (2004), *Desert Islands and Other Texts 1953–1974*, trans. M. Taormina, ed. D. Lapoujade , New York: Semiotext(e).

Deleuze, G. and F. Guattari (1984), *Anti-Oedipus*, trans. R. Hurley, M. Seem and H. R. Lane, London: Athlone.

Deleuze, G. and F. Guattari (1988), *A Thousand Plateaus*, trans. B. Massumi, London: Athlone.

Deleuze, G. and F. Guattari (1994), *What is Philosophy?*, trans. H. Tomlinson and G. Burchell, London: Verso.

Genosko, G. (ed.) (1996), *The Guattari Reader*, Oxford: Blackwell.

Goodchild, P. (1996), *Deleuze and Guattari: An Introduction to the Politics of Desire*, London: Sage.

Lambert, G. (2006), *Who's Afraid of Deleuze and Guattari?*, New York: Continuum.

Ley, G. and J. Milling (2001), *Modern Theories of Performance: From Stanislavski to Boal*, New York: Palgrave.

Morfee, A. (2005), *Antonin Artaud's Writing Bodies*, Oxford: Oxford University Press.

Scheer, E. (ed.) (2004), *Antonin Artaud: A Critical Reader*, London: Routledge.

Schumacher, C. (ed.) (1989), *Artaud on Theater*, London: Methuen.

Sontag, S. (ed.) (1976), *Antonin Artaud: Selected Writings*, New York: Farrar, Straus and Giroux.

Stastney, P. (1998), "From Exploitation to Self-Reflection: Representing Persons with Psychiatric Disabilities in Documentary Film," *Literature and Medicine*, 17:1, 68–90.

Thévenin, P. (1993), *Antonin Artaud, ce désespéré qui vous parle*, Paris: Editions du Seuil.

Notes

1. I would like to thank John Mullarkey, Tim Clark, and Dan Smith for their helpful comments in response to earlier drafts of this essay.
2. Deleuze expands upon the nature of this personal suffering somewhat, arguing that: "Nietzsche moved like a condemned man from room to room, against which he set a grandiose defiance; Lawrence lived under the accusations of immoralism and pornography that were brought against the least of his water-colors; Kafka showed himself to be 'diabolical in all innocence' in order to escape from the 'tribunal in the hotel' where his infinite engagements were being judged" (Deleuze 1998: 126).
3. Deleuze gives the specific example of the character of *Ajax* here – presumably referring to the early play by Sophocles, although this is not made clear.
4. Aside from the reference to the body without organs at the end of the radio play as it was performed, Artaud had hoped to include an additional poem, "The Theater of Cruelty," which expands upon the idea as follows:

    The body is the body,
    it is alone
    and needs no organs,
    the body is never an organism,
    organisms are the enemies of the body . . .

    Reality has not yet been constructed because the real organs of the
      human body have not yet been formed and deployed.
    The theater of cruelty has been created to complete this deployment,
      and to undertake, by a new dancing of man's body, a diversion
    from this world of microbes which is merely coagulated nothingness . . .
    (Artaud in Schumacher 1989: 173)

    However, according to Schumacher, the poem "had to be left out because of lack of air time" (Schumacher 1989: 172).
5. As Claude Schumacher (1989) reports, the radio program was recorded

November 22–9, 1947 by Artaud and his collaborators. Originally commissioned by Fernand Pouey, the program was censored by Wladimir Porché, the director-general of the radio station on the day before it was scheduled for broadcast: February 2, 1948 (Schumacher 1989: 189). As Marc Dachy (1995) tells us in a short introductory essay in the cover notes of the recording, the broadcast had two private hearings for Artaud's friends and colleagues. The first was held on February 5, 1948, in the hope of changing Porché's mind about the ban. Those who attended – including Jean-Louis Barrault and Roger Vitrac – passed a favorable verdict on the recording, but the ban was maintained, resulting in Pouey's resignation. The second private hearing was held on February 23, 1948 "in a disused cinema" (sleeve notes to Artaud 1996).

6. A fuller articulation of this argument, and of the concepts of a "theater without organs" and a "destratified voice" can be found in Cull 2009.

7. As is well known, Artaud was forcibly institutionalised in a number of French "asylums" for nine years from 1937 (Atteberry 2000: 715), and it is this issue of involuntary commitment that continues to focus much of the ethical debate around schizophrenia and mental health service provision more broadly. Unfortunately, it is beyond the scope of this chapter to address these debates, the ethics of Guattari's call for the "depsychiatrization of madness" (Guattari in Genosko 1996: 478) or his argument that "the true scandal is the existence of incarcerative structures which literally exterminate the mentally ill and the personnel who work there, in the place of creating living systems" (Guattari in Genosko 1996: 485). However, I hope what follows provides some indirect stimulus for reflecting on these matters, and on how academia might relate to the "mad," through a direct consideration of Deleuze and Guattari's complex and changing treatment of Artaud.

8. This is my own translation of a quotation that Attebury gives in the original French: "D'emblee, Gilles Deleuze, tombant dans le piege majeur, identifie Antonin Artaud a la schizophrenie" (Thévenin 1993: 200).

9. Thévenin republished her essay in 1993 as part of a collection of writings on Artaud (Thévenin 1993). As Attebury (2000) reports, the collection's introduction includes an apology of sorts to Deleuze from Thévenin, which Attebury reads as an acknowledgement of the inherent difficulty of reading Artaud. Here, Thévenin refers to her early critique of Deleuze as "a little bit exaggerated" (Thévenin, translated in Scheer 2004: 27).

10. For example, Julian Bourg suggests that the problem was that "even if *Anti-Oedipus* did not make the claim for limitless liberated desire, it did not make a clear case against it" (Bourg 2007: 120). As such, Bourg argues that "Despite their continual efforts to explain that they were not merely advocating a free-for-all celebration of unfettered desire, it was not merely by chance that their work was judged in that light" (Bourg 2007: 121). Ultimately, he argues, *Anti-Oedipus*' desire is "lawless."

11. Likewise, this chapter has constituted only a very early attempt to construct some kind of connection between my own research into Deleuze's philosophy and a place outside this book (and indeed Deleuze's books) which we might designate the realm of mental health: understood as including a diverse range of embodied experiences, therapeutic practices, medical professional/patient dynamics and as a site for fraught disputes over rights and ethics, particularly with respect to the issue of involuntary containment. Clearly, there is a great deal more work to be done here, perhaps particularly regarding what we might call the minor literature of mental health, which includes the work of Artaud. In terms of filmic practice, there is an extensive history of experimental documentary which might also be construed as invoking a "mad" people-to-come,

including: Raymond Depardon's *Urgences* (1987), which Guattari described as "working upon our own lines of fragility"; Allie Light's *Dialogues with Madwomen* (1994); and Nicholas Philibert's *La Moindre des Choses* (1997). See Stastney 1998 for a more extensive list of films that might be considered to belong to this minor literature on mental health.

12. Clearly, I am asking these questions as much of myself as a scholar-artist as I am of any interested readers. Just as this is an early theoretical response to Artaud, I have also performed some initial practical responses. One example of this can be found in the performance "Manifesto" (2008) which responds to Artaud, alongside Deleuze, Allan Kaprow, John Cage, and Goat Island. "Manifesto" was presented at the ICA in London as part of the exhibition *Nought to Sixty*, and can be watched on YouTube at http://www. youtube.com/ user/lauramullarkey#p/a/u/2/WN9TG5fg5Gc

Chapter 4

Responsive Becoming: Ethics between Deleuze and Feminism

Erinn Cunniff Gilson

This chapter explores the possibility of an alliance between Deleuze's philosophy and feminist philosophy with respect to ethics. I begin by specifying some of the general points of convergence between Deleuzian ethics and feminist ethics. In the second section, I turn away from feminist ethics in particular to consider feminist engagement with Deleuze's (and Deleuze and Guattari's) work; in this section, I describe the central criticisms of Deleuze offered by feminist philosophers and point out the aspects of his thought that have been valuable for feminist theorizing. In order to respond to what I take to be the overarching concern feminists have about Deleuze's philosophy, the third section develops a proposal for a Deleuzian conception of ethics that is able to do (much of) what feminists require of an ethical theory.

Ethics Away from Tradition

Feminist ethics emerged as a unique subdiscipline in the 1970s and 1980s in particular through the work of Nel Noddings and Carol Gilligan.[1] While it has become a diverse field with various perspectives and threads of interest, I will attempt briefly to draw a general picture of the concerns that animate it so that we might see in what ways Deleuzian ethics and feminist ethics may coincide. Central to feminist ethics is both a critical perspective, criticizing gender bias and the attendant gender-associated dualisms within mainstream ethics and the history of ethics, and a reconstructive endeavor to provide a more adequate ethical theory (Held 1990). This simultaneously critical and constructive approach developed in diverse ways: some theorists focused on bringing to light issues and domains of moral concern that had previously been overlooked because of their association with women (the home, mothering and domestic work, sexual violence, abortion, etc.); some charted and criticized the gender-bias present in traditional ethical theories; while others worked to elaborate "what was now beginning to be claimed as a distinctively feminine moral experience of sensibility" (Jaggar 1991: 81). Ultimately, most feminist ethicists came to focus on the inadequacy of these traditional paradigms and to construct new models with varying degrees of continuity with the tradition.[2] Deleuze's approach to ethics is likewise both critical, following the Nietzschean trajectory that rejects transcendent moral norms in favor of immanent and plastic principles, and constructive, especially in its emphasis on creativity and novelty. Thus, both Deleuzian and feminist ethics share a strong critical perspective on traditional ethical theories and develop alternative understandings of ethics and ethical thinking that operate as counter-movements to this tradition.[3]

Beyond this fundamental yet broad commonality, Deleuzian and feminist ethics converge in at least four other respects. These four points of convergence will enable us to discern in more specific terms how Deleuzian ethics and feminist ethics are simultaneously critical and constructive, as well as in what ways they may be in tension with one another. Although the overarching aim of this section is to elaborate a picture of ethics that addresses both Deleuzian and feminist concerns, in the process of delineating these commonalities I will also point out how their orientations differ and will not seek to minimize these differences. Such differences may ultimately be fruitful for developing alternative ways of using both Deleuzian and feminist concepts.

Firstly then, both approaches articulate an understanding of ethics that is rooted in and grows out of experience rather than being purified of experiential elements. From a feminist perspective, the desire is to remedy the occlusion of women's experiences throughout the history of ethics by developing an understanding of ethics that either significantly encompasses or is even grounded in women's ethical experiences (Brennan 1999). In Deleuze's thought, ethics is itself a matter of experiencing the world and the self in a certain way. In terms of historical influence, Deleuze's conception of ethics is formed primarily through readings of the Stoics, Spinoza, and Nietzsche. In his book on Spinoza's practical philosophy, he defines ethics as "a typology of immanent modes of existence," a definition that emphasizes that he regards ethics not as supplying standards for judgment but as a practice through which one invents for oneself better ways of living (Deleuze 1988: 23). Following Nietzsche, he considers valuing and evaluating as the primary ethical activities: through living, one values, and how one lives defines what one values. Ethics consists of distinguishing between those affects, relations, ways of thinking, and, ultimately, ways of living that are life-affirming, joyous, and active and those that are life-negating, sad, and reactive. Thus, it is fundamentally a matter of experience and experimentation. Only through experimentation is one able to discern the differences between those things that can be said to be good for us and those that are bad for us, and devise for oneself such a typology of ways of living. For Deleuze, then, ethics is a question of ethology in the sense that it has to do with studying bodies – both animal and human – in terms of what they are capable of doing and undergoing, and evaluating those changes from within the experience of affecting and being affected (Deleuze 1988: 125).

Second, and related to the criteria that ethical valuation be grounded in experience, both are concerned to understand ethical comportment in terms of practices rather than in terms of adherence to abstract rules and forms of moral reasoning. One instance of this focus, although certainly not the only one, is the development of a feminist ethic of care.[4] In her overview of care ethics, Virginia Held emphasizes two sides of care: care as a practice and care as a value. The value of care is one that originates to a certain extent in caring relations, namely those that are formative of us as individual subjects; we care and we value care because others have cared for us. The value of care, which incorporates other related values such as trust, sensitivity, and mutual concern, is a value that must be embodied in actual caring practices and relationships (Held 2004: 65). To hold care as a value and decline to incorporate it into one's activities is really to fail to care. The domain of experience that is of particular concern for the care ethicist is similar to that of concern for Deleuze: concrete individuals in their singularity and in relations with other unique individuals. One clear point of difference is the role pre-individual singularities plays in Deleuze's philosophy; while feminist care ethics is certainly interested in the constitutive nature of relations, its emphasis is on the constituted subject rather than the singularities that constitute it. Another dissimilarity concerns the care. While care is one of the central values in feminist ethics, it is absent from Deleuze's ethics, which center on transformative relationships rather than caring ones per se.

A third commonality is a shared line of critique that focuses on a conventional understanding of ethical subjectivity that emphasizes autonomy, rationality, independence, impartiality, and self-mastery. For both Deleuze and feminist thinkers, this form of subjectivity is one that demands submission: submission to a norm of what it means to be a "good" person, which implicitly determines the qualities of the virtuous as being masculine, as well as obedience to the moral law itself. For feminist philosophers, this ideal of a moral subject is both gender-biased and specious, and a comprehension of the centrality of relations in shaping ethical subjectivity is crucial to altering it. Deleuze's critique of the subject also shifts the focus from the subject as autonomous substance to the relations that constitute it, whether these relations generate a molar identity or a "fascinated self" in a process of becoming. Likewise, his work continually seeks to upset the dualist thinking that underlies oppression, fabricating oppositional categories, constituting subjects in accordance with them, and elevating, for instance, men over women, rationality over emotion, or autonomy over heteronomy. In both cases, constructively criticizing such conventional norms involves undermining dualism and doing so via a focus on constitutive relations rather than ready-made beings.

Lastly, both Deleuze and feminist theorists approach ethics in a way that is inherently political; the question of how to live ethically is fundamentally a political question. This point is closely connected to the previous one insofar as the conception of subjectivity under dispute is a political one; that is, one that advances the ends and interests of some at the expense of others. Consequently, both Deleuzian and feminist approaches to ethics are able to expand the scope of ethical concern not merely in the sense of "moral extensionism" – extending moral consideration to nonhuman animals and nature, for instance – but in the sense of treating ethics as ethos, as a matter of a way of living rather than a discipline that sets about solving a discrete set of problems. Alison Jaggar makes this claim on behalf of feminist ethics: "rather than being limited to a restricted ethical domain, feminist ethics has *enlarged* the traditional concerns of ethics" (Jaggar 1991: 86). A Deleuzian approach does likewise. There is, then, some basis for thinking that Deleuze and feminism might ally when it comes to ethics.

Feminism Contra Deleuze?

To determine what form an alliance between Deleuze and feminism might take with respect to ethics, it will also be important to consider how feminist thinkers have directly appropriated and/or addressed Deleuze's work. This section thus centers on the concept that has evoked the most debate and skepticism from feminist readers of Deleuze: becoming-woman. The feminist reception of Deleuze's work in terms of this concept indicates that it is a potential roadblock to any alliance. Many feminist thinkers have been skeptical about the value of

Deleuze and Deleuze and Guattari's work for feminism because of the implications of the idea of "becoming-woman." This notion, along with the view of desire with which it is paired, is regarded as both quite problematic and as indicative of the usefulness of Deleuze's work as a whole, perhaps because it is one of the few points in his work where he addresses sex, sexuality, women, and femininity. The charges made against Deleuze and Guattari with respect to becoming-woman are varied: first, that they overemphasize a rather stereotypical rendering of femininity; second, that they appropriate femininity for the purposes of men's becoming; third, that they consequently neglect women's specificity by depicting femininity in this way; and, fourth, that they further disregard the lives of actual women by focusing on a level of change that is abstract and detached from women's experiences.[5] These criticisms are quite serious: if the most significant treatment of women, sex, and sexuality in Deleuze's work amounts to an effacement of women, then his thought is likely to be of little use to feminists.

Here, I will take Elizabeth Grosz's summation of these feminist criticisms as a starting point for assessing the basic objections. Grosz identifies three unresolved problems with Deleuze and Guattari's work: 1) their apparent inattentiveness to the specificity of women and lack of awareness of their own masculine subject position; 2) the possibility that their account of desire and becoming still allows women to be taken as "the vehicles, the receptacles of men's becomings"; and 3) the fact that their account may, in effect, reterritorialize or restrict women's progressive becomings by making them "part of a more universalist movement of becoming" (Grosz 1994: 182). The third problem can be broken down into two parts. One reason for feminists to be apprehensive about "becoming" is the possibility that women's becomings in particular would get swept away in a greater flow of change and destabilization.[6] It is worth noting that this particular worry appears to be less that women would get lost, overlooked, or hindered in processes of untrammelled becoming, and more a worry about how women's becomings and becomings in relation to femininity are configured in theory by Deleuze and Guattari. It is essentially a concern about the insensitivity of the philosopher and thus much akin to the first problem. The other aspect of this third problem is the idea of "a more universalist movement of becoming" and the role played by such a movement. The concern here centers on what is taken to be the privileged role of the universal or absolute in relation to what appears to be a limited interest in the particular and concrete (especially the particularity of women). Thus, in conclusion, Grosz suggests that it will have to become "clearer what becoming-woman means for those beings who are women, as well as for those beings who are men," if the value of Deleuze and Guattari's work for feminism is to become apparent (Grosz 1994: 182). In the context of these skeptical assessments, I offer an alternative account of the process of becoming-woman that aims to do just that.

Much has been written about this concept and its peculiar status in the chain of becomings that Deleuze and Guattari sketch in plateau ten of *A Thousand Plateaus*, and I do not intend to rehash well-covered terrain by speculating as to what kind of priority they accorded becoming-woman.[7] Rather than defining it negatively by emphasizing what it is not, I will focus on what becoming-woman means as a positive process by elaborating three distinctive components of the concept. The main concern will be to consider how it might pertain to women's particularity: Is becoming-woman a process that ignores the specificity of women or is it rather a process that attends to that specificity? And, if the latter, in what ways might it so attend?

One component of becoming-woman is Deleuze and Guattari's concept of "becoming-minoritarian" and the distinction they make between the major and the minor. Since "all becoming is a becoming-minoritarian," becoming always occurs in relation to a minor molar term – a woman or animal, for instance – that functions to destabilize the major molar term, a man or human being, correspondingly (Deleuze and Guattari 1987: 291; 1980: 356). The identity categories that are "major" (for instance, human, male, adult, white, rational) are defined as such in virtue of their dominance, the way they set the standards for the hierarchical terms of identity; they distribute and maintain binaries that reinforce their dominance. All molar subjectivities, both those of major and minor terms, are formed in relation to this "man-standard," as Deleuze and Guattari call it. The consequence of the constitutive force of this "man-standard" is that even those who are part of a minority group must still become minoritarian in order to break with it. Becoming, then, is a process of departing from the standard, the norm, and the dominant pattern, a transformation not just of majoritarian identity but of the minor, which has been defined in relation to it. So, becoming-minoritarian in the form of becoming-woman is not a revaluation of the degraded minor side of the binary, "woman," but a break from such rigidly dualist terms altogether, which are themselves a product of and in the service of the "man-standard."

In this context, Deleuze and Guattari's contentious claim that "in a way, it is always 'man' who is the subject of becoming" appears less divisive and more explicable; as they go on to clarify, "he is only this subject when he enters into a becoming-minoritarian that tears him away from his major identity" (Deleuze and Guattari 1987: 291; 1980: 357). "Man" is always the subject of becoming not because only men can become or only men need to undergo such transformative engagements, but rather because it is always with respect to the "man-standard" that defines molar identities that one must deterritorialize. The subject that desubjectifies itself, undoes its constitution in relation to the dominant paradigm, is a subject that has been defined in relation to "man."[8] As a molar woman, one has been defined in relation to, indeed in opposition to, man, one's femininity in contrast with masculinity.[9] Becoming-woman, therefore, is a process that ruptures the dominance of the "man-standard" around which are constructed our molar identities, which in their oppositionality and rigidity constitute oppressive hierarchies. Consequently, it cannot be undertaken by trying to become like the group "women" by developing ostensibly "feminine" traits; as Deleuze continually emphasizes, becoming bears little relation to resemblance or imitation.

Paul Patton's characterization of becoming-woman elaborates on this point quite clearly while also portraying becoming-woman in a way that might bolster some of the criticisms mentioned above. Accordingly, it is worth quoting his account at length:

> Becoming-woman should be understood as a becoming of the same type as becoming-animal, in the sense that it involves a virtual alliance with the affects and powers that have been traditionally assigned to women. The reality of the becoming has little to do with a relation to real women, but everything to do with a relation to the incorporeal body of woman as it figures in the social imaginary. This body might be defined in terms of the affects associated with the nurture and protection of others, or the affects associated with dependent social status such as a capacity for dissimulation or for cultivating the affection of others, delight in appearances and role-play. Becoming-woman does not involve imitating or assuming the forms of femininity but rather creating a molecular or micro-femininity in the subject concerned by reproducing the characteristic features, movements or affects of what passes for "the feminine" in a given form of patriarchal society. (Patton 2000: 81)

Many aspects of this account are quite apt: becoming is a matter of virtual alliance rather than imitation; as a result, it is a question of alliance through impersonal affects rather than personal identification; and, consequently, becoming-woman necessarily involves a relation to "the incorporeal body of woman . . . in the social imaginary" rather than relationships with particular, actual women. Yet, it remains unclear what it would mean to "reproduce the characteristic features, movements or affects of what passes for 'the feminine' in a given form of patriarchal society" in a way that does not simply reproduce molar femininity in a masculine subject. Likewise, this account leaves unanswered what it would mean for women to enter into becoming-woman: how would becoming-woman be a meaningful process of transformation for women if it consisted in reproducing, albeit perhaps as a parody, typical feminine traits?[10]

If the first component of the process of becoming-woman is its status as a type of becoming-minoritarian, then the second key component of this concept is the body and the relationship between the body and the constitution of normalized subjectivity. This aspect of becoming-woman will shed light on the questions just raised. As recounted above, becoming-woman is a process that departs from the dominant paradigm of man and woman, masculine and feminine, for alternative ways of being gendered creatures. Thus, it diverges from standard gender/sex models. The concept of becoming-woman, then, must be understood as a response to the way molar sexed subjectivity is formed through the theft of the body and the domestication of bodily affects.

The sex/gender system that shapes us into molar men and women functions through bodily normalization, that is, through the enforcement of sexual dimorphism (that there are two sexes: male and female) and concomitantly binary systems of gendered meaning (that there are two corresponding sets of gendered roles, attitudes, characteristics: masculine and feminine). Such a system involves taming the body so that it falls in line with the appropriate one of these two options. This "theft" of the body – the teleological organization of its sexual organs, the restriction and channeling of its forces, the molding of its capacities into acceptable patterns – sexes and sexualizes it. According to Deleuze and Guattari, the body – with all its free-flowing affects and uncontained movements – is stolen first from the little girl, who subsequently can be held up as model of good behavior and a desirable object to the little boy.[11] A vital part of this normalizing organization is the organization of the sexual organs, the proper codification of the erogenous zones of the body. When the genitals are deemed the appropriate erogenous zones, erotic and sexual activity is both limited to activity between the two sexes and subordinated to reproductive ends.

As a process that deterritorializes molar men and women, becoming-woman is a way of stealing back the body, stealing it away from the organization that invested it with the forms and norms of sexed subjectivity. If the body has been stolen, becoming-woman is a return to the body and a way of de-structuring the body. By undoing oppositional patterns of sexed corporeality and subjectivity, becoming-woman also unhinges sexuality from the normative and teleological paradigm to which it is confined, promoting the eroticization of other parts of the body.[12]

This last point leads us to the third key idea that helps explicate the concept of becoming-woman. Throughout *A Thousand Plateaus*, Deleuze and Guattari thematize becoming as a matter of alliance, contagion, and involution in contrast to filiation, heredity, and evolution: what is at stake in becoming is production rather than reproduction. As a matter of alliance rather than filiation and heredity, the "nuptials" of becoming are unnatural in the sense that they do not follow the prescribed pattern for sexual reproduction: an association between man and woman that produces offspring. In filial relations and the relations between the sexes for sexual reproduction, "the only differences retained are a simple duality between the sexes within the same species, and small modifications across generations" (Deleuze and Guattari 1987: 242; 1980: 296). In contrast to this conception, which reduces productive relations to those that take place between two fixed and opposed sexes, the alliances that constitute becoming-woman demand that we think sexual differences and their production differently. If our ways of being sexed and sexualized creatures exceed the binary relations that have structured sexed subjectivity, then the idea of sexual difference need not be thought as binary (male/female) but as a multiplicity of sexual differences. As Deleuze and Guattari put it, there are "n sexes" that are all the myriad ways of living one's sexuality in one's body in relation to other bodies (Deleuze and Guattari 1987: 277; 1980: 340).[13] Lastly, for becoming to be involution rather than evolution entails that it be a process of simultaneous deformation and recreation rather one of progressive formation and development. Becoming-woman thus is a generative process because in forming alternate "unnatural nuptials" it unweaves oppositional and reproductively oriented forms of sexuality and sexed subjectivity.

These last two points – that becoming-woman is a matter of loosening the grip of normative sex/gender arrangements on the body and that becoming-woman creates sexual differences outside of these arrangements through its "unnatural nuptials" – clarify the relationship of actual women to this process of becoming-woman. Indeed, if bodily subjection is what is contested and undone through becoming-woman, then it is clear that the concept speaks directly to the conditions in which actual women live rather than viewing them as vehicles for men's becomings or sweeping them up in a broader movement of transformation. While, as Patton implies, the becoming-woman of a man need not happen in relation to an actual woman (and certainly not in relation to her identity as such), and need not involve a relationship between a man and a woman, the reality of becoming-woman appears to have *everything* to do with real women. The reality of becoming-woman has to do with women's bodies and the bodies of men, in relation to whom they are defined, as well as with the capacity of those bodies to experience different connections, to allow bodily affects to flourish in ways unaccounted for by dualist conceptions of sex and sexuality.

In light of this conceptual contextualization, it appears that the feminist criticism that Deleuze and Guattari are inattentive to women's specificity is mistaken in at least one respect: the constitution of sexed subjectivity. Although becoming-woman is an abstract concept, it is one through which Deleuze and Guattari intend to embrace singularity precisely by eschewing the generality of two sexes.[14] Likewise, given the way becoming-woman functions in response to the injustice done to women by the theft of the body, it seems unlikely that it would be a concept permitting women to serve as vehicles for men's becomings.[15] I have offered an account of becoming-woman that demonstrates how Deleuze and Guattari evince an awareness of and sensitivity to the socio-historical conditions that have shaped female subjectivity, making it in particular the trap they consider all molar identities to be. For this reason as well as for others, the focus on corporeality in becoming-woman should make Deleuze and Guattari's work more appealing to their critics. Indeed, corporeality has been the aspect of their work that feminist theorists have found most valuable, so it is to this theme, the body, that I now turn in order to investigate in what ways and for what reasons feminist thinkers have found that work to be of value.

To a significant extent, feminist appropriations of Deleuze's work have focused on the conceptions of the body and desire it offers and the resources found therein for rethinking sex, sexuality, and gender. In her essay on the unique "Australian" feminism of Moira Gatens, Elizabeth Grosz, and Genevieve Lloyd, Claire Colebrook isolates features of the Spinozist-Deleuzian understanding of the body that is adopted by all three. The picture they draw is one that enables them to depart from the essentialism/constructivism dichotomy in thinking about sex, gender, and sexuality. The (sexed) body is neither a natural given nor is its meaning merely constructed via representations or ideological systems. Instead, the body is a positive, active force, itself productive of meaning, "a becoming meaningful"; it is "the site of the distribution whereby it becomes *as a body*" (Colebrook 2000: 86, 89). The body is not just the locus of becoming but is a becoming and, as such, is an opening to incalculable linkages and transformations. This conception of the body is quite valuable in devising an alternative understanding of the genesis and status of the sexed body, as is evident in the work of Gatens in particular. Colebrook summarizes this contribution by noting that "masculinity and femininity are *more* than mental or cultural representations; but at the same time they cannot be appealed to as self-present substances or essences given once and for all *through* certain attributes and qualities" (Colebrook 2000: 87). In the Deleuzian alternative to subjects/substances and attributes, fixed forms and modes of organization, one finds the resources for thinking the reality of sexed subjectivity and for thinking its future otherwise.

This way of thinking sex and sexuality otherwise is enacted by Grosz in much of her work, but especially in the essays collected in *Space, Time, and Perversion*. In the essay, "Refiguring Lesbian Desire," she proposes abandoning the conception of desire that has prevailed throughout the history of philosophy as well as in contemporary work in feminist and queer theory – desire conceived as lack, and the psychoanalytic paradigm that is its chief advocate – in favor of the Deleuzian view of desire as "a force of positive production" (Grosz 1995: 179). Grosz explains this decision to turn to Deleuze and Guattari's model by noting "that their work does not have to be followed faithfully to be of use in dealing with issues [such as lesbian desire] that they do not . . . deal with themselves" (Grosz 1995: 180). Indeed, insofar as they give us notions that make experimentation central to thought and life, we ought not to follow them faithfully but errantly. Their concepts are valuable "because they enable desire to be understood not just as feeling or affect, but also as doing and making" (Grosz 1995: 180). Since female desire has been severely circumscribed by an account of desire (as lack) as implicitly male and even ultimately a relation between men, feminists cannot but find useful an alternative that regards desire as creative. Grosz's subsequent description of how such desire works reveals several other aspects that are of interest to feminists.

Desirous becomings operate at the level of the singular; they are unique not just to individuals but to the becoming itself, which brings into play parts of individuals, fragments of their bodies, affects that take hold of them, and movements that flow through them. As Grosz notes, "becomings then are not a broad general trajectory of development, but always concrete and specific" (Grosz 1995: 184). Becoming, therefore, cannot overlook the specificity of women since it is precisely a process of engaging various aspects of that specificity. Moreover, a focus on singularity alleviates some of the difficulty feminists have when it comes to theorizing identity. The notion of "intersectionality" in feminist thought expresses the idea that sex or gender is not the only relevant form of difference and that other modes of difference such as race, ethnicity, nationality, and class cannot simply be aggregated, added on top of gender as other discrete factors, but rather intersect and overlap in complex ways. This picture of difference as "intersectional" rather than additive or aggregative coincides significantly with the Deleuzian picture of how difference is generated through the becoming of multiplicities in relation with one another. Indeed, one might claim that Deleuze's model could add more nuance to feminist thinking about difference because of the way the logic of becoming traverses various levels of social organization – engaging groups, social meanings, sub-individual affects, in addition to individuals – rather than being confined to one (the identity of the individual).[16]

Relatedly, becoming is always a matter of relation and connection with otherness. It is, thus, in a sense always "intersubjective."[17] Such intersubjective assemblages are oriented towards creating new ways of living. As Grosz puts it with respect to "becoming-lesbian":

> the question is not am I – or are you – a lesbian, but rather, what kinds of lesbian connections, what kinds of lesbian-machine, we invest our time, energy, and bodies in, what kinds of sexuality we invest ourselves in, with what other kinds of bodies, and to what effects? What it is that together, in parts and bits, and interconnections, we can make that is new, exploratory, opens up further spaces, induces further intensities, speeds up, enervates, and proliferates production (production of the body, production of the world)? (Grosz 1995: 184)

This view of the body and its creative becomings inaugurates, as Colebrook states, "an ethics of desire; affirming one's own becoming is maximized in the affirmation of the becoming of others" (Colebrook 2000: 88). Such an ethics is one that is oriented towards experimentation, towards inventing more fulfilling, enlivening, and intense ways of thinking, feeling, and relating. Yet, it is not solipsistic – the sovereignty of the self is put into question – nor is it resistant to attentiveness to others; becoming only happens together.

We have seen what feminist thinkers find appealing about Deleuze's philosophy.[18] While points of affinity between Deleuze and feminism are to be found in the focus on corporeality and bodies as a locus of transformation and resistance to the oppressive demands of normalized subjectivity and the associated demands of conventional moral-ity, one apparent incompatibility arises given that many feminists espouse the need to pay heed to the experience of women qua women while Deleuzian becoming dismantles molar identities such as that of "woman."[19] In light of the aforementioned critiques and worries, some of the aspects of Deleuze's thought embraced by feminist Deleuzians appear to be precisely those that others might still regard warily. The emphasis placed on creation, experimentation, and the production of novelty, and on the sub- or pre-personal level at which becoming oper-ates, might seem to take Deleuze's concepts "out of this world."[20] In this way, his thought could be deemed unresponsive to particularity, understood as the particularity of subjects: it goes beneath it and thus undermines it. The concern here is not, perhaps, the absence of the con-crete, but the nearly exclusive interest in what surpasses and underlies the personal: "a more universalist movement of becoming." These spe-cific tensions, I believe, are encompassed by a broader worry on the part of feminist thinkers, which is that the ethos of Deleuze's philosophy does not advocate responsibility and lacks attentiveness to social, historical context because the insistence on creative deterritorialization and the production of novelty precludes such contextualization and responsive-ness.[21] The third and final section of this chapter will contest this con-clusion by elaborating how a Deleuzian ethic might entail the kind of responsiveness feminists (and others) seek.

Mapping a Deleuzo-Feminist Ethics

The key, I believe, to mapping a Deleuzian ethics that may be of use to feminism is to reveal his work to contain both an ethos and a concept of responsiveness, and one that has the sense both of responsiveness to socio-historical context and of responsiveness to others. Indeed, such a sense of responsiveness is not foreign to Deleuze's thought, which con-tinually emphasizes it in some form or another, and several instances of this responsiveness will be explored throughout this section.

The first major instance of this emphasis is the dynamic of the problem and solution. In its earliest formulation in *Difference and Repetition*, the problem is an internally differentiated multiplicity the contours of which must be determined in order to generate a solution. Deleuze develops this conception of the problem in response to the sixth postulate of the dogmatic image of thought: that designation or reference is the privi-leged domain of truth (and falsity). This understanding grounds truth in sense: for a proposition to be judged true or false it must have sense. The domain of sense and of propositions that have sense, however, extends beyond the limits of the true; false statements have sense – they must in order for us to deem them false – as do nonsense words. Yet, the image of thought that locates truth in propositions and takes sense to be the necessary, if not sufficient, condition of truth, also reduces sense to a sterile condition. Sense is an ideality reducible to an attribute of a proposition and the object to which the proposition refers, which are said to *have* sense. Thus, "sense appears here, as the outcome of the most powerful logical effort, but as Ineffectual, a sterile incorporeal, deprived of its power of genesis" (Deleuze 1994: 156; 1985: 203). The consequence is that, as the locus of sense, the problem is conceived as merely propositional, as drawn from propositions that might serve as solutions. On this model, the problem is not genuinely productive precisely because it is fixed in the domain of propositions and set up in terms of already comprehensible possible responses.[22]

However, for the problem truly to operate as ground and condition, it must be genuinely productive; it must generate responses rather than itself "be traced from the corresponding propositions that serve, or can serve, as responses" (Deleuze 1994: 157; 1985: 204). For Deleuze, the problem as virtuality is such that it exceeds and persists beyond any particular case of solution to which it gives rise. Problems are not resolved but are that with which we experiment by venturing responses.[23] By seeking to conceive the problem as generative in its own right, as properly transcendental rather than traced from empirically given conditions, and by in effect inverting the relation between the problem and the proposition, Deleuze invests the dynamic of the problem and solution with a mode of responsiveness. Since they are not determined in advance, solutions function as genuine responses and must always be responsive to the problem precisely because they take it as their condition. The constant relation to the problems from which they arise is a necessary feature of responses or cases of solution, a necessary feature that prevents them from falling back into the generality of propositions and losing their sense. Deleuze writes, "Once we 'forget' the problem, we have before us no more than an abstract general solution, and since there is nothing to support that generality, there is nothing to prevent the solution from fragmenting into the particular propositions that form its cases" (Deleuze 1994: 162; 1985: 211). Thus, it is through their very responsiveness to problems that instances of solution retain their meaningfulness.

Since the problem is a problematic-*Idea* and responses attest to it in its *ideality* or *virtuality*, it might seem that such a notion is far detached from any form of responsiveness to socio-historical conditions or actual others. Yet this set of ideas regarding the problem and solution finds its ethical correlate in Deleuze's comment concerning ethics and the event in *The Logic of Sense*.[24] In this text, responsiveness to the problem becomes responsiveness to the event and is thus explicated further. Here, inspired by the Stoics, Deleuze makes one of his most direct pronouncements concerning ethics: "either ethics makes no sense at all, or this is what it means and has nothing else to say: not to be unworthy of what happens to us" (Deleuze 1990: 149; 1969: 174). Occurring as it does in the twenty-first series in the text, that concerning the event, this statement explicates not being unworthy in terms of being worthy of the event, which is to say, willing and expressing it. The event is here understood in its duality: it is both what happens, the actual event, and it is the event of sense, a virtual or incorporeal event, not an actual state of affairs or "that which occurs," but that from which "that which occurs" derives its meaning. Thus, there are two aspects to not being unworthy of what happens. Not to be unworthy is both to refrain from *ressentiment*, instead affirming each event, and to refer "that which occurs" back to the potential for change inherent in the incorporeal event, which imbues "that which occurs" with a sense that exceeds it and that constitutes us, the bearers of the event, as open to the future. These two sides of the event and two aspects of willing it are not separate but concurrent. For an individual to will the event is always to will "the embodiment, the actualization of the pure incorporeal event in a state of affairs and in his or her own body, own flesh," and thus to make the potential of the event operative. The incorporeal event – the event that is "the pure expressed" – demands to be actualized (Deleuze 1990: 146, 149; 1969: 172, 175).

In what sense is willing the event, embodying it, a responsive endeavor? First of all, the event or the problem calls for creation and activity. It demands not passive acceptance of what happens but engagement with the sense of what occurs in such a way that out of an understanding of this sense one creates something new that speaks to what has been. To express the power of the event, one cannot merely repeat what has happened. To do so is indeed to be unworthy insofar as it is to reject the generative aspect of the event, to ignore the opening onto the future that it entails. Therefore, an ethical relation to the event is a responsive one precisely because not being unworthy can be defined as creating a new mode of living that grows out of and speaks to the event in its duality.

These two notions – problem and event – find a synthesis of sorts in *What is Philosophy?*, in which philosophical concepts are understood as expressive of the event and as responding to problems by determining and formulating them as well as comprising cases of solution.[25] Philosophy, as the practice of creating concepts, is an ethical activity because it seeks to attest to the event. Concepts are composed as responsive to events and to problems. Crucial to Deleuze and Guattari's development of the concept of the concept in *What is Philosophy?* is the idea that ethical modes of life and thought – that is, concept-creation – and must bear a certain relation to the present, to actuality, to the socio-historical conditions in which we find ourselves. This emphasis serves to contextualize the ethos of responsiveness contained in the ideas of expressing the event and responding to the problem.

The account they give of what defines political philosophy and, in particular, the concept of utopia is exemplary of this emphasis on responsiveness to the present. The political notion of utopia is not on Deleuze and Guattari's account an ideal to which to aspire, but constitutes a form of revolution. More specifically, the concept of "*utopia is what links* philosophy with its own epoch" and is that through which philosophy "takes the criticism of its own time to its highest point" (Deleuze and Guattari 1994: 99; 1991: 95). The idea of utopia binds the transformative power of the virtual – the event – to that which it transforms; it joins the force of undoing of absolute deterritorialization to the socio-historical conditions of the present. As Deleuze and Guattari note, utopia means "absolute deterritorialization but always at the critical point at which it is connected with the present relative milieu, and especially with the forces stifled by this milieu" (Deleuze and Guattari 1994: 100; 95–6). The becomings that utopia inspires are thus responsive ones, modes not just of creativity but also of critique and resistance. Such becomings can only be creative, can only be critical, because they are responsive, because they productively react against the limiting conditions of the present. Becoming-woman, therefore, is a creative way of taking up, inventing, or resisting modes of sexed corporeality because there are modes of sexed subjectivity to which to respond.

On this understanding, becoming responds to historical conditions and the conditions of the present, but is not and cannot itself be historical. History traffics only in states of affairs, that which has occurred, while becoming is openness to the future and experimentation, which "is always that which is in the process of coming about – the new, the remarkable, and interesting" (Deleuze and Guattari 1994: 111; 1991: 106). As Dorothea Olkowski puts it: "Although it is true ... that Deleuze is not 'doing' history, he is not doing it because he insists upon philosophical and concrete specificities, whereas history demands generalities" (Olkowski 1999: 52). Thus, the critique of becoming-woman that contends that it is too general a concept, one that cannot account for or encompass women's history and the particularity of their experiences, is not mistaken about Deleuze's regard for history. Rather, the criticism is mistaken because it fails to acknowledge that for Deleuze there is a quite particular conception of history and historical temporality at stake, and it thus equates concreteness with a generic sense of history. Concreteness is present in Deleuze's work even in the absence of the temporal fixity that he takes to define history: one need not fix an experience, a process, an event in a determinate moment in time in order to achieve concreteness. It is not that history is irrelevant for Deleuze, but that it is important only as a "set of almost negative conditions that make possible the experimentation of something that escapes history" (Deleuze and Guattari 1994: 111; 1991: 106).[26]

While the concept of utopia illuminates for us the way Deleuze's concept of becoming entails responsiveness to historical conditions, the notion of responsibility he and Guattari briefly sketch in *What is Philosophy?* illuminates how becoming is a process that engages us with others and calls for us to be responsive to them. In the context of a criticism of human rights, which "say nothing about the immanent modes of existence of people provided with rights," they write, "We are not responsible for the victims but responsible before [*devant*] them" (Deleuze and Guattari 1994: 107, 108; 1991: 103). Responsibility is not absent from Deleuzian ethics, but takes a different form. One is not responsible *for* others, or rather the preposition "for" does not mean "'for their benefit,' or yet 'in their place.' It is 'before.' It is a question of becoming" (Deleuze and Guattari 1994: 109; 1990: 105). Responsibility is not a matter of acting for others or acting as if one were the other, of taking upon oneself the task of assuming the other's projects as if they were one's own; such modes of responsibility would presume that the self is set off from the other, as an autonomous and discrete subject, consciously taking on responsibility. Instead, one is responsible before others, facing them, and in relation to them. As Leonard Lawlor observes, the sense conveyed by the preposition "before" in the phrase being "responsible before" others is that of being *among* and *within* the singularities of a multiplicity: "I find myself fascinated *before* something I cannot recognize, before something that has lost its molar form, something singular" (Lawlor 2008: 176). As a question of becoming, responsibility both involves and demands a certain mode of relationship and engagement with others, and not simply with them as molar entities but with that which composes them. One is responsible because one is in the midst of, linked to, and becoming through something within the other.

If responsibility is "a question of becoming" and becoming involves the kind of relation that is constitutive of responsibility, then the linkage between these two concepts entails that becoming is an ethical endeavor. In becoming, one expresses, augments, and transforms the capabilities of one's body through its relation to those of another body; yet, as Paul Patton notes, this assemblage is formed without "involving [the] appropriation of those powers" or hindering the other's ability to express itself (Patton 2000: 79). Deleuze's comments concerning the problem of evil in Spinoza's ontology of bodies clarify this point:

> What is positive or good in the act of beating? Spinoza asks. What is good is that this act (raising my arm, closing my fist, moving rapidly and forcefully) expresses a power of my body; it expresses what my body can do in a certain relation. What is bad in this act? The bad appears when the act is associated with the image of a thing whose relation is decomposed by that very act (I kill someone by beating him). The same act would have been good if it had been associated with the image of a thing whose relation agreed with it (e.g., hammering iron). Which means that an act is bad whenever it directly decomposes a relation, whereas it is good whenever it directly compounds its relation with other relations. (Deleuze 1988: 35)

To be responsible, on this understanding, is to refrain from connecting one's body with other bodies in ways that decompose the relations that constitute them or diminish their powers, and instead to find compositions with others that enhance the powers of both. Becoming, therefore, involves a measure of responsiveness to others that precludes it from rendering women the mere vehicles of men's becomings. The responsibility inherent in becoming requires, rather, that men become-woman in a way that does not reterritorialize women's bodies and selves but that facilitates women's own becomings.

While one conception of response and responsiveness lies in the conceptual nexus of the problem-event and response, and another in the associated understanding of responsive becoming, another instance of responsiveness in Deleuze's work lies in the emergence of the themes of caution, sobriety, and meticulousness in *A Thousand Plateaus*. The idea that caution and sobriety are a vital part of becoming further demonstrates how it is a responsive process. In plateau six, "How Do You Make Yourself a Body Without Organs," Deleuze and Guattari note that "three great strata . . . directly bind us: the organism, significance, and subjectification" (Deleuze and Guattari 1987: 159; 1980: 197). These layers of structure organize the body into its purportedly natural organization, language and meaning into pregiven forms of understanding (via interpretation), and the self into normative modes of subjectivity. Becoming or making oneself a body without organs is a way of disordering the body, breaking dominant patterns of meaning, and desubjectifying the self. Yet, Deleuze and Guattari claim that "caution is the art common to all three," the art that prevents these processes of becoming from turning dangerously destructive, from "sinking into the unreal, the illusory, the unmade, the unprepared," and from losing the thread that connects them to reality (Deleuze and Guattari 1987: 160; 1980: 198).

Becoming, they imply, is not haphazard or uncontrolled, but cautious and, in certain ways, planned and deliberate. Since a telos is absent from the concept of becoming, it is not planned in the sense in of being mapped out in advance in order to achieve some particular end. Rather, to avoid "sinking into . . . the unprepared," becoming must involve preparation in the sense of planning a mode of attack, a style, a form of engagement. One knows not where the process will lead or what affects it will produce, but one must know in relation to which strata and which forms of organization one seeks to become. Deleuze and Guattari make this point by noting that "you have to keep small supplies of signifiance and interpretation, if only to turn them against their own systems when the circumstances demand it, when things, persons, even situations, force you to; and you have to keep small rations of subjectivity in sufficient quantity to enable you to respond to the dominant reality" (Deleuze and Guattari 1987: 160; 1980: 199). As a process of construction, of making rather than descending into the entirely "unmade," becoming is laying out and following a "meticulous relation" with this dominant reality (Deleuze and Guattari 1987: 161; 1980: 199). Only through such a relation with the norms and forms of subjectivity that one seeks to evade and subvert is one able to do just that. This type of relation is one in which "you respond to the dominant reality." Ignoring it, moving away from it too quickly or too incautiously, is a recipe for a destructive rather than constructive becoming. Thus, we see that becoming presents a response to actual conditions, precluding obliviousness to them.

This inflection of Deleuzian ethics responds to the feminist concern that women's becomings will be subordinated to and undermined by a "more universalist movement of becoming" because it demonstrates that Deleuze and Guattari are aware of, and indeed even wary of, the sweeping force of absolute deterritorialization. Their construal of becoming as a mode of resistance and ethical relation draws a picture in which the process is not one in which individuals are swept up, desubjectified, and dispossessed of their "being" by the force of a movement external to them, but one in which courting desubjectification is itself a tactical practice. We might, consequently, understand "a more universalist movement of becoming" in a different sense, one that implies not an overwhelming and, indeed, undermining force of change but a power of transformation into which we tap in order to construct strategic forms of resistance. So, for instance, although Jane Drexler suggests that Deleuze and Guattari's "conceptual frameworks . . . sometimes seem too far removed from real social situations" from the perspective of a concerned feminist thinker, she also contends that "because the carnival of becoming occurs within the cracks of an existent system of relations, it serves as a site for experimentation without the threat of disappearing. Becoming-woman, then, is an ongoing creative practice rather than a question of being or not-being" (Drexler 2000: 233). While the "carnival" to which she refers is a concept gleaned from Bakhtin, and Drexler's assessment of Deleuze and Guattari's concept involves synthesizing these different theorists, her evaluation pertains to Deleuze's work in general: becoming-woman is not a decontexualized, ahistorical process, but is an eruption from within the dominant reality and is responsive to it. Becoming-woman, in particular, is more fruitfully understood by feminist thinkers as a conceptual tool to be used in the construction of new ways of living within (and against) a sex/gender system rather than as a foil against which to protest. As we have seen in the previous section, becoming-woman is actually an embodiment of a meticulous relation with dominant reality; it amounts to a protest against naturalized sex/gender norms and the way those norms for subjectivity tame and domesticate bodily forces, creating sexed types of "docile bodies."

Conclusion

A Deleuzian ethos, therefore, does not necessarily entail an unconcerned and detached mode of creativity, one that lacks attentiveness to the exigencies of present-day life and the specificity of sexed experience in particular. By reconsidering Deleuze's work from the perspective of a sympathetic feminist critic, we can emphasize alternate webs of concepts and devise new points of connection that reveal different ways of thinking about Deleuze's ethics. While many feminist readers of Deleuze have embraced and adopted his (and Guattari's) way of conceiving the body and desire precisely because these conceptions allow for an openness and creativity that other models of desire and sexed corporeality do not, I have tried to emphasize another array of concepts that may also be of value to feminists. In particular, the theme of responsiveness, which is subtly emphasized throughout Deleuze's work, may alleviate feminists' concerns about the character of becoming-woman by revealing becoming to be not a detached process of self-creation that authorizes obliviousness to others but a process that is grounded in relations with others and that enables us to transform those relations.

These instances of responsiveness in Deleuze's thought, however, do more than indicate that his work ought not to be objectionable from a feminist perspective. Beyond assuaging the aforementioned worries, the notion of responsiveness also provides the basis for an understanding of Deleuzian ethics that resonates more soundly with feminist aims. In this light, a Deleuzo-feminist ethics is simultaneously both responsive and creative, an ethics in which these features – creativity and responsiveness – are necessarily paired: for the creation of the new to be constructive (rather than haphazard or destructive), it must be responsive, and for responsibility or responsiveness to be forward-looking (rather than merely retroactive), it must be creative. Returning briefly to the four points of convergence between feminist and Deleuzian ethics outlined above, we can see that this pairing of creativity and responsiveness that defines Deleuzian ethics is vital to all four concerns. If ethics is a critical endeavor that contests the dominant norms of subjectivity for their oppressive sexism and rigidity, and is thus an inherently political enterprise, then it is necessarily responsive to present conditions. Yet, as a matter of experience and experiencing, engaging in certain kinds of practices in certain ways, ethics is also necessarily creative, moving beyond the limits of those present practices to venture into new ones that expand the contours of our experience. It is such a picture of ethical engagement as an oscillation between critique and construction that Deleuze and feminism can jointly embrace.

References

Braidotti, R. (1994), *Nomadic Subjects: Embodiment and Sexual Difference in Contemporary Feminist Theory*, New York: Columbia University Press.

Braidotti, R. (2003), "Becoming Woman: or Sexual Difference Revisited," *Theory, Culture, & Society*, 20:3, 43–64.

Brennan, S. (1999), "Recent Work in Feminist Ethics," *Ethics*, 109:4, 858–93.

Buchanan, I., and C. Colebrook (2000), *Deleuze and Feminist Theory*, Edinburgh: Edinburgh University Press.

Cixous, H. and C. Clément (2001), *The Newly Born Woman*, trans. B. Wing, Minneapolis: University of Minnesota Press.

Colebrook, C. (2000), "From Radical Representations to Corporeal Becomings: The Feminist Philosophy of Lloyd, Grosz, and Gatens," *Hypatia*, 15:2, 76–93.

Deleuze, G. (1969), *Logique du sens*, Paris: Minuit.

Deleuze, G. (1985), *Différence et repetition*, Paris: Presses Universitaries de France.

Deleuze, G. (1988), *Spinoza: Practical Philosophy*, trans. R. Hurley, San Francisco: City Lights Books.

Deleuze, G. (1990), *The Logic of Sense*, trans. M. Lester and C. Stivale, ed. C. Boundas, New York: Columbia University Press.

Deleuze, G. (1994), *Difference and Repetition*, trans. P. Patton, New York: Columbia University Press.

Deleuze, G. (1997), *Essays Critical and Clinical*, trans. D. W. Smith and M. A. Greco, Minneapolis: University of Minnesota Press.

Deleuze, G. and F. Guattari (1980), *Mille plateaux*, Paris: Minuit.

Deleuze, G. and F. Guattari (1987), *A Thousand Plateaus*, trans. B. Massumi, Minneapolis: University of Minnesota Press.

Deleuze, G. and F. Guattari (1991), *Qu'est-ce que la philosophie?*, Paris: Minuit.

Deleuze, G. and F. Guattari (1994), *What is Philosophy?*, trans. H. Tomlinson and G. Burchell, New York: Columbia University Press.

Derrida, J. (1985), "Choreographies," in J. Derrida, *The Ear of the Other*, trans. C. McDonald, Lincoln: University of Nebraska Press, 163–85.

Diprose, R. (2000), "What is (Feminist) Philosophy?" *Hypatia*, 15:2, 115–32.

Drexler, J. (2000), "Carnival: The Novel, Wor(l)ds, and Practicing Resistance," in D. Olkowski (ed.), *Resistance, Flight, Creation: Feminist Enactments of French Philosophy*, Ithaca: Cornell University Press, 216–34.

Gatens, M. (1996a), "Through a Spinozist Lens: Ethology, Difference, Power," in P. Patton (ed.), *Deleuze: a Critical Reader*, Oxford: Blackwell, 162–87.

Gatens, M. (1996b), *Imaginary Bodies: Ethics, Power and Corporeality*, New York: Routledge.

Gatens, M. (2000), "Feminism as 'Password': Re-thinking the 'Possible' with Spinoza and Deleuze," *Hypatia*, 15:2, 59–75.

Gilson, E. C. (2009), "Review of Peter Hallward's *Out of this World: Deleuze and the Philosophy of Creation*," *Continental Philosophy Review*, 42:3, 429–34.

Goulimari, P. (1999), "A Minoritarian Feminism?" *Hypatia*, 14:2, 97–120.

Grosz, E. (1994), *Volatile Bodies: Toward a Corporeal Feminism*, Bloomington: Indiana University Press.

Grosz, E. (1995), *Space, Time, and Perversion: Essays on the Politics of Bodies*, New York: Routledge.

Grosz, E. (2004), *The Nick of Time: Politics, Evolution, and the Untimely*, Durham: Duke University Press.

Hallward, P. (2006), *Out of this World: Deleuze and the Philosophy of Creation*, London: Verso.

Held, V. (1990), "Feminist Transformations of Moral Theory," *Philosophy and Phenomenological Research*, 50: Supplement, 321–44.

Held, V. (2004), "Taking Care: Care as Practice and Value," in C. Calhoun (ed.), *Setting the Moral Compass*, New York: Oxford University Press, 59–71.

Irigaray, L. (1985), *This Sex Which Is Not One*, trans. C. Porter and C. Burke, Ithaca: Cornell University Press.

Jaggar, A. M. (1991), "Feminist Ethics: Projects, Problems, Prospects," in C. Card (ed.), *Feminist Ethics*, Lawrence: University Press of Kansas, 78–104.

Jaggar, A. M. (1995), "Caring as a Feminist Practice of Moral Reason," in V. Held (ed.), *Justice and Care: Essential Readings*, Boulder: Westview Press, 179–99.

Lawlor, L. (2008), "Following the Rats: Becoming-Animal in Deleuze and Guattari," *SubStance*, 37:3, 169–87.

Lorraine, T. (1999), *Irigaray and Deleuze: Experiments in Visceral Philosophy*, Ithaca: Cornell University Press.

Marrati, P. (2006), "Time and Affects: Deleuze on Gender and Sexual Difference," *Australian Feminist Studies*, 21:51, 313–25.

Marsden, J. (2004), "Deleuzian Bodies, Feminist Tactics," *Women: A Cultural Review*, 15:3, 308–19.

Olkowski, D. (1999), *Gilles Deleuze and the Ruin of Representation*, Berkeley: University of California Press.

Olkowski, D. (2007), *The Universal (In the Realm of the Sensible): Beyond Continental Philosophy*, New York: Columbia University Press.

Patton, P. (2000), *Deleuze and the Political*, New York: Routledge.

Sellars, J. (2006), "An Ethics of the Event: Deleuze's Stoicism," *Angelaki*, 11:3, 157–71.

Tong, R. (2009), "Feminist Ethics," *Stanford Encyclopedia of Philosophy*, May 4, 2009, http://plato.stanford.edu/entries/feminism-ethics (accessed September 1, 2009).

Tronto, J. (1987), "Beyond Gender Difference to a Theory of Care," *Signs*, 12:4, 644–63.

Notes

1. As Rosemarie Tong's *Stanford Encyclopedia of Philosophy* entry on "Feminist Ethics" elaborates, feminist ethics has a history that predates contemporary thought. See the section on "Feminist Ethics: Historical Background" in Tong 2009.

2. Alison Jaggar's "Feminist Ethics: Projects, Problems, Prospects" clearly details the history, the central concerns, and the animating questions of the field of feminist ethics. See Jaggar 1991.

3. Pragmatist approaches to ethics would also likely fit this general description (especially regarding the first two points mentioned below), yet, as I intend to elucidate in what follows, Deleuzian and feminist ethics may have certain critical concerns in common that pragmatism – broadly construed – does not necessarily share. Likewise, Deleuzian approaches and pragmatic approaches may share a focus on the value of experimentation that many feminists would not automatically adopt. These further parallels in method and concern are the subject for a different study, however.

4. For many, feminist ethics is "synonymous with an ethics of care," but given that many feminist ethicists are critical of care ethics, or seek to prioritize concepts besides "care," I will treat care ethics as one dimension of feminist thinking about ethics (see Jaggar 1991: 83). For critical accounts of care ethics, see Tronto 1987 and Jaggar 1995.

5. See Irigaray 1985: 140–1 for an oft-referenced version of these criticisms. See Goulimari 1999 for a valuable assessment of these critiques as they are exemplified in the work of Alice Jardine and Rosi Braidotti. Chapter 2, "Can a Feminist Read Deleuze and Guattari?," of Olkowski 1999 also addresses Jardine's criticisms and those of Judith Butler in her *Subjects of Desire* quite well.

6. Grosz herself expresses this concern a few pages earlier with respect to Deleuze and Guattari's use of the figure of the girl: "The girl's specificity, her body, is once again robbed, this time not by the anonymous 'they' of the earlier passage but by Deleuze and Guattari who render it equivalent to a generalized and indeterminate in-betweenness, a transgressive movement in itself" (Grosz 1994: 175).

7. If we were to speculate about this, we might say that becoming-woman is accorded a unique role – as "the key to all the other becomings" – precisely because it is a process that undoes the bodily subjection that produces two diametrically opposed forms of sexed subjectivity – male and female – by normalizing a certain reproductively oriented organization of sexed bodies (Deleuze and Guattari 1987: 277; 1980: 340). This account of becoming-woman will be elaborated upon in what follows. It is perhaps in this respect that becoming-woman must be the first becoming, the process through which all others must pass; for any other becoming (becoming-animal, becoming-molecular, becoming-imperceptible), one must first become less rigidly lodged in one's subjectivity and, correspondingly, in one's body taken as an organism with specific purposes and proper ways of functioning in accord with those purposes.

8. When they further note, "There is no subject of becoming except as a deterritorialized variable of the majority, and there is no medium of becoming except as a deterritorialized variable of the minority," it is clear that subject of becoming is not necessarily a man but rather the elements of our identities that are "variable[s] of the majority" (Deleuze and Guattari 1987: 292; 1980: 357).

9. Feminist thinkers of various stripes, most notably Simone de Beauvoir and Luce Irigaray, have long made the point that female identity has always been understood and defined (by both men and women) in opposition and as lacking in relation to male identity, and thus that women have not genuinely had their own identity.

10. Nor does it seem that becoming-woman by "becoming-stereotypically-feminine" is the best way to contest the seeming givenness of oppositional sex/gender difference and create a sensibility able to disrupt a binary sex/gender system (indeed, it would seem to buy into the idea that nurture, superficiality, docility, coyness, and playfulness are proper to women, and can be taken up by men only in an unnatural process of alteration).

11. Regardless of whether or not it is developmentally accurate to claim that female children are subjected to this kind of training before male children, it does seem to be the case that normative gender development is a harder route for girls than it is for boys. The psychoanalytic story of the female child's development illustrates this point: on Freud's account, the female child has particular developmental difficulties because of the necessity of shifting her primary object choice from the mother to a male in order to accord with a norm of heterosexuality. Since the first object of attachment for both male and female children is female (the mother), male children take a woman as an analogous love object fairly easily whereas female children must shift from loving a woman to loving a man. The female body must also be reterritorialized so that the primary erotic zone is the vagina, not the clitoris; no such reterritorialization of the male body is required. De Beauvoir's account of female development in *The Second Sex* also clearly describes the troublesome nature of becoming a (molar) woman. The restrictions on movement, emphasis on "proper" behavior and dress, and limits on envisaging and undertaking creative endeavors all make female subjectivity perhaps more restrictive than male. Iris Marion Young's essay "Throwing Like a Girl" updates this kind of account from a Merleau-Pontyian perspective.

12. Paola Marrati also reads Deleuze on sexuality in this way. See the last section, "On Sexual Difference," in Marrati 2006.

13. In relation to the second point central to understanding becoming-women (the body as the terrain for normalizing subjectivity), the myriad ways of living one's sexuality in one's body are tied neither to reproductively oriented sexual nor to genitally focused activity. Eroticism is decoupled from purpose – reproduction or, equally teleological, orgasm – and proper locale, although it may remain

localized in particular bodily zones. In this context, sexual differences multiply to the extent that diverse modes of desire and sensation proliferate; there are "n sexes" because the configurations of bodies, desires, sensations, movements, etc., are innumerable, indeed, incalculable. This idea of a multiplicity of sexual differences, "n sexes," also finds expression in the work of Cixous and Derrida. See Cixous' essay "Sorties" in Cixous and Clément 2001, and Derrida 1985: 167, 183–5.

14. It is abstract in Deleuze and Guattari's sense of abstract as a virtual movement linking diverse features; the "abstract machine," for instance, "connects a language to the semantic and pragmatic contents of statements, to collective assemblages of enunciation, to a whole micropolitics of the social field" (Deleuze and Guattari 1987: 7; 1980: 14, cf. 252; 308).

15. The third concern – about a more universal movement of becoming – will be addressed in the next section.

16. To pursue this claim fully would require an entirely different paper, so I can only mention it here.

17. Something like "inter-sub-subjective" might be a more accurate albeit more unwieldy term, since we are not talking about connections between subjects per se, but among the more minute parts of those constituted subjects.

18. This brief synopsis cannot do justice to the diversity and richness of feminist work on Deleuze or influenced by him. For further Deleuzian inspired feminist thought consider, among others, the following: Braidotti 1994; Buchanan and Colebrook 2000; Gatens 1996a and 1996b, 2000; Grosz 2004; Lorraine 1999; Marrati 2006; Marsden 2004; Olkowski 1999, 2007.

19. Deleuze and Guattari acknowledge the necessity of feminist politics organized around a molar identity: "It is, of course, indispensable for women to conduct a molar politics, with a view to winning back their own organism, their own history, their own subjectivity" (Deleuze and Guattari 1987: 276; 1980: 338). Yet, they also warn of the danger of remaining within such an identity.

20. As Peter Hallward claims in his recent book, *Out of this World: Deleuze and the Philosophy of Creation*. My review of Hallward's book contests this claim. See Hallward 2006, Gilson 2009.

21. On this point see Hallward 2006 and Braidotti 2003. Rosalyn Diprose suggests that Deleuze and Guattari's understanding of the concept and the becoming of the concept via the philosopher in *What is Philosophy?* entails "little consideration of how the history of the philosopher's social experiences (their encounters with other social beings) informs the production of concepts" (Diprose 2000: 120).

22. This claim is a more general version of Deleuze's analysis, which elaborates both natural and philosophical illusions of the seventh postulate of the dogmatic image: "We always find the two aspects of the illusion: the natural illusion that involves tracing problems from supposedly preexistent propositions, logical opinions, geometrical theorems, algebraic equations, physical hypotheses, transcendental judgments; and the philosophical illusion that involves evaluating problems according to their 'solvability' – in other words, according to the extrinsic and variable form of their possibility of solution" (Deleuze 1994: 161; 1985: 209–10).

23. Thus, he shifts truth and falsity from the realm of designation or reference to that of problems themselves, as productive instances: "Far from being concerned with solutions, truth and falsity primarily affect problems" (Deleuze 1994: 159; 1985: 206). Poorly posed problems are themselves false, generating false solutions while original, creative problems are true problems that generate corresponding kinds of solutions: "A solution always has the truth that it merits

according to the problem to which it responds, and the problem always has the solution that it merits according to *its own* truth or falsity, that is to say, according to its sense" (Deleuze 1994: 159; 1985: 206).

24. John Sellars presents a very clear explanation of the ethics of the event, emphasizing the link Deleuze makes between Stoicism and Nietzschean *amor fati* and assessing the extent to which Deleuze's version of Stoicism is consonant with Stoic ethics itself. See Sellars 2006.

25. On the relation between the concept and event, Deleuze and Guattari state: "It is a concept that apprehends the event, its becoming, its inseparable variations. . . . In its production and reproduction, the concept has the reality of a virtual, of an incorporeal, of an impassible . . ." (Deleuze and Guattari 1994: 158–9; 1991: 150). Regarding the problem and concept, they note that "all concepts are connected to problems without which they would have no sense and which can themselves only be isolated or understood as their solution emerges" (Deleuze and Guattari 1994: 16; 1991: 22).

26. Thus, Deleuze and Guattari conceive the relationship between change – in the form of becoming – and history as one in which processes of becoming pull away from the determinacy of history, turning away from it not in order to dispense with it but to exceed it, reinvigorating the present with "an unhistorical element." They write, for instance, that "Philosophy cannot be reduced to its own history, because it continually wrests itself from this history in order to create new concepts that fall back into history but do not come from it. How could something come from history? Without history, becoming would remain indeterminate and unconditioned, but becoming is not historical. . . . The event itself needs becoming as an unhistorical element" (Deleuze and Guattari 1994: 96; 1991: 92).

Chapter 5

Deleuze, Values, and Normativity

Nathan Jun

This chapter is concerned with two distinct but related questions: (a) does Deleuzian philosophy offer an account of moral norms (i.e., a theory of normativity)? (b) does Deleuzian philosophy offer an account of moral values (i.e., a theory of the good)? These are important questions for at least two reasons. First, the moral- and value-theoretical aspects of Deleuzian philosophy have tended to be ignored, dismissed, overlooked, or otherwise overshadowed in the literature by the ontological, historical, and political aspects. Second, Deleuze – along with other alleged "postmodernists" such as Foucault and Derrida – has occasionally been accused of moral relativism, skepticism, and even nihilism. The aim of what follows is to demonstrate the value and importance of Deleuze's (and Guattari's) contributions to ethics and to defend Deleuzian philosophy from the charges just mentioned.

Between 1933 and 1945, Nazi Germany systematically dismantled German democracy, violated international law, and perpetrated countless horrific crimes against humanity – chief among them the extermination of 11 million people, approximately 6 million of whom were Jews. Between 1948 and 1994, Nelson Mandela and other activists engaged in a bloody but ultimately successful battle against the racist government of South Africa in an effort to abolish apartheid. Most people would regard the actions of the Nazis as morally reprehensible and the actions of the anti-apartheid freedom fighters as morally praiseworthy. Although both used violence in the pursuit of political ends, only the latter were allegedly morally justified in doing so. Why is this the case? On what grounds do we morally condemn the Nazis but morally praise the freedom fighters?

These and similar questions are questions about *political normativity* – the moral criteria by which we judge the actions, policies, and, in some instances, the very *existence* of political entities. Politico-normative criteria often involve moral concepts such as justice, rights, and equality which, though related to other moral concepts such as the right and the good, apply specifically to political entities rather than individual persons. The overarching concern of political normativity, therefore, is: *how ought political institutions to conduct themselves?* This includes *internal* questions (e.g., what laws, policies, or principles ought states to implement?) as well as *external* questions (e.g., how ought states to act with regard to other states?). Theories of political normativity often attempt to provide answers to the sorts of questions mentioned above in terms of *justice*, which is without a doubt the pre-eminent value of modern political philosophy. Generally speaking, a state is regarded as "just" if it implements just laws, policies, and social norms and acts justly towards its own citizens as well as those of other states. But this merely begs a further question, one that lies at the heart of the Western political tradition: namely, *what is justice?* Answers to this question are, of course, many and varied, but all of them take for granted that justice is the fundamental value in determining how political entities ought to conduct their affairs.

Although this approach to political philosophy is hardly new (Plato and Aristotle, not to speak of countless other ancients, were all preoccupied with questions of justice[1]), it did not "come of age," as it were, until the Enlightenment. For thinkers such as Immanuel Kant, normativity (both moral and political) was inexorably connected to related liberal concepts such as universal rationality and autonomous subjectivity. By the middle of the nineteenth century, however, such concepts had fallen prey to severe criticisms from the likes of Marx and Nietzsche. Since that time, philosophers such as Gilles Deleuze have pushed these criticisms to their limit, completely jettisoning the ontological, epistemological, and moral presuppositions upon which much of Enlightenment thought was founded. At the same time, it is clear that Deleuze – both in his work as a philosopher and as a political activist – believed that certain political institutions are to be recommended and others rejected.[2] How is this possible given Deleuze's wholesale rejection of Enlightenment concepts such as justice, autonomy, and transcendental normativity? In this chapter, my aim is to provide an answer to this question by exploring Deleuze's political philosophy. Although Deleuze rejects certain conceptions of normativity – most importantly the transcendental and universalizable normativity underlying liberal thought – I shall argue that he does not reject normativity *tout court*. Rather, he formulates an entirely new concept of normativity which is categorical without being transcendental – in other words, an *immanent* conception of normativity.

Writ large, normativity refers to imperatives, duties, obligations, permissions, and principles which do not describe the way the world is but rather prescribe the way it ought to be (Korsgaard 1996: 8–9; cf. Kagan 1997; Dancy 2000; Gert 2004; Sosa and Villanueva 2005). Morality, which may be regarded as coextensive with normativity, concerns laws, principles, and norms which prescribe how human beings ought and ought not to act (Korsgaard 1996: 8–9). To this extent, it is principally concerned with expressing what is *right* (i.e., what ought to be done) as distinct from what is *good* (i.e., what is worth being valued, promoted, protected, pursued, etc.). The latter is the purview of *axiology* or *ethics* – the study of what is good or valuable for human beings and, by extension, what constitutes a good life (Korsgaard 1996: 1–4; cf. Crisp and Slote 1997; MacIntyre 1997; Hursthouse 2002). For the ancients, the *ethical* question of "how one should live" (i.e., what constitutes a good life) was of primary importance. Life is judged vis-à-vis its relationship to the cosmological order – the "great chain of being" – in which it is situated. At the summit of this order is the Form of the Good (for Plato) or the specifically human *telos* known as *eudaimonia* (for Aristotle) to which human lives must conform. The good or the valuable transcends the realm of human experience because it is, in some sense, *more real*. Consequently, the things of this world are always striving not only to become *better* but to *be* – that is, to exist in the fullest and most real sense (Korsgaard 1996: 2). In the case of human beings, success in this striving is manifested in *arête* – that is, excellence or virtue.

The ethical question (*how should one live?*) was gradually replaced by the moral or normative question (*how should one act?* or *how should one behave?*). Enlightenment philosophers such as Bentham and Kant were no longer concerned with the good life so much as the moral righteous action. In truth, the origins of this shift can be traced to a much earlier period – namely, the Christian Middle Ages.[3] During that time, the classical concept of virtue is at first eclipsed by but ultimately fused with the Hebraic concept of *law*. In medieval Christianity, material (hence human) reality is no longer considered good (even in the less-than-ideal sense of "not as good as the realm of the Forms") but fallen. Consequently, material things – including human beings – are "reluctant, recalcitrant, [and] resistant" to the good (Korsgaard 1996: 4). They must be compelled through the force of laws, prescriptions, imperatives, and commandments which are given directly by God or else embedded in human nature itself.[4] Despite its emphasis on law rather than excellence, the Christian concept of normativity nonetheless maintains the assumption of a hierarchical cosmological order. Modern moral philosophers like Kant, Bentham, and Mill repudiate this idea in two crucial ways: first, by shifting the focus of moral judgment to individual subjects, as opposed to the relation of human life in general to a larger cosmological whole; and second, by rejecting the idea of a "great chain of being" – i.e., a qualitative ontological hierarchy with God (or the Forms) at the top and brute matter at the bottom. Consequently, morality is no longer concerned with the shape lives take; rather, it establishes the moral boundaries or limits of human action. As long as one acts within said boundaries, the direction one's life as a whole takes is entirely up to the individual. Morality becomes an exteriorized and transcendent concept, estranged from ordinary human life. Whether its ultimate foundation is the divine commandments of God or the dictates of an abstract moral law (e.g., Kant's categorical imperative or Bentham's principle of utility), it is no longer situated in our world or woven into the fabric of our experiences.

Much of this changes in the nineteenth century with Nietzsche. As Lewis Call notes, Nietzsche's "dispersed, nonlinear, aphoristic style combines with his powerfully destabilizing genealogical method to produce a thinking which calls everything into question ... [which] lays waste to every received truth of the modern world, including those of science, politics, and religion" (Call 2002: 2). Nietzsche's most radical moves are without question his announcement of the death of God[5] and his systematic critique of traditional morality.[6] In one fell swoop, Nietzsche not only destroys the very idea of God, but with it the transcendent foundation of conventional Judeo-Christian morality. This gives rise to a new question: not *how should one live?* or *how should one act?* but rather *how might one live?* In lieu of any transcendent "outside" to constrain our actions or establish what sorts of lives are worthwhile for us to pursue, we are free to pursue new ambitions and projects, to explore new ways of being – in short, to discover with Spinoza "what a body is capable of" (Deleuze 1990b: 226). The trend in philosophy known as "postmodernism," of which Deleuze is a part, is often said to begin with Nietzsche (as well as Freud and Marx). This claim is not without warrant, since all of the typical postmodern gestures – e.g., "incredulity towards metanarratives, a suspicious attitude towards the unified and rational self characteristic of much post-Enlightenment philosophy ... a powerfully critical stance towards any and all forms of power ... a critical awareness of the ways in which language can produce, reproduce, and transmit power [etc.]" – were first made by Nietzsche (Call 2002: 13–14). Todd May has suggested that the question of *how might one live?* is the cornerstone of Deleuze's philosophy (May 2005: 3). Far from merely reiterating Nietzsche's answers to this question, however, Deleuze systematically *reinvents* them.

The primary focus of Deleuze's early works is metaphysics and the history of philosophy. Nevertheless, a few ideas from these works are worth noting in brief detail in order to understand Deleuze's later, more explicitly moral-theoretical endeavors. The first is Deleuze's critique of the subject. Liberal political philosophy – not to speak of modern philosophy more generally – begins with the concept of the individual, self-identical subject (as opposed to non-subjective concepts such as essences, substances, or, in the political realm, sovereigns). Within this framework, the subject is not only conceptually distinct from the world but *substantially* distinct; it is, in a word, *beyond* or *transcendent* of it. This is because the subject (which is immaterial and active) *constitutes* the world (which is physical and passive). To this extent, moreover, the subject is superior to the world because it gives form and content to an otherwise empty and inert "prime matter." Deleuze denies this dualistic picture of reality. Following Spinoza, he instead claims that there is only one Being or substance which *expresses* itself differentially through an infinite number of attributes (chief among them thought and extension) which are in turn expressed through an infinite number of modes. Because Being is univocal, the world and everything it contains – from physical objects to mental constructions – cannot be articulated in terms of relations of self-contained identity (Deleuze 1994: 36–40). It does not follow from anything, it is not subordinated to anything, and it does not resemble anything; it expresses and is expressed in turn:

> Expression is on the one hand an explication, an unfolding of what expresses itself, the One manifesting itself in the Many ... Its multiple expression, on the other hand, involves Unity. The One remains involved in whatever expresses it, imprinted in what unfolds it, immanent in whatever manifests it. (Deleuze 1990b: 16)

All being is immanent; there is no transcendence, thus there are no self-contained identities outside the world (gods, values, subjectivities, etc.) that determine or constitute it (Deleuze 1983: 147). Furthermore, substance is at root a *difference* that exists virtually in the past and is actualized in various modes in the present.[7] These modes are not stable identities but multiplicities, differences, complicated intersections of forces. As Daniel Smith notes: "There is no universal or transcendental subject, which could function as the bearer of universal human rights, but only variable and historically diverse 'processes of subjectivation'" (Smith 2003: 307).

The Cartesio-Kantian subject which underlies modern politico-philosophical thought is therefore a fiction. It neither transcends the world nor is transcended by anything else in turn. But there is another key concept that underlies much modern thought – the concept of *rationality*. Simply put, rationality involves an alleged direction of fit between our thoughts and the world (theoretical rationality) or between our desires/moral beliefs and our actions (practical rationality). Both conceptions involve the idea of *representation* – our thoughts are rational to the extent that they accurately represent the world (i.e., are *true*); our actions, in turn, are rational to the extent that they accurately represent our desires/moral beliefs.[8] Ever since Kant, moral philosophers have tended to regard rationality as the foundation of normativity. As Christine Korsgaard puts it:

> Strictly speaking, we do not disapprove the action because it is vicious; instead, it is vicious because we disapprove it. Since morality is grounded in human sentiments, the normative question cannot be whether its dictates are true. Instead, it is whether we have reason to be glad that we have such sentiments, and to allow ourselves to be governed by them. (Korsgaard 1996: 50)

The point here is that an immoral action – one which we *ought not* to perform – is one which we have a *rational reason* not to perform. What distinguishes normativity from conventional modes of practical reasoning is the universalizable or categorical nature of the rational reason in question – i.e., the fact that in all relevantly similar circumstances it applies equally to all moral agents at all times. Typically this rational reason has taken the form of a universal moral principle, such as Kant's categorical imperative ("so act on that maxim which you can at the same time will to be a universal law") or Bentham's principle of utility ("act so as to bring about the greatest happiness for the greatest number"). It is precisely this universal and abstract character which makes normativity "transcendent" in the sense outlined earlier.

Deleuze regards this concept of rationality, no less than the concept of the subject, as a fiction: "Representation fails to capture the affirmed world of difference. Representation has only a single center, a unique and receding perspective, and in consequence a false depth. It mediates everything, but mobilizes and moves nothing" (Deleuze 1994: 55–6). The problem with this "dogmatic image of thought" is that it relies on representation, and difference (read: substance) cannot be represented through linguistic categories. This is because linguistic categorization assumes that the things it aims to represent are fixed, stable, and self-identical, which, as we noted above, they are not. The difference at the heart of being is fluid, constantly overflowing the boundaries of representation.[9] In the place of representational language, Deleuze offers what he calls a "logic of sense" (which, for the sake of brevity, we shall not explore here.)[10] Deleuze's political philosophy, as outlined in the two volumes of *Capitalism and Schizophrenia* co-authored with Guattari,[11] may be seen as an extension of his earlier ontology. Like all of Deleuze's works, the *Capitalism and Schizophrenia* volumes are so formidably dense and complicated that we cannot begin to do justice to them in an essay of this size. Instead we will limit ourselves to a brief "thematic overview" of those ideas and concepts which are relevant to understanding the role of normativity in Deleuzian philosophy.

Just as Deleuze replaces the foundational modern concept of identity with the concept of difference, so does he replace the concept of the individual subject with other concepts such as the *machine*. In Deleuze's ontology, individuals, communities, states, and the various relations that obtain among them are all understood as machines or machinic processes. Unlike an organism, which is "a bounded whole with an identity and an end," and unlike a mechanism, which is "a closed machine with a specific function," a machine is "nothing more than its connections; it is not made by anything, and has no closed identity" (Colebrook 2002: 56; cf. Deleuze and Guattari 1977: 1). Whereas liberalism regards the relation between individuals and society mechanistically (i.e., as a "specific set of connections") or organically (i.e., "as a self-organizing whole"), Deleuze regards this relation *machinically* (i.e., "as only one level of connections that can be discussed") (May 2005: 123). Unlike the static, self-contained, and transcendental subject of liberal theory, machines are fluid, mobile, and dynamic; they are capable of changing, of connecting and reconnecting with other machines, they are immanent to the connections they make, and vice versa. In creating these connections, moreover, machines produce and are produced by desires (hence "desiring-machines"). The liberal subject consents to be governed because it lacks the ability to realize its own interests independently of the state. Machines, in contrast, "do not operate out of lack. They do not seek to fulfill needs. Instead they produce connections. Moreover, the connections they produce are not pre-given ... Machines are productive in unpredictable and often novel ways" (May 2005: 125).

There are different types of machines which can be distinguished according to how they operate. In all cases, machines are driven by fuel, which Deleuze variously describes as power (especially in Deleuze 1988) or, more typically, in terms of *forces*. Deleuze distinguishes between two types of force to which he assigns different names in different books. On the one hand there is what he refers to as "reactive force" in his book on Nietzsche and as "social" or "oedipal" force in *Capitalism and Schizophrenia*. On the other hand there is what he refers to as "active force," "forces of desire," or "schizophrenic" force. What are these forces and how do they operate according to Deleuze? In one decidedly aphoristic passage, Deleuze claims there are only forces of desire (i.e., active or schizophrenic forces) and social (i.e., reactive or oedipal) forces (Deleuze and Guattari 1977: 29). A force of desire or active force is one which "goes to the limit of its power," i.e., which expresses itself creatively to the fullest extent of its ability, which produces rather than represses its object (Deleuze 1983: 59). Social or reactive forces, in contrast, "decompose; they separate active force from what it can do; they take away a part or almost all of its power . . . they dam up, channel, and regulate" the flow of desire (Deleuze 1983: 33, 66). In making this distinction, Deleuze does not mean to suggest that there are two distinct *kinds* of forces which differentially affect objects exterior to themselves. On the contrary, there is only a single, unitary force which manifests itself in particular "assemblages" (Deleuze 1983: 66). Each of these assemblages, in turn, contains within itself both desire (active force) and various "bureaucratic or fascist pieces" (reactive force) which seek to subjugate and annihilate that desire (Deleuze and Guattari 1986: 60; cf. Deleuze and Parnet 1987: 133). Neither force acts or works upon pre-existent objects; rather everything that exists is alternately created and/or destroyed in accordance with the particular assemblage which gives rise to it.

As May notes by way of summary, "power does not suppress desire; rather it is implicated in every assemblage of desire" (May 1994: 71). Machines are constituted ("assembled") by forces that are immanent to them; "concrete social fields" are therefore affects of complex movements and connections of forces which vary in intensity over time (Deleuze and Guattari 1977: 135). For Deleuze, forces are principally distinguished according to their affects, which in turn are distinguished according to whether they are *life-affirming* or *life-denying* at the level of *life itself* (Deleuze 1990b: 102, 218). Unlike the concept of "coercive power," which has a kind of built-in normativity, the concepts of life-affirming/life-denying are, in the first instance at least, *purely descriptive*; that is, they describe the way forces produce reality and nothing else. Given the ubiquitous and ontologically constitutive nature of force, it goes without saying that force *simpliciter* cannot be "abolished" or even "resisted." As we shall see, this does not mean that *repressive* social forces (or machines) cannot be opposed. It does imply, however, that for

Deleuze (as for Spinoza) the question is not whether and how resistance is possible, but rather how and why desire comes to repress and ultimately destroy itself in the first place (Deleuze and Guattari 1977: xiii). This requires, among other things, an analysis of the various assemblages that come into being over time (vis-à-vis their affects) as well as the experimental pursuit of alternative assemblages at the level of praxis.

According to Deleuze, repressive forces do not emanate from a unitary source but rather within multiple sites. The complex interconnection of these sites, moreover, is precisely what gives rise to the various machines that inhabit the social world (this is what he means when he suggests that power is "rhizomatic" as opposed to "arboreal"). This is not to say that power does not become concentrated within certain sites; indeed, much of *Capitalism and Schizophrenia* is given over to an analysis of such concentrations as they manifest themselves in particular political and economic forms. What this analysis reveals is a constant conflict between reactive machines (e.g., the State-form) which seek to "overcode" and "territorialize" desire, and various desiring-machines (e.g., the nomadic war machine), which seek to "reterritorialize" themselves along "lines of flight." Similar analyses could no doubt be afforded of the "Church-form," the "gender-form," and countless other sites of concentrated power. In all such cases, however, one and the same force is simultaneously seeking to escape and re-conquer itself, and it is precisely this tension which allows ostensibly "revolutionary" or "liberatory" movements (e.g., Bolshevism) to occasionally metamorphose into totalitarian regimes (e.g., Stalinist Russia).

For Deleuze, then, political power is multifarious and rhizomatic in nature. Unlike Marxism and other "strategic" political philosophies which identify a unitary locus of repressive power, the "tactical" political philosophy of Deleuze "perform[s] [its] analyses within a milieu characterized . . . by the tension between irreducible and mutually intersecting practices of power" (May 1994: 11). In older radical philosophies such as anarchism, manifestations of power are distinguished according to their *effects*. These effects, in turn, are distinguished according to their relative *justifiability* within a universalizable normative scheme that is both prior and exterior to power itself. Repressive power, again, is only a species of "power to," which is at least analogous if not identical to Deleuze's all-encompassing "force." The only real difference is that "repressive power" in the classical paradigm involves the forcible or even violent compulsion of bodies (what Foucault calls "biopower") whereas repressive forces in the Deleuzian scheme principally work to subjugate *desires*.

This brings us to the question of how Deleuze reinvents the concept of normativity. Some thinkers, most notably Paul Patton and Todd May, have attempted to situate Deleuze's thought within the normative paradigm of classical liberalism. May, for example, tries to found Deleuze's political philosophy on a pair of normative principles which, he thinks, are intimated below the surface of Deleuze's writings. In the final chapter of *The Political Philosophy of Poststructuralist Anarchism*, May rehearses the oft-repeated accusation that poststructuralism engenders a kind of moral nihilism (May 1994: 121–7). Such an accusation is a product, May thinks, of the poststructuralists' general unwillingness to "refer existence to transcendent values," which, as we noted, is the dominant strategy of much traditional moral philosophy in the West (May 1994: 127). Strangely, May goes to great lengths to explain why Deleuze rejects classical "ethics," only to argue that certain of Deleuze's other commitments implicitly contradict this rejection. As he notes, Deleuze

> praises Spinoza's *Ethics*, for instance, because it "replaces Morality . . ." For Deleuze, as for Nietzsche, the project of measuring life against external standards constitutes a betrayal rather than an affirmation of life. Alternatively, an ethics of the kind Spinoza has offered . . . seeks out the possibilities life offers rather than denigrating life by appeal to "transcendent values." Casting the matter in more purely Nietzschean terms, the project of evaluating a life by reference to external standards is one of allowing reactive forces to dominate active ones, where reactive forces are those which "separate active force from what it can do." (May 1994: 127)

In the same breath, however, May argues that Deleuze provides no explicit means by which to distinguish active forces from reactive ones beyond a vague appeal to "experimentation" (May 1994: 128). Such a means, he thinks, can only be discovered by extracting "several intertwined and not very controversial ethical principles" from the hidden nooks of the Deleuzian corpus.

The first such principle, which May terms the "anti-representationalist principle," is that "practices of representing others to themselves – either in who they are or in what they want – ought, as much as possible to be avoided" (May 1994: 130). The second, which he calls the "principle of difference," holds that "alternative practices, all things being equal, ought to be allowed to flourish and even to be promoted" (May 1994: 133). In both cases, May provides ample textual evidence to demonstrate that Deleuze (inter alia) is implicitly committed to the values underlying these principles. I think his analysis in this regard is very astute, as it is very clear from the foregoing that (for example)

"Gilles Deleuze's commitment to promoting different ways of thinking and acting is a central aspect of his thought" (May 1994: 134). What I take issue with is the idea that the avowal of such values, implicit or otherwise, is *a fortiori* an avowal of *nomological* (i.e., law-, principle-, or rule-based) normative principles.

As we noted above, the defining characteristics of nomological normativity are precisely abstraction, universality, and exteriority to life, all of which Deleuze seeks to undermine in his analysis of power. Although May argues that Deleuze's unwillingness to prescribe universalizable norms is itself motivated by a commitment to the aforesaid principles, this amounts to claiming that Deleuze is self-referentially inconsistent; it does not lead, as May thinks, to a general absolution of the charge of moral nihilism. If it is true that Deleuze scorns representation and affirms difference – and I think it is – the operative values cannot be articulated and justified by means of representation or the suppression of difference except on pain of dire contradiction. This is precisely the opposite of what May wishes to argue.

Paul Patton offers a much more promising idea – namely, that the "the overriding norm [for Deleuze] is that of deterritorialization" (Patton 2000: 9). In shifting the focus of political philosophy from static, transcendent concepts like "the subject" and "rationality" to dynamic, immanent concepts such as "machinic processes," "processes of subjec-tification," etc., Deleuze also shifts the focus of normativity from extensive to intensive criteria of normative judgment. As Patton notes, "What a given assemblage is capable of doing or becoming is determined by the lines of flight or deterritorialization it can sustain" (Patton 2000: 106). Thus normative criteria will not only demarcate the application of power by a given assemblage but, as Smith points out, "will also find the means for the critique and modification of those norms" (Smith 2003: 308). Put another way, political normativity must be capable not only of judging the activity of assemblages, but also of judging the norms to which said assemblages gives rise. Such normativity is precisely what prevents the latent "micro-fascism of the avant-garde" from blossoming into full-blown totalitarianism.

The normative principles which May attributes to Deleuze are prob-lematic not because they are categorical but because they are tran-scendent – they stand outside of any and all particular assemblages and so cannot be self-reflexive. It is easy to see how such principles, however radical they may seem on the surface, can become totalitar-ian. To take a somewhat far-fetched but relevant example, the principle of anti-representationalism would effectively outlaw *any* processes of majoritarian representation, even in banal contexts such as homecoming competitions or bowling leagues. Likewise, the principle of difference would permit, or at least does not obviously prohibit, morally odious "alternative practices" such as thrill-killing or rape. A year after the publication of *Poststructuralist Anarchism*, May amended his views somewhat, expanding them into a comprehensive moral theory (May 1995). The foundation of this theory is a revised version of the anti-representationalist principle, according to which "people ought not, other things being equal, to engage in practices whose effect, among others, is the representation of certain intentional lives as either intrinsically superior or intrinsically inferior to others" (May 1995: 48). The principle of difference drops out of the picture altogether.

May buttresses the revised anti-representationalist principle with what he calls a "multi-value consequentialism" (May 1995: Chapter 3). After suggesting that "moral values" are "goods to which people ought to have access" (May 1995: 87), he proceeds to argue that the "values" entailed by the anti-representationalist principle include "rights, just distributions, and other goods" (May 1995: 88). May's theory judges actions as "right" to the extent that (a) they do not violate the anti-representationalist principle nor (b) result in denying people goods to which they ought to have access. Whatever substantive objections one might raise against this theory would be quite beside the point. The problem, as we have already noted, is that the very idea of a "moral theory of poststructuralism" based on universalizable normative principles is oxymoronic. What distinguishes normativity from conventional modes of practical reasoning is the universalizable or categorical nature of the rational reason in question – i.e., the fact that in all relevantly similar circumstances it applies equally to all moral agents at all times. Typically this rational reason has taken the form of a universal moral principle, and to this extent, May's "principle of anti-representationalism" is no different from Kant's categorical imperative or Bentham's principle of utility. It is precisely this universal and abstract character that makes normativity "transcendent" in the sense outlined earlier, and poststructuralism is nothing if not a systematic repudiation of transcendence.

Some would suggest that normativity of this sort is attractive precisely because it provides us with a reliable means by which to guide our actions. It is not at all clear, however, that this requires transcendental moral principles, especially if ordinary practical reasoning will suffice. Take, for example, the so-called prefigurative principle, which demands that any means employed be morally consistent with the desired ends; this is a practical principle or hypothetical imperative of the form "if you want X you ought to do Y." Anarchism, a political theory whose adherents have historically affirmed the prefigurative principle, has long argued that incongruity between the means and the end is not pragmatically conducive to the achievement of the end. As such, it is not the case that one ought to do Y because it is the "morally right" thing to do, but because it is the most sensible course of action given one's desire to achieve X. A principle of this sort can be regarded as categorical or even universalizable, but it is scarcely "transcendental." Its justification is immanent to its purpose, just as the means are immanent to the desired end. It provides us with a viable categorical norm without any concept of transcendence.

Transcendental normativity generates norms that do not and cannot take account of their own deterritorialization or lines of flight. Because the norms follow from, and so are justified by, the transcendental ground, they cannot provide self-reflexive criteria by which to question, critique, or otherwise act upon themselves. The concept of normativity as deterritorialization, on the contrary, does not generate norms. Rather, it stipulates that "what 'must' always remain normative is the ability to critique and transform existing norms, that is, to create something new ... [o]ne cannot have preexisting norms or criteria for the new; otherwise it would not be new, but already foreseen" (Smith 2003: 308). Absolute deterritorialization is therefore categorical, insofar as it applies to every possible norm as such, but it is not transcendent; rather, it is immanent to whatever norms (and, by extension, assemblages) constitute it. (There can be no deterritorialization without a specific assemblage; thus normativity of deterritorialization both constitutes and is constituted by the particular norms/assemblages to which it applies.) Considered as such, normativity as deterritorialization is ultimately a kind of "pragmatic" normativity. It determines what norms ought or ought not to be adopted in concrete social formations according to a pragmatic consideration – namely, whether the norm adopted is capable of being critiqued and transformed. This further entails that a norm cannot be adopted if it prevents other norms from being critiqued and transformed. We might say, then, that for Deleuze a norm must (a) be self-reflexive and (b) its adoption must not inhibit the self-reflexivity of norms. Because normativity is a process that constitutes and is constituted by other processes, it is dynamic, and to this extent we should occasionally expect norms to become perverted or otherwise outlive their usefulness. Pragmatic normativity provides a meta-norm that is produced by the adoption of contingent norms but stands above them as a kind of sentinel; to this extent it is categorical without being transcendent.

Such a view of normativity, while interesting and promising, is not without its problems. Among other things, it does not specify when it is advisable or acceptable to critique or transform particular norms; rather, it only stipulates that any norm must in principle be open to critique and transformation. For example, suppose I belong to a society that adopts vegetarianism as a norm. The adoption of this norm obviously precludes other norms, such as carnivorousness. Is this a reason to reject it? Not necessarily. As long as we remain open to other possibilities, the norm is at least *prima facie* justified. But this by itself does not explain (a) what reasons we may have to adopt a vegetarian rather than a carnivorous norm in the first place; and (b) what reasons we may have to ultimately reject a vegetarian norm in favor of some other norm. Such an explanation would require a theory of value – that is, an axiological criterion that determines what things are worth promoting or discouraging vis-à-vis the adoption of normative principles.

As Spinoza noted, the alternative to morality (and, by extension, normativity) is *ethics* – i.e., the study of value and the good life. The Deleuzian distinction between "life-affirming" and "life-denying" practices, not to speak of related concepts such as Foucault's "care of the self," are replete with ethical content. It is clear, after all, at least implicitly, that pursuing "life-affirming" practices or engaging in the "care of the self" are in some sense "valuable" or constitutive of a "good life." The question, of course, is how Deleuze would go about defining "value" or "the good life." We already know that ethics is to be distinguished from morality on the basis of its concreteness, particularity, and interiority to life itself. Rather than posing universal codes of conduct grounded in abstract concepts like "rationality," ethics is instead concerned with the myriad ways in which lives can be led. To this extent, the traditional notion that ethics is concerned with *values* rather than *norms* is not entirely unfitting. Clearly values can be and often are universalized and rendered transcendent, as in the case of natural law theory. Even the Greeks, for whom value was a function of particular standards of excellence proper to particular things, believed that such standards were uniform for all human beings.

There are at least two ways to understand the concept of value. On the first, which we can call the "descriptive" reading, "X is valuable" means "X is something which I happen to value," which in turn means "X is something of which I happen to approve, or which I happen to regard positively." On the second, which we can call the "normative" reading, "X is valuable" means "X is something which I *ought to* value" (regardless of whether I actually value X or not), which in turns means

"X is something of which I *ought* to approve, or which I *ought to* regard positively" (regardless of whether I actually approve of or regard X positively or not). The problem with the descriptive reading is that seems to confuse the *concept of value* with the *act of valuing*. (Surely not everything that I happen to value is *actually* valuable?) On the other hand, the normative reading appears circular. How do I know whether I *ought* to value something or not? Well, presumably I ought to value it just in case it is valuable. But it is valuable just in case I ought to value it, and so on. (It is precisely this sort of conundrum that led G. E. Moore to postulate that "goodness" or "value" is an irreducible and non-natural property of things.)

A. C. Ewing famously suggested that to value something, to treat it as good, is to treat it as something "we ought to welcome, [to] rejoice in if it exists, [to] seek to produce if it does not exist ... to approve its attainment, count its loss a deprivation, hope for and not dread its coming if this is likely, [and] avoid what hinders its production" (Ewing 1947: 149). It is worth noting at the outset that Deleuze isn't as interested in the question of "what is good" or "what is valuable" as he is in the capacity of human beings to *value* things (or, if you like, to "create values"). Every human being is both a product of a unique and complicated multiplicity of forces, including the inward-directed forces of self-creation, as well as a producer of difference, change, movement, and transformation. These are the processes – which collectively, following Deleuze, we can simply call "life" or "being alive" – through which human beings experience value. Life, understood in this sense, is what interests Deleuze. There is little doubt that Deleuze values life – or, rather, that Deleuzian philosophy regards life as valuable, i.e., as something that is in some sense worthy of being valued. On the other hand, could life or anything else be "intrinsically good" in a Deleuzian universe, if by this we mean that the value of life obtains independently of its relations to other things, or that life is somehow worthy of being valued on its own account, etc.? For Deleuze, after all, it would not make sense to speak of life, or anything else, in this way, since by its very nature life is relational and dynamic. Thus if life is *worthy* of being protected, pursued, promoted, etc., it cannot be because of traditional distinctions between intrinsic and instrumental value.

Deleuze's valorization of "difference" and scorn of "representation" surely hint at, if they do not altogether reveal, a solution to this issue. Time and again Deleuze, like Nietzsche, emphasizes the importance of loving and affirming life. It is likewise clear that this *"Leben-liebe"* is both a condition and a consequence of creativity, experimentation, the pursuit of the new and the different. To the extent that representation and its social incarnations are opposed to life, they are condemnable, marked by "indignity." This strongly suggests that for Deleuze, again, life is loveable, valuable, and good; that it is worthy of being protected and promoted; that whatever is contrary to it is worthy of disapprobation and opposition. At the same time, however, we must recall that *the life of which he speaks is something virtual, and there is no guarantee that its actualizations will be affirmative and active.* Of course, this is simply one more reason why Deleuze emphasizes experimentation, on the one hand, and eternal vigilance, on the other. Our experiments may lead to positive transformations, they may lead to madness, they may lead to death. What starts out as a reckless and beautiful affirmation of life can result in a death camp. It is not enough, therefore, to experiment and create; one must be mindful of, and responsible for, one's creations. The process requires an eternal revolution against life-denial wherever and however it arises – eternal because without a *telos*, and without a *telos* because life-denial as such can never be completely stopped. It can only be contained or, better, outrun. Whatever goodness is created along the way, Deleuze thinks, will always be provisional, tentative, and contingent, but this is hardly a reason not to create it.

Deleuzian value theory, then, aspires to be an eternal revolution against representation which is itself an eternal process of creation and transformation, an eternal practice of freedom. The good or ethical life is both a goal as well as the infinite network of possibilities we travel in its pursuit. Ethics traces the multiple locations at which means and ends overlap or blur together, the multiple sites at which our desires become immanent to their concrete actualizations, the multiple spaces within which the concrete realizations of our desire become immanent to those desires. For Deleuze, such sites and spaces are constantly shifting into and out of focus, moving into and out of existence. Concrete moral and political goals sought as an end are constituted by our seeking them. Thus the process of seeking freedom or justice is a process of eternal movement, change, becoming, possibility, and novelty which simultaneously demands eternal vigilance, and endurance. There is neither certainty nor respite at any point. There are no stable identities, no transcendent truths, no representations or images. There are only the variable and reciprocal and immanent processes of creation and possibility themselves. Deleuze thinks every human being is the product of a unique and complicated multiplicity of forces. Consequently only individuals are in a position to discover, through processes of experimentation, what is valuable in their lives, what they ought to pursue and avoid, etc., in a particular set of circumstances. Only through the process of pursuing alternative practices can one begin to discover the manifold possibilities of life. Deleuze's explicitly rejects the idea that there is any sort of "natural" hierarchy of values among individuals. As he notes time and again in *Capitalism and Schizophrenia*, the authority of oppressive assemblages is always justified by assuming that certain peoples' values are, in some sense, *weightier* than those of others, and it is precisely the function of normativity to conceal the arbitrary and artificial nature of this assumption under the guise of universalizability and transcendence.

The process of creating value therefore requires an *eternal* revolution against the forces of repression wherever and however they arise. It lacks any kind of *telos* or end goal, since there is always a micro-fascism lurking at the heart of every system of personal value-construction which can, and often will, reterritorialize and overcode that system. Again, such a micro-fascism is every bit as instrumental in producing value as, say, the desire for freedom. It is not the case, therefore, that we *ought* to oppose what is anti-life, but rather that we *must* if we are to ever achieve value at all. The fact that the discovery of value is always provisional, tentative, and contingent is hardly a reason not to pursue it. In the end, there may be no ultimate means by which to distinguish one way of living from another, but it is precisely our inability to secure such a means which necessitates an ongoing commitment to ethical life.

References

Aristotle (1998), *Nichomachean Ethics*, trans. J. L. Ackrill et al., New York: Oxford University Press.

Call, L. (2002), *Postmodern Anarchism*, Lanham: Lexington Books.

Celano, A. J. (2000), *From Priam to the Good Thief: The Significance of a Single Event in Greek Ethics and Medieval Moral Teaching*, Toronto: Pontifical Institute of Medieval Studies Press.

Colebrook, C. (2002), *Gilles Deleuze*, New York: Routledge.

Crisp, R. and M. Slote (1997), *Virtue Ethics*, New York: Oxford University Press.

Dancy, J. (2000), *Normativity*, London: Blackwell.

Deleuze, G. (1983), *Nietzsche and Philosophy*, trans. H. Tomlinson, New York: Columbia University Press.

Deleuze, G. (1988), *Bergsonism*, trans. H. Tomlinson and B. Habberjam, New York: Zone.

Deleuze, G. (1990a), *The Logic of Sense*, trans. M. Lester and C. Stivale, ed. C. Boundas, New York: Columbia University Press.

Deleuze, G. (1990b), *Expressionism in Philosophy: Spinoza*, trans. M. Joughin, New York: Zone.

Deleuze, G. (1994), *Difference and Repetition*, trans. P. Patton, New York: Columbia University Press.

Deleuze, G. and C. Parnet (1987), *Dialogues*, trans. H. Tomlinson and B. Haberjam, New York: Columbia University Press.

Deleuze, G. and F. Guattari (1977), *Anti-Oedipus: Capitalism and Schizophrenia*, trans. R. Hurley, M. Seem, and H. R. Lame, New York: Viking Press.

Deleuze, G. and F. Guattari (1986), *Kafka: Toward a Minor Literature*, trans. D. Polan, Minneapolis: University of Minnesota Press.

Deleuze, G. and F. Guattari (1987), *A Thousand Plateaus: Capitalism and Schizophrenia*, trans. B. Massumi, Minneapolis: University of Minnesota Press.

Ewing, A. C. (1947), *The Definition of Good*, London: Macmillan.

Gert, J., et al. (2004), *Brute Rationality: Normativity and Human Action*, Cambridge: Cambridge University Press.

Hursthouse, R. (2002), *On Virtue Ethics*, New York: Oxford University Press.

Kagan, S. (1997), *Normative Ethics*, Westview Press.

Korsgaard, C. (1996), *Sources of Normativity*, Cambridge: Cambridge University Press.

May, T. (1994), *The Political Philosophy of Poststructuralist Anarchism*, University Park: Pennsylvania State University Press.

May, T. (1995), *The Moral Theory of Poststructuralism*, University Park: Pennsylvania State University Press.

May, T. (2005), *Gilles Deleuze: An Introduction*, Cambridge: Cambridge University Press.

MacIntyre, A. (1997), *After Virtue*, London: Duckworth.

Nietzsche, F. (1969), *On the Genealogy of Morals*, trans. W. Kaufmann and R. J. Hollingdale, New York: Vintage Books.

Nietzsche, F. (1988), *Thus Spake Zarathustra*, trans. W. Kaufmann, New York: Penguin.

Nietzsche, F. (1990), *The Gay Science*, trans. W. Kaufmann, New York: Vintage Books.

Nietzsche, F. (1991), *Daybreak*, trans. R. J. Hollingdale, Cambridge: Cambridge University Press.

Patton, P. (2000), *Deleuze and the Political*, New York: Routledge.

Plato (1992), *The Republic*, trans. G. M. A. Grube and C. D. C. Reeve, Indianapolis: Hackett.

Smith, D. (2003), "Deleuze and the Liberal Tradition: Normativity, Freedom, and Judgment," *Economy and Society*, 32:2, 299–324.

Sosa, E. and E. Villanueva (2005), *Normativity*, London: Blackwell.

Notes

1. See, for example, Plato 1992: 433a–c; Aristotle 1998, esp. Book V.
2. Unlike his longtime friend and collaborator Félix Guattari, who had been involved in radical activism since the early 1960s, Deleuze did not become especially politically active until after 1968. "From this period onward," writes Paul Patton, "he became involved with a variety of groups and causes, including the *Groupe d'Information sur les Prisons* (GIP) begun by Foucault and others in 1972" (Patton 2000: 4). More importantly, Deleuze's prior commitment to speculative metaphysics gave way to a deep interest in political philosophy as he attempted to make sense of the political practices he encountered in 1968.
3. Hence the development in the Middle Ages of casuistry – the systematic application of general moral principles to concrete moral cases – which remained the dominant form of moral reasoning in the West until at least the Renaissance. See, for example, Raymund of Pennafort, *Summa de Poenitentia et Matrimonia* (c.1235); Bartholomew of San Concordio, *Summa Pisana* (c.1317); Sylvester Prierias (d.1523), *Summa Summarum*; St. Antoninus of Florence (d.1459),

Summa Confessionalis and *Summa Confessorum*. For more on the history of medieval casuistry see Celano 2000.

4. This is the context in which St. Thomas Aquinas formulates his natural law theory in *Summa Theologiae* I–II (Q. xc–cviii).
5. See Nietzsche 1988, esp. Prologue, section 2; and 1990, esp. Book 9, section 125.
6. See Nietzsche 1991, esp. section 3; Nietzsche 1988, esp. "On the Old and New Tablets" and "On Self Overcoming"; and Nietzsche 1969, esp. essay 2, sections 11–20.
7. For more on the temporality of substance, see Deleuze 1988.
8. Some philosophers claim that an action is rational if and only if it satisfies a *rational* desire. This is an ongoing debate within contemporary analytic moral philosophy which I shall not discuss here.
9. Derrida articulates a similar view; the difference is that for him this fluidity is a feature of language rather than a feature of reality itself.
10. See Deleuze 1990a.

Chapter 6

Ethics and the World without Others

Eleanor Kaufman

There are numerous ways in which the thought of Gilles Deleuze might be aligned with a generally recognizable form of ethics: from Deleuze's beautiful Nietzschean meditations in *Spinoza: Practical Philosophy* on the *ethics* of good and bad forces as opposed to the *morality* of Good and Evil (Deleuze 1988: 17–29), to Foucault's famous designation of Deleuze and Guattari's *Anti-Oedipus* as a "book of ethics, the first book of ethics to be written in France in quite a long time" (Deleuze and Guattari 1983: xv), to the late profoundly ethical reflections on conceptual personae, philosophical friendship, and even an ethics of "life" (Deleuze and Guattari 1994). This is not to mention the Stoic dictum from *The Logic of Sense* "not to be unworthy of what happens to us" (Deleuze 1990: 149). While it is specifically the early single-authored work from the late 1960s that will be under consideration here, at issue is a notion of ethics that arguably might not be recognized as such at all, or as in any way resonant with Deleuze. The ethics in question here – what will at times be labeled an "*anethics*" – is stranger and darker than the more palatable examples listed above, an ethics more in resonance with Lacan as well as with a certain structuralist imperative.

Lacan will propose a counter-intuitive if not perverse definition of ethics in his 1959–60 seminar *The Ethics of Psychoanalysis*: "And it is because we know better than those who went before how to recognize the nature of desire, which is at the heart of this experience, that a reconsideration of ethics is possible, that a form of ethical judgment is possible, of a kind that gives this question the force of a Last Judgment: Have you acted in conformity with the desire that is in you? ... Opposed to this pole of desire is traditional ethics" (Lacan 1992: 314). If the Lacanian model of ethics is thus to not "give ground relative to one's desire," (Lacan 1992: 319) I would propose that the Deleuze of the late

1960s – and arguably the Deleuzian oeuvre in its entirety – twists that dictum into the following formulation without ever stating it as such: *to not give ground relative to that place where desire is stopped in its tracks.* In his extended consideration of *Antigone* in the ethics seminar, Lacan emphasizes the way in which Antigone's "strange beauty" stops desire in its tracks,[1] and similarly it will be emphasized here the way in which the Deleuze who with Guattari would seem to be preoccupied with desire is in fact equally preoccupied with those zones where desire is arrested, and more often than not arrested at that point where it resonates with a higher notion of structure itself.

The structure in question takes on different forms, which I will attempt to delineate in what follows. But all such forms hinge on what Deleuze characterizes as an "extreme formality," and it is this combination of the formal and the extreme that will be central to the alternative Deleuzian ethics – or anethics – proposed here. This combination of formal and extreme is perhaps best articulated in the disjunction Deleuze repeatedly emphasizes between sadism and masochism, and beyond that the disjunction inherent in the structure of sadism itself, one side of which is precisely that place where desire is stopped in its tracks, a place entirely above and beyond the structure of masochism, or even the first order of sadism.

Deleuze's 1967 essay "Coldness and Cruelty" first appeared in the context of a work devoted to Leopold von Sacher-Masoch and featuring the latter's *Venus in Furs*, yet it nonetheless brings a particular, and particularly acute, attention to outlining the structure of sadism. Of course it might be argued that such attention is critical to an understanding of masochism, and to some extent this is the case; but if the two forms do not rely on each other for their definition, why is it that Deleuze keeps returning to the question of sadism in his exposition of masochism? It will be claimed in this chapter that the structure of sadism, above and beyond that of masochism, is in strong resonance with a series of terms that traverse, in subterranean fashion, Deleuze's work from the late 1960s, and that all in their way point to a modality of ethics that is more nearly akin to an anethics, insofar as it eschews the categories of the human and even of life, focusing instead on the highest structural order that can be reached within a given system (in this sense, it is not so far removed from Foucault's 1966 *The Order of Things*). Thus, Deleuze's concepts of sadism, the world without others, the third synthesis of time, and the death instinct all mirror each other and reveal not only an extreme formalism but an extreme state of stasis and non-becoming at the heart of Deleuze's early work.

I have argued previously that Deleuze has a somewhat fraught relation to the question of movement (Kaufman 2006). Although he and Guattari are always careful to insist that there need not be actual physical movement for flights or becomings or nomad thought to take place, there is nonetheless a privilege accorded to becoming and the implicit movement it entails, so that a certain dialectic of movement and stasis tends to result, with movement being the favored term. This might be mapped onto Deleuze's privileging of the time of Aion in *The Logic of Sense*, which is that of the past–future conjunction that he opposes to Chronos, the time of the present. In his discussion of the event, we see an implicit premium placed on the movement of becoming:

> The event in turn, in its impassibility and impenetrability, has no present. It rather retreats and advances in two directions at once, being the perpetual object of a double question: What is going to happen? What has just happened? The agonizing aspect of the pure event is that it is always and at the same time something which has just happened and something about to happen; never something which is happening. (Deleuze 1990: 63)

In the realm of the Aion, what counts is what has just happened, and what is about to happen. There is a movement in two directions at once, but it is not a movement of cancellation. It appears that even in the intemporal form of time which is Aion, there is still a hint of movement – and this, as we shall see in what follows, is what distinguishes the Aion from Deleuze's third synthesis of time in *Difference and Repetition*.

I have tried to suggest that, by contrast, Maurice Blanchot embraces more fully than Deleuze, at least in the twentieth-century French tradition, a being of pure inertia and immobility, so that, for Blanchot, movement or action ultimately leads to a more radical state of inertia, an *inertia of being* (as opposed to a seemingly more Deleuzian notion of becoming) (Kaufman 2006). Blanchot's fictional works present, much like those of Franz Kafka, Samuel Beckett, and Herman Melville's "Bartleby," characters who remain stuck in a hemmed-in interior space, a hotel room or apartment or concentrationary universe from which there is no escape, even if in some instances it would seem that the characters are free simply to walk away. This Blanchotian state of arrestation surpasses even the intemporality of Deleuze's Aion, and invokes an interminable and immobile present over and above a convergence of past and future. Such an endless present marks a radical dwelling in being that in no way resembles the *parousia* of being or presence that is often under assault by Jacques Derrida and others. (Indeed, Derrida's *Demeure*, in addition to a series of writings on Blanchot throughout his career, captures this Blanchotian modality of dwelling, of remaining, or living on – but as *désoeuvrement* rather than *parousia* – as perhaps nobody else has done, though without an open embrace of its ontological ramifications.[2])

Thus, in comparing Deleuze and Blanchot, it is not difficult to affirm that Blanchot has a more developed notion of stasis, immobility, and inertia, especially compared to the Deleuze of becoming over being, of nomadology, of lines of flight, deterritorialization, and so forth. But I want to suggest that there is a register in Deleuze's early texts that runs entirely against this divide and is often best discerned by signaling which terms receive a positive or a negative valence in Deleuze's thought. (Of course, that does sometimes change.) So, for example, in "Coldness and Cruelty," when Deleuze writes: "while Sade is spinozistic and employs demonstrative reason, Masoch is platonic and proceeds by dialectical imagination" (Deleuze 1991: 22), any reader remotely familiar with Deleuze's philosophical trajectory would know that Spinoza is always cast on the side of the good and Plato more nearly (though not uniformly) on that of the bad. Similarly the dialectic (here associated with Masoch) is for Deleuze generally, though not exclusively, cast on the side of the bad. Of course, it is never this simple: Deleuze has some surprisingly good things to say about Plato (this reader would even claim that Deleuze and Alain Badiou are the two most Platonic philosophers in the twentieth-century French tradition, but that will be left aside). Still, we have to take note, when seeing Sade so blatantly tethered to Spinoza and Spinozist ethics, that there must be something of enormous appeal for Deleuze in the structure of sadism, which, as he emphasizes at practically every juncture in "Coldness and Cruelty," is fundamentally different in kind from masochism. For Deleuze argues that sadism and masochism are not complementary structures, and to lump them together is conceptually inaccurate.

I will return to "Coldness and Cruelty" in what follows, but for now I ask the reader simply to consider the hypothesis that there may be something that Deleuze finds particularly compelling about sadism in terms of its structural purity – and it must be emphasized that sadism and masochism here are impersonal structures above and beyond anything else, more than they are attributes of individuals. This is in no way to claim that Deleuze unilaterally *disfavors* the structure of masochism, for in fact sometimes masochism (as well as the neurotic, to take another somewhat comparable example) is described with epithets to which Deleuze gives negative valence (Platonic, dialectic, etc.) and at other times with epithets that are favored (humor, suspense, suspended gestures). To this end, masochism is the harder structure to pin down because it goes in several directions at once, whereas sadism has a purity to which masochism can only aspire. And, as we shall see, sadism and its attendant ethics, or anethics, has a remarkable affinity with at least three other distinctive structures in Deleuze's early works, works written in the late 1960s, and concentrated in the year 1967.

Published that year is an essay on Michel Tournier's rewriting of the Robinson Crusoe story in his acclaimed novel *Friday*, entitled "Michel Tournier and the World without Others." The essay provides a crucial if indirect elaboration of the structure of sadism, which is also a structure or space of extreme intemporality and stasis (and such a space recurs in Deleuze's single-authored works from the 1960s and even appears to some degree in the joint works with Guattari, above all *Anti-Oedipus*). Here, Deleuze describes the world that the protagonist Robinson comes to inhabit on the desert island, which is the world without others. It is not simply that the other is missing from the desert island, which it is, but at stake is the opening that this absence provides, an opening onto an impersonal and inhuman perceptual space that is entirely beyond the realm of other people. Deleuze writes:

> In the Other's absence, consciousness and its object are one . . . Consciousness ceases to be a light cast upon objects in order to become a pure phosphorescence of things in themselves. Robinson is but the consciousness of the island, but the consciousness of the island is the consciousness the island has of itself – it is the island in itself. We understand thus the paradox of the desert isle: the one who is shipwrecked, if he is alone, if he has lost the structure-Other, disturbs nothing of the desert isle; rather he consecrates it. (Deleuze 1990: 311)[3]

Evoked here is something akin to a pre-Kantian notion of the thing-in-itself, a notion precluded by what Quentin Meillassoux will term the "correlationism" that is inaugurated by Kant, in short the idea that everything must be described as *relative* to the perceiving consciousness and not in and of itself (Meillassoux 2008). But here we see something like the *thing-in-itself*, or even like Jean-Paul Sartre's *in-itself*, a level of pure being or essence that is not usually equated with Deleuze. And this vision of thing-being, of island-consciousness, is also an opening to an ontology of non-relation. If ethics might be said to be about relations, and human relations at that, then the particularly Deleuzian ethology of this period is an ethics beyond being and relation, an ethics beyond ethics, indeed what I am also calling an anethics.

This realm of the world without others is notably intemporal yet also eternally present. In this regard, it is hard to know where to fit it into the temporalities mapped out in *The Logic of Sense*, whether it would fall into the past–future conjunction of becoming which is Aion, or the disfavored chronological time of the present which is Chronos. Ultimately, it is not clear that the world without others fits into either of these temporalities. Deleuze notes that, under the regime of the structure-Other (which is a highly Lacanian, if not Hegelian and Sartrean, model of the other as a structural field, one that is endemic to language, and falls under the register of the possible – which, again, any good Deleuzian will recognize as a pejorative term), spatial and temporal distribution and organization dominate the field, but in the absence of the structure-Other they no longer obtain. As Deleuze writes: "How could there still be a past when the Other no longer functions?" (Deleuze 1990: 311). It would seem that the past, or even the past–future conjunction of Aion, is something like a preliminary stage that is then subsumed by the world without others.

Furthermore, this world without others is curiously described as an "eternal present." Deleuze writes: "lacking in its structure, [the Other's absence] allows consciousness to cling to, and to coincide with, the object in an eternal present" (Deleuze 1990: 311). Such a notion of the present is decidedly not the time of Chronos, which is another kind of present, but rather an eternal present. It is worth noting in passing that Thomas Aquinas, one of Deleuze's proclaimed enemies, evokes a divine temporality that has striking affinities with Deleuze's eternal present. In God's time, there is no past or future, and no succession. For Aquinas, God cannot be the result of anything, since he is the prime mover, inhabiting an intemporal eternal present that is very much like the world without others.[4] The crucial point of difference between Aquinas's eternity and Deleuze's notion of the "eternal present" as accessed in the world without others resides in the centrality of Deleuze's concept of difference. Because the world without others is itself generated through a process of difference (it is not itself the primary substance, or first mover), and is itself the *product* of genesis, it is formed by an entirely different process than Aquinas's divinity, which by definition cannot be preceded by anything. It is this that distinguishes Deleuze's intemporal eternal present from a purely theological one: for Deleuze the world without others (or third synthesis of time) is not a primary order but a secondary one, which for Deleuze generally makes it better (and this is not the case for Aquinas).

Therefore, unlike Aquinas, Deleuze's eternal present is not primary but secondary or tertiary. While Deleuze is critical of a certain dualism present in modern psychology, and even in Husserl – a dualism, for example, "between the matter of the perceptual field and the pre-reflective syntheses of the ego" (Deleuze 1990: 308) – he affirms the dualism inherent in the workings of the structure-Other, one that is produced through a genetic process that stems from a difference in kind. Thus he insists, apropos of dualism, that:

> The true dualism lies elsewhere; it lies between the effects of the "structure Other" of the perceptual field and the effects of its absence (what perception would be were there no Others). We must understand that the Other is not one structure among others in the field of perception . . . *It is the structure which conditions the entire field* and its functioning . . . [It is] the a priori principle of the organization of every perceptual field . . . Real dualism then appears with the absence of the Other. (Deleuze 1990: 308–9)

Again, we have this second-order dimension: the structure-Other is primary, whereas the world without others, which is the higher order for Deleuze, is secondary. One might think that the world without others would be some sort of primordial, chaotic state from which the proper structural relation to the other would emerge (like an elemental Imaginary from which the Symbolic order emerges, or something of the sort, though Lacan is never that straightforward). But that is not the case, for the principle of ordering or genesis is crucial to the understanding of the concept, and the world without others is a product, and a higher product, of the structure-Other.[5]

We see this same ordering in *The Logic of Sense* with respect to the "incorporeal," which is at a higher level than the corporeal but also issuing from it, and the same holds with the rather elaborate hierarchies of art in the Proust book (these are notably all works from this same period in the 1960s).[6] Almost invariably in early Deleuze it is the second order, or the third order if there are three, that is the higher one, the more intemporal, immaterial and pure order, and the one generated from the preceding order or orders. Deleuze writes in *Difference and Repetition* of "the formless as the product of the most extreme formality" (Deleuze 1994: 115) and this is the relentless if not cruel logic that connects all the examples at issue here.[7] It is thus the recognition and description of this higher level that takes on its own sort of anethical imperative in early Deleuze.

Such a logic traverses *Difference and Repetition*, and does so more systematically than in *The Logic of Sense*, where it appears at its most acute in the appendices. If the time of the Aion in *The Logic of Sense* might still fall under the category of a generalized movement or becoming, the third synthesis of time in *Difference and Repetition* falls squarely outside of it, and resonates in profound fashion with the description of "the world without others" that concludes *The Logic of Sense*. Moreover, if *The Logic of Sense* anticipates some of the major thematics of *Anti-Oedipus*, above all in the early formulation of the "body without organs," then *Difference and Repetition* reads as a paean to Sigmund Freud in a fashion that is no longer operative in *Anti-Oedipus*.

To begin with the third synthesis, it is delineated in opposition to the first synthesis, which is that of habit and the more Chronos-like present, and even to the second synthesis which is that of memory and the past (and to a certain degree resembles the time of Aion in *The Logic of Sense*). By contrast, Deleuze characterizes the third synthesis, invoking Hamlet, as "time being out of joint":

> [T]ime out of joint means demented time or time outside the curve which gave it a god, liberated from its overly simple circular figure, freed from the events which made up its content, its relation to movement overturned; in short, time presenting itself as an empty and pure form ... [Time] ceases to be cardinal and becomes ordinal, a pure *order* of time ... We can then distinguish a more or less extensive past and a future in inverse proportion, but the future and the past here are not empirical and dynamic determinations of time: they are formal and fixed characteristics which follow *a priori* from the order of time, as though they comprised a static synthesis of time. The synthesis is necessarily static, since time is no longer subordinated to movement; time is the most radical form of change, but the form of change does not change. (Deleuze 1994: 88–9)

Of import here, in addition to the articulation of the concepts, is the order of their presentation. Just as the cinema books might be said to be ordered according to the overcoming of movement by time, so too the height of Deleuzian genesis entails first a surpassing of movement and secondly a surpassing of time. The ultimate attainment is an empty and pure form, which is also a pure order, and with that, static. Time at its most radical is divorced from movement, and is static. As we proceed, then, through the Deleuzian syntheses of time, we ascend to the higher, intemporal, static, third order.[8] Indeed, if much of what is considered to be Deleuzian ethics revolves around a type of becoming that avoids the stasis of morality, then at stake here is a rarefied kind of stasis that approximates *being* above and beyond *becoming* yet also in its formless (*informe*) quality escapes the realm of morality and its attendant judgments. It is the triumph of Kant's second critique, which Deleuze himself alludes to in select moments in his writings on Kant, and which will be taken up in what follows.

It is in this context that I wish to come full circle (though Deleuze's notion of the circle in *Difference and Repetition* is ambivalent at best[9]) and return to "Coldness and Cruelty," because it is through Freud, of all unlikely Deleuzian models, that we can see formulated most clearly the connection between the third synthesis, the world without others, the structure of sadism, and the question of ethics. This connection is made via Freud's notion of the death instinct, as outlined in *Beyond the Pleasure Principle*, which "masterpiece," according to Deleuze, "is perhaps the one where he engaged most directly – and how penetratingly – in specifically philosophical reflection" (Deleuze 1991: 11). In *Difference and Repetition*, Deleuze clearly links the third synthesis of time to the Freudian death instinct, where he writes in the above-mentioned discussion of the three syntheses of time that:

> Time empty and out of joint, with its rigorous formal and static order, its crushing unity and its irreversible series, is precisely the death instinct. The death instinct does not enter into a cycle with Eros, but testifies to a completely different synthesis ... [It is] a death instinct desexualised and without love. (Deleuze 1994: 111)

These are precisely the terms used to characterize Robinson on the desert island. In the third synthesis, we see all at once the alignment of: (1) time out of joint; (2) a rigorous, formal and static order; and (3) the death instinct. Rather than dwelling on *Difference and Repetition* and the complexities of its syntheses of time, which have been capably treated elsewhere,[10] I wish to use this alignment of concepts to argue that, despite the neutrality of tone and evenhandedness with which sadism and masochism are taken up in "Coldness and Cruelty," it is above all the structure and the anethics of sadism that resonate most fully with this extreme space of stasis and intemporality in Deleuze's work from the late 1960s.

Although Deleuze links both sadism and masochism simultaneously to the pleasure principle and to the death instinct, he takes care to distinguish between, on the one hand, death or destructive instincts which are in a *dialectical* relation to Eros and governed by the unconscious, and, on the other, the Death Instinct (which he puts in capital letters), which is a pure, silent, and absolute negation that is not connected to the unconscious, since, as Freud puts it, there is no big No (or pure negation) in the unconscious.[11] Deleuze links such an absolute negation to the second-order negation in Sade. The first order is a personal form of Sadean negativity that is imperative and descriptive (good sense?), and the second and related but higher order is one that is impersonal and absolute, even delusional (Deleuze 1991: 19). Deleuze writes that

> the second and higher factor represents the *impersonal* element in sadism and identifies the impersonal violence with an Idea of pure reason, with a terrifying demonstration capable of subordinating the first element. In Sade we discover a surprising affinity with Spinoza – a naturalistic and mechanistic approach imbued with the mathematical spirit. (Deleuze 1991: 19–20)

As indicated above, for Deleuze one cannot surpass "the Christ of philosophers" and author of the *Ethics*, and it seems that this passage must be read, above all, as an extraordinary paean to the second level of sadism and its surprising Spinozisms.

In a similar vein, we also see the gesture towards an absolute if not divinely violent form of pure reason that in its extremity might explode and overcome reason's law, and here it is not insignificant that Deleuze cites Lacan's 1963 essay "Kant with Sade" in the footnotes (Deleuze 1991: 137). Deleuze develops this idea in the section of "Coldness and Cruelty" on "Humor, Irony, and the Law," when he notes that Kant's second critique is more revolutionary than the first, for if the first weds us to the subject, the second establishes the law at such a level of pure form that it opens the path – a formal one – to its overturning. I quote this passage in its entirety:

> The Copernican revolution in Kant's *Critique of Pure Reason* consisted in viewing the objects of knowledge as revolving around the subject; but the *Critique of Practical Reason*, where the Good is conceived as revolving around the Law, is perhaps even more revolutionary. It probably reflected major changes in the world. It may have been the expression of the ultimate consequences of a return beyond Christianity to Judaic thought, or it may even have foreshadowed a return to the pre-Socratic (Oedipal) conception of the law, beyond to the world of Plato. However that may be, Kant, by establishing that THE LAW is an ultimate ground or principle, added an essential dimension to modern thought: the object of the law is by definition unknowable and elusive. (Deleuze 1991: 81)[12]

This passage sets up the paradox of the form or structure that, when pushed to its extreme, is static and formless, essentially the claim that Deleuze will make about Lévi-Strauss's "empty square" in his essay "How Do We Recognize Structuralism?" from this same period

(Deleuze 2004a). Are there not so many occasions when one does something out of principle, out of a strange and possibly even self-destructive loyalty to the form something should take, above and beyond the content or value? If push comes to shove, can it be explained *why* the principle is held to with such tenacity, even if its difference in outcome matters little? It is that imperative to hold to form, and the attendant stasis or dissolution that may be produced – quite literally stuck on the formality – that Deleuze explains on an ontological level. But following Lacan, can such an imperative be divorced from desire, and when in fact it is divorced from any desire for content, does it not become a sort of ethics of form, one which then leaves desire itself somewhat stranded and by the wayside?

Deleuze continues his discussion of Kant and law with an analysis of the way in which masochism and sadism, each in their way, subvert the law. In masochism this is done through humor, through the downward movement of exploding the law from within by observing its very letter to the point that its absurdity is brought into full relief. But with sadism it is an issue of principle and the overturning is transcendental. Through Sadean institutional anarchy, Evil subverts Platonism and transcends the law from on high. Whereas the masochist is "the logician of consequences," the ironic sadist is "the logician of principles" (Deleuze 1991: 13). While the relation between heights and depths is indeed a fraught one, above all in *The Logic of Sense*, I would claim that, without ever stating this as such (indeed Deleuze writes that "[the masochist] overthrows law as radically as the sadist, though in a different way" [Deleuze 1991: 34]), it is hard to come away from a thorough reading of Deleuze's work from this period without remarking on the Deleuzian proclivity for heights over depths, for the superego over the ego, for the raging molecules over the agrarian, for thought over imagination, and for the thinker over the visionary. The former terms are all used to describe sadism, the latter terms masochism. Admittedly, there may be some ambivalence in the terms, and certainly they are not simple opposites of one another, to return to the oft-reiterated central thesis of "Coldness and Cruelty." It may be contentious to claim that the thinker or philosopher takes precedence over the visionary or artist, but is anything ever higher than thought for Deleuze?[13] Even in the book on Proust where art would take on the loftiest space in all of Deleuze's works, it is art's formality and purity, things accessed by the philosopher, that gives it its high status. Creativity, after all, may proceed dialectically, but pure form, and pure thought, do not. Pure thought is the product, and the higher project, of an initial and more primary structure.[14]

It is also notable that in his brief discussion of Kant, Deleuze introduces a rare form of speculation as to what produced this shift between the first and second critiques, making the second more revolutionary. Leaving aside the Judeo-Christian hypotheses, which might be mapped more decisively onto thinkers such as Derrida, Agamben, and even Badiou, it is notable simply that Deleuze makes a fleeting reference to "forces in the world," for the world is *decidedly not* the realm that serves as the backdrop for his analysis. Indeed, like the Libertine sequestered in his "*tour abolie*," Deleuze does not present a program for "applying" the structures of sadism and masochism to the "real world," not that they cannot be so applied in his wake. Rather, he focuses on the question of structure as such, at least in the work from this period, and on this count alone, sadism, in its purer and more absolute structural logic, must necessarily be the higher form.[15]

On the concluding page of "Michel Tournier and the World without Others," Deleuze writes that in Sade's work, "victims are not at all grasped as Others" (Deleuze 1990: 320) and he goes on to note that

> the world of the pervert [which is Robinson on his desert island, with his "desert sexuality" as Deleuze calls it] is a world without Others, and thus a world without the possible [again, the possible is almost always bad for Deleuze, so this seems to be a pure tribute to the world without Others]. This is a strange Spinozism from which "oxygen" is lacking, to the benefit of a more elementary energy and a more rarefied air. (Deleuze 1990: 39)

This state lacking in oxygen is the extreme state of negation, death, purity, sadism, intemporality, incorporeality, and an eschewal of the other and of communication and relation that traverses the work from the late 1960s and forms the hidden kernel of Deleuze's philosophical project, which is on some level quite a dark one (think of the dark precursor[15]), and is not so clearly visible from the vantage point of the later work or the joint work with Guattari. It does not present a palatable ethics in the form of *Spinoza: Practical Philosophy* or some of the late writings. In fact it presents something quite contrary to these easier ethics, but something that is nonetheless an ethics of relation, if not to others then to the forces of the impersonal, the law, and structure itself.

References

Aquinas, Thomas (1914–38), *Summa contra Gentiles*, trans. Fathers of the English Dominican Province, London: Washbourne.

Aquinas, Thomas (1981), *Summa theologica*, trans. Fathers of the English Dominican Province, Notre Dame: Christian Classics.

Blanchot, M. and J. Derrida (2000), *The Instant of My Death* and *Demeure: Fiction and Testimony*, trans. E. Rottenberg, Stanford: Stanford University Press.

Bryant, L. R. (2008), *Difference and Givenness: Deleuze's Transcendental Empiricism and the Ontology of Immanence*, Evanston: Northwestern University Press.

Deleuze, G. (1968), *Différence et répétition*, Paris: Presses Universitaires de France.

Deleuze, G. (1972), *Proust and Signs*, trans. R. Howard, New York: Braziller.

Deleuze, G. (1988), *Spinoza: Practical Philosophy*, trans. R. Hurley, San Francisco: City Lights Books.

Deleuze, G. (1990), *The Logic of Sense*, trans. M. Lester with C. Stivale, ed. C. Boundas, New York: Columbia University Press.

Deleuze, G. (1991), *Masochism*, trans. J. McNeil, New York: Zone.

Deleuze, G. (1994), *Difference and Repetition*, trans. P. Patton, New York: Columbia University Press.

Deleuze, G. (2004a), "How Do we Recognize Structuralism?," in *Desert Islands and Other Texts 1953–1974*, trans. M. Taormina, Los Angeles and New York: Semiotext(e).

Deleuze, G. (2004b), "The Idea of Genesis in Kant's Esthetics," in *Desert Islands and Other Texts 1953–1974*, trans. M. Taormina, Los Angeles and New York: Semiotext(e).

Deleuze G. and F. Guattari (1983), *Anti-Oedipus*, trans. R. Hurley, M. Seem, and H. R. Lane, Minneapolis: University of Minnesota Press.

Deleuze G. and F. Guattari (1994), *What is Philosophy?*, trans. H. Tomlinson and G. Burchell, New York: Columbia University Press.

Deleuze, G. and L. von Sacher-Masoch (1967), *Présentation de Sacher-Masoch*, Paris: Minuit.

Faulkner, K. W. (2006), *Deleuze and the Three Syntheses of Time*, New York: Lang.

Freud, S. (1961), *Beyond the Pleasure Principle*, New York: Norton.

Hallward, P. (2006), *Out of this World: Deleuze and the Philosophy of Creation*, London: Verso.

Hughes, J. (2008), *Deleuze and the Genesis of Representation*, London: Continuum.

Kaufman, E. (2002), "Why the Family is Beautiful (Lacan Against Badiou)," *diacritics*, 32:3–4, 135–51.

Kaufman, E. (2006), "Midnight, or the Inertia of Being," *parallax*, 12:2, 98–111.

Kaufman, E. (2007), "Lévi-Strauss, Deleuze, and the Joy of Abstraction," *Criticism*, 49:4, 429–45.

Lacan, J. (1992), *The Ethics of Psychoanalysis*, trans. Dennis Porter, New York: Norton.

Marks, J. (forthcoming), "Ethics," in *The Deleuze Dictionary: Revised Edition*, ed. Adrian Parr, Edinburgh: Edinburgh University Press.

Meillassoux, Q. (2008), *After Finitude: An Essay on the Necessity of Contingency*, trans. R. Brassier, London: Continuum.

Melville, H. (1986), *Billy Budd and Other Stories*, New York: Penguin.

Nguyen, C. (n.d.) "Recycling Time: Time in Deleuze's *Difference and Repetition*," unpublished.

Notes

1. See my extended discussion of this in Kaufman 2002.
2. See Blanchot and Derrida 2000.
3. Originally published as "Une Théorie d'autrui (Autrui, Robinson et le pervers): Michel Tournier: *Vendredi ou les limbes du pacifique*," *Critique*, 241, 1967,

503–25. Translated as "Michel Tournier and the World without Others" as an appendix to Deleuze 1990.

4. See Aquinas 1981: Ia, q. 10, and 1914–38: I.15, II.19. Interestingly, in another strange affinity with Aquinas – strange because, given his adherence to Scotus' model of univocity, Deleuze, in *Difference and Repetition* and in some of his course lectures, is always at pains to attack Aquinas's model of analogy – he will note in "Coldness and Cruelty," apropos of the distinction between sadism and masochism, that: "The concurrence of sadism and masochism is fundamentally one of analogy only, their processes and formations are entirely different" (Deleuze 1991: 46). So here, analogy is not so terrible, and in fact partakes of a logic of difference. For a damning discussion of Thomas in the course lectures, see Gilles Deleuze, "Seminar on Scholasticism and Spinoza," January 14, 1974, available at www.webdeleuze.com

5. For a tour de force mapping of the workings of genesis in *Difference and Repetition* and *The Logic of Sense*, see Hughes 2008. See also Bryant 2008 on the static genesis and the structure-Other, esp. pp. 220–62.

6. Deleuze uses the same phrasing when he writes that "The extreme formality is there only for an excessive formlessness (Hölderlin's *Unförmliche*)" (Deleuze 1994: 91). ("L'extrême formalité n'est là que pour un informel excessif" [Deleuze 1968: 122].) As John Marks (forthcoming) writes with regards to judgment and cruelty: "This means that the doctrine of judgement is only apparently more moderate than a system of 'cruelty' according to which debt is measured in blood and inscribed directly on the body, since it condemns us to infinite restitution and servitude. Deleuze goes further to show how these four 'disciples' [Nietzsche, D. H. Lawrence, Kafka, Artaud] elaborate a whole system of 'cruelty' that is opposed to judgment, and which constitutes the basis for an ethics. The domination of the body in favour of consciousness leads to an impoverishment of our knowledge of the body. We do not fully explore the capacities of the body, and in the same way that the body surpasses the knowledge we have of it, so thought also surpasses the consciousness we have of it. Once we can begin to explore these new dimensions – the *unknown* of the body and the *unconscious* of thought – we are in the domain of ethics."

7. There are, nonetheless, points of confusion in the above passage such as the claim that the future and past "follow *a priori* from the order of time." How does one follow *a priori*? Is there then a second order of past and future that follows from a third synthesis of time?

8. This chapter has benefited from an unpublished essay by Catherine Nguyen on the ambivalent figure of the circle in the three syntheses of time: "Recycling Time: Time in Deleuze's *Difference and Repetition*."

9. See especially Faulkner, who distinguishes empty time from eternity in the following fashion: "unlike eternity, empty time retains events" (Faulkner 2006: 103). I am not entirely convinced that events indeed survive empty time, but it does seem quite plausible that they could be generated from empty time, in a fashion pertaining to the questions raised in note 7.

10. Deleuze gives a similar gloss on the deep ontology of Freud's death instinct at a later point in "Coldness and Cruelty" when he writes that "Thanatos *is*; it is an absolute. And yet the 'no' does not exist in the unconscious because destruction is always presented as the other side of a construction" (Deleuze 1991: 116).

11. Faulkner notes that "the practical law itself signifies nothing other than the empty form of time" (Faulkner 2006: 106) and that Deleuze reads Kant's second critique through the lens of Freud's death instinct, which is also linked to the body without organs. For a succinct overview of Deleuze's reading of Kant's three critiques with respect to the problem of genesis, see Deleuze 2004b.

12. Deleuze writes that "the thinker is necessarily solitary and solipsistic" (Deleuze 1994: 282), and evokes solitude with respect to sadism (Deleuze 1991: 19).
13. In this regard, I would take issue with Peter Hallward's focus on creativity as the motor force behind Deleuze's thought. See Hallward 2006.
14. For an extended example of this premium placed on the question of structure, see Deleuze 2004a. See my analysis of this in Kaufman 2007.
15. Deleuze writes in *Difference and Repetition* that "the dark precursor is not a friend" (Deleuze 1994: 145).

Chapter 7

Deleuze and the Question of Desire: Towards an Immanent Theory of Ethics

Daniel W. Smith

My title raises two questions, each of which I would like to address in turn. What is an *immanent* ethics (as opposed to an ethics that appeals to transcendence, or to universals). And what is the philosophical question of desire? My ultimate question concerns the link between these two issues: What relation does an immanent ethics have to the problem of desire? Historically, the first question is primarily linked with the names of Spinoza and Nietzsche (as well as, as we shall see, Leibniz), since it was Spinoza and Nietzsche who posed the question of an immanent ethics in its most rigorous form. The second question is linked to names like Freud and Lacan (and behind them, to Kant), since it was they who formulated the modern conceptualization of desire in its most acute form – that is, in terms of *unconscious* desire, desire as unconscious. It was in *Anti-Oedipus*, published in 1972, that Deleuze (along with Félix Guattari, his co-author) attempted to formulate his own theory of desire – what he would call a purely *immanent* theory of desire. In his preface to *Anti-Oedipus*, Michel Foucault claimed, famously, that "*Anti-Oedipus* is a book of ethics, the first book of ethics to be written in France in quite a long time" (Foucault 1977: xiii) – thereby making explicit the link between the theory of desire developed in *Anti-Oedipus* and the immanent theory of ethics Deleuze worked out in his monographs on Nietzsche and Spinoza.

The chapter falls into three parts. In the first, I want to make some general comments about the nature of an immanent ethics. In the second part, I would like to examine in some detail two sets of texts from Nietzsche and Leibniz, which will flesh out some of the details of an immanent ethics. Finally, I will conclude with some all-too-brief comments on the nature of desire in relation to some of the themes in *Anti-Oedipus*.

On the Nature of an Immanent Ethics

Let us turn to the first question: What is an immanent ethics? Throughout his writings, Deleuze has often drawn a distinction between "ethics" and "morality" – a distinction that has traditionally been drawn to distinguish modes of reflection that place greater emphasis, respectively, on the good life (such as Stoicism) or on the moral law (such as Kantianism). Deleuze, however, uses the term "morality" to define, in very general terms, any set of "constraining" rules, such as a moral code, that consists in judging actions and intentions by relating them to transcendent or universal values ("This is Good, that is Evil").[1] What he calls "ethics" is, on the contrary, a set of "facilitative" (*facultative*) rules that evaluates what we do, say, and think according to the immanent mode of existence that it implies. One says or does this, thinks or feels that: *what mode of existence does it imply?* "We always have the beliefs, feelings, and thoughts we deserve," writes Deleuze, "given our way of being or our style of life" (Deleuze 1983: 1).[2] Now according to Deleuze, this immanent approach to the question of ethics was developed most fully, in the history of philosophy, by Spinoza and Nietzsche, whom Deleuze has often identified as his own philosophical precursors.[3] Both Spinoza and Nietzsche were maligned by their contemporaries not simply for being atheists, but, even worse, for being "immoralists."[4] A potent danger was seen to be lurking in Spinoza's *Ethics* and Nietzsche's *Genealogy of Morals*: without transcendence, without recourse to normative universals, we will fall into the dark night of chaos, and ethics will be reduced to a pure "subjectivism" or "relativism." Both Spinoza and Nietzsche argued, each in his own way, that there are things one cannot do or say or think or feel except on the condition of being weak, base, or enslaved, unless one harbors a vengeance or *ressentiment* against life (Nietzsche), unless one remains the slave of passive affections (Spinoza); and there are other things one cannot do or say except on the condition of being strong, noble, or free, unless one affirms life, unless one attains active affections.[5] Deleuze calls this the method of "dramatization": actions and propositions are interpreted as so many sets of symptoms that express or "dramatize" the mode of existence of the speaker. "What is the mode of existence of the person who utters a given proposition?" asks Nietzsche, "What mode of existence is *needed* in order to be able to utter it."[6] Rather than "judging" actions and thoughts by appealing to transcendent or universal values, one "evaluates" them by determining the mode of existence that serves as their principle. A pluralistic method of explanation by immanent modes of existence is in this way made to replace the recourse to transcendent values: in Spinoza and Nietzsche, the transcendent moral opposition (between Good and Evil) is replaced by an immanent ethical difference (between noble and base modes of existence, in Nietzsche; or between passive and active affections, in Spinoza).

In Spinoza, for instance, an individual will be considered "bad" (or servile, or weak, or foolish) that remains cut off from its power of acting, that remains in a state of slavery with regard to its passions. Conversely, a mode of existence will be considered "good" (or free, or rational, or strong) that exercises its capacity for being affected in such a way that its power of acting increases, to the point where it produces active affections and adequate ideas. For Deleuze, this is the point of convergence that unites Nietzsche and Spinoza in their search for an immanent ethics. Modes are no longer *judged* in terms of their degree of proximity to or distance from an external principle, but are *evaluated* in terms of the manner by which they "occupy" their existence: the intensity of their power, their "tenor" of life.[7] It is always a question of knowing whether a mode of existence – however great or small it may be – is capable of deploying its capacities, of increasing its power of acting to the point where it can be said to go to the limit of what it "can do" (see Deleuze 1994: 41). The fundamental question of ethics is not "What *must* I do?" (which is the question of *morality*) but rather "What *can* I do, what am I *capable* of doing?" (which is the proper question of an ethics *without* morality). Given my degree of power, what are my capabilities and capacities? How can I come into active possession of my power? How can I go to the limit of what I "can do"?

What an ethics of immanence will criticize, then, is anything that *separates* a mode of existence from its power of acting – and what separates us from our power of acting is, ultimately, the illusions of transcendence. (We should immediately point out that the illusions of transcendence go far beyond the transcendence of God; in the *Critique of Pure Reason*, Kant had already critiqued the concepts of the Self, the World, and God as the three great illusions of transcendence; and what he calls the "moral law" in the second critique is, by Kant's own admission, a transcendent law that is unknowable.) When Spinoza and Nietzsche criticize transcendence, their interest is not merely theoretical or speculative – exposing its fictional or illusory status – but rather practical and ethical.[8] This is no doubt the point that separates Deleuze most from the ethical thinking of Emmanuel Levinas – the great philosopher of transcendence, insofar as the Other is the paradigmatic concept of transcendence – as well as Jacques Derrida, who was much closer to

Levinas than Deleuze on this score. The ethical themes one finds in transcendent philosophies like those of Levinas and Derrida – an absolute responsibility for the other that I can never assume, or an infinite call to justice that I can never satisfy – are, from the Deleuzian point of view of immanence, imperatives whose effect is to separate me from my capacity to act. From the viewpoint of immanence, in other words, *transcendence, far from being our salvation, represents our slavery and impotence reduced to its lowest point*: the demand to do the impossible is nothing other than the concept of impotence raised to infinity.

But this is precisely why the question of desire is linked with the theme of an immanent ethics, and becomes a political question. For one of most difficult problems posed by an immanent ethics is the following: if transcendence represents my impotence (at the limit, my power reduced to zero), then under what conditions can I have actually been led to *desire* transcendence? What are the conditions that could have led, in Nietzsche's words, to "the inversion of the value-positing eye" – that is, to the whole history of nihilism that Nietzsche analyses (and nihilism, for Nietzsche, is nothing other than the triumph of transcendence, the point where life itself is given a value of nil, *nihil*)? This is the fundamental political problem posed by an immanent ethics: How can people reach a point where they actually desire their servitude and slavery *as if it were their salvation* – for those in power have an obvious interest in separating us from our capacity to act? How can we *desire* to be separated from our power, from our capacity to act? As Deleuze and Guattari write, following Reich: "The astonishing thing is not that some people steal or that others occasionally go out on strike, but rather that all those who are starving do not steal as a regular practice, and all those who are exploited are not continually out on strike" (Deleuze and Guattari 1983: 29). In other words, whereas other moral theories see transcendence as a necessary principle – the transcendence of the moral law in Kant, for instance, or the transcendence of the Other in Levinas – for Deleuze transcendence is the fundamental *problem* of ethics, what prevents ethics from taking place, so to speak.

We have thus isolated two aspects of an immanent ethics: it focuses on the differences between modes of existence, in terms of their immanent capabilities or power (active versus reactive, in Nietzsche; active versus passive, in Spinoza), and it poses, as one of its fundamental problems, the urge towards transcendence that effectively "perverts" desire, to the point where we can actually desire our own repression, a separation from our own capacities and powers.

Nietzsche and Leibniz: The Theory of the Drives

With these two aspects in mind, let me turn to the second – and largest – part of this chapter, which deals with the question of how Deleuze in fact characterizes modes of existence, with their powers and capacities. The answer is this: Deleuze approaches modes of existence, ethically speaking, not in terms of their will, or their conscious decision-making power, nor even in terms of their interests, but rather in terms of their *drives*. For Deleuze, conscious will (Kant) and preconscious interest (Marx) are both subsequent to our unconscious drives, and it is at the level of the drives that we have to aim our ethical analysis. Here, I would like to focus on two sets of texts on the drives taken, not from Nietzsche and Spinoza, but rather from Nietzsche and Leibniz (Leibniz being one of the first philosophers in the history of philosophy to have developed a theory of the unconscious).

The first set of texts comes from Nietzsche's great early book entitled *Daybreak*, published in July 1881. Nietzsche first approaches the question of the drives by giving us an everyday scenario:

> Suppose we were in the market place one day and we noticed someone laughing at us as we went by: this event will signify this or that to us according to whether this or that drive happens at that moment to be at its height in us – and it will be a quite different event according to the kind of person we are. One person will absorb it like a drop of rain, another will shake it from him like an insect, another will try to pick a quarrel, another will examine his clothing to see if there is anything about it that might give rise to laughter, another will be led to reflect on the nature of laughter as such, another will be glad to have involuntarily augmented the amount of cheerfulness and sunshine in the world – and in each case, a drive has gratified itself, whether it be the drive to annoyance, or to combativeness or to reflection or to benevolence. This drive seized the event as its prey. Why precisely this one? Because, thirsty and hungry, it was lying in wait. (Nietzsche 1982: 120, §119)

This is the source of Nietzsche's doctrine of *perspectivism* ("there are no facts, only interpretations"), but what is often overlooked is that, for Nietzsche, it is our *drives* that interpret the world, that are perspectival – and not our egos, not our conscious opinions. It is not that I have a different perspective on the world than you; it is rather that each of us has multiple perspectives on the world because of the multiplicity of our drives – drives that are often contradictory among themselves. "*Within ourselves*," Nietzsche writes, "we can be egoistic or altruistic, hard-hearted, magnanimous, just, lenient, insincere, can cause pain or give pleasure" (Nietzsche cited in Parkes 1994: 291–2).[9] We all contain such "a vast confusion of contradictory drives" (Nietzsche 1967: 149, §259) that we are, as Nietzsche liked to say, multiplicities, and not unities. Moreover, these drives are in a constant struggle or combat with each other: my drive to smoke and get my nicotine rush is in combat with (but also coexistent with) my drive to quit. This is where Nietzsche first developed his concept of the will to power – at the level of the drives. "Every drive is a kind of lust to rule," he writes, "each one has its perspective that it would like to compel all the other drives to accept as a norm" (Nietzsche 1967: 267, §481).

To be sure, we can combat the drives, fight against them – indeed, this is one of the most common themes in philosophy, the fight against the passions. In another passage from *Daybreak* (Nietzsche 1982: 109, §109), Nietzsche says that he can see only six fundamental methods we have at our disposal for combating the drives. For instance, if we want to fight our drive to smoke, we can avoid opportunities for its gratification (no longer hiding packs of cigarettes at home for when we run out); or we can implant regularity into the drive (having one cigarette every four hours so as to at least avoid smoking in between); or we can engender disgust with the drive, giving ourselves over to its wild and unrestrained gratification (say, smoking non-stop for a month) to the point where we become disgusted with it. And so on. But then Nietzsche asks: *Who* exactly is combating the drives in these various ways? His answer:

> [The fact] *that* one *desires* to combat the vehemence of a drive at all, however, does not stand within our own power; nor does the choice of any particular method; nor does the success or failure of this method. What is clearly the case is that in this entire procedure our intellect is only the blind instrument of *another* drive which is a *rival* of the drive whose vehemence is tormenting us ... While "we" believe we are complaining about the vehemence of a drive, at bottom it is one drive *which is complaining about the other*; that is to say: for us to become aware that we are suffering from the *vehemence* [or *violence*] of a drive presupposes the existence of another equally vehement or even more vehement drive, and that a *struggle* is in prospect in which our intellect is going to have to take sides. (Nietzsche 1982: 110, §109)

What we call thinking, willing, and feeling are all "merely a relation of these drives to each other" (Nietzsche 1992a: 237, §36).

Thus, what do I mean when I say "I am trying to stop smoking" – even though that same I is constantly going ahead and continuing to smoke? It simply means that my conscious intellect is taking sides and associating itself with a particular drive. It would make just as much sense to say, "Occasionally I feel this strange urge to stop smoking, but happily I have managed to combat that drive and pick up a cigarette whenever I want." Almost automatically, Nietzsche says, we take our *predominant* drive and for the moment turn it into the *whole* ego, placing all our weaker drives perspectively *farther away*, as if those other drives weren't *me* but rather an *it* (hence Freud's idea of the "id," the "it" – an idea he admitted was derived from Nietzsche). When we talk about the "I," we are simply indicating which drive, at the moment, is sovereign, strongest; "the feeling of the I is always strongest where the preponderance [*Übergewicht*] is," flickering from drive to drive. But the drives themselves remain largely unknown to what we sometimes call the conscious intellect. In another aphorism of *Daybreak*, Nietzsche concludes, "However far a man may go in self-knowledge, nothing however can be more incomplete than his image of the totality of *drives* which constitute his being. He can scarcely name the cruder ones: their number and strength, their ebb and flood, their play and counterplay among one another – and above all the laws of their *nutriment* – remain unknown to him" (Nietzsche 1982: 118, §119). In other words, there is no struggle of reason against the drives; what we call "reason" is itself nothing more than a certain "system of relations between various passions" (Nietzsche 1967: 208, §387), a certain ordering of the drives.

This, however, is where the question of morality comes in for Nietzsche, for one of the primary functions of morality is to establish an "order of rank" among the drives or impulses: "Wherever we encounter a morality," Nietzsche writes, "we also encounter valuations and an order of rank of human impulses" (Nietzsche 1974: 174, §116). "Now one and now another human impulse and state held first place and was ennobled because it was esteemed so highly" (Nietzsche 1974: 174, § 115). Consider any list of impulses – in our present morality, industriousness is ranked higher than sloth; obedience higher than defiance; chastity higher than promiscuity, and so on. One can easily imagine – and indeed find – other moralities that make a different selection of the drives, giving prominence, for instance, to impulses such as aggressiveness and ferocity (a warrior culture). When Nietzsche inquires into the *genealogy* of morality, he is inquiring into the *conditions* of any particular moral ranking of the impulses: why certain impulses are selected *for* and certain impulses are selected *against*. Behind this claim is the fundamental insight that there is no distinction between nature and artifice at the level of the drives: it is not as if we could simply remove the mechanisms of morality and allow the drives to exist in a "free" and "unbound" state: there is no such thing, except as an Idea.

Kant liked to say that we can never get beyond our representations of the world; Nietzsche surmises that what we can never get beyond is the reality of the drives (Nietzsche 1992a: 237, §36). In fact, the drives and impulses are always *assembled* or *arranged*, *from the start*, in different ways, in different individuals, in different cultures, in different eras – which is why Nietzsche always insisted that there are a plurality of moralities (and what he found lacking in his time was an adequate *comparative* study of moralities.)

In *On the Genealogy of Morals*, Nietzsche attempts to show that what *we* call "morality" arose when one particular drive came to the fore and dominated the selection and organization of all the others. He uses a French word to describe this drive – *ressentiment* – because the French verb *ressentir* means primarily not "to resent" but rather "to feel the effects of, to suffer from." In a sense, morality is not unlike aesthetics: much aesthetic theory is written, not from the viewpoint of the artist who creates, but rather from the viewpoint of a spectator who is making judgments about works of art they did not and could not create; similarly, morality is undertaken, not from the viewpoint of those who act, but rather the viewpoint of those who feel the effects of the actions of others. Both are driven by a mania to judge: this is why philosophers are obsessed with analyzing "aesthetic judgments" and "moral judgments." The person whose fundamental drive is *ressentiment* is what Nietzsche calls a "reactive" type: not only to they do not act, but their re-action to the actions of others is primarily felt (*sentir*) and not acted. This is the point Nietzsche is making in his famous parable about the lambs and birds of prey:

> That lambs dislike great birds of prey does not seem strange; only it gives no ground for reproaching these birds of prey for bearing off little lambs. And if the lambs say among themselves "these birds of prey are evil; and whoever is least like a bird of prey, but rather its opposite, lamb – would he not be good?" there is no reason to find fault with this institution of an ideal, except perhaps to say that birds of prey might view it a little ironically and say: "*we* don't dislike them at all, these good little lambs; we even love them: nothing is more tasty than a tender lamb." (Nietzsche 1992b: 480–1, Essay I, §13)

In this parable, the lambs are reactive types: not being able to act, or re-act, in the strict sense, their reaction can only take the form of a feeling or affect, which, in the moral realm, Nietzsche describes as an affect of resentment against those who act: I suffer; you who act are the cause of my suffering, it's your fault that I suffer; and I therefore condemn your activity. Nietzsche's puzzle in *On the Genealogy of*

Morals is this: How did a morality derived from this fundamental drive of *ressentiment* come to dominate all others? How did reactive drives triumph over active drives?

In the first essay of the *Genealogy*, Nietzsche gives his answer: reactive forces triumph by positing the fiction that we are subjects endowed with free will. This is what Deleuze calls "the fiction of a force separated from what it can do," which is in part derived from the subject-predicate grammar of language. When we say "lightning flashes," for instance, we separate in language the lightning from the flash, as if the flash were an action or operation undertaken by a subject called lightning – as if the lightning were separate from the flash, and could perhaps have decided not to flash had it so chosen. But this is obviously a fiction: there is no lightning behind the flash; the lightning and the flash are one and the same thing. Yet it is precisely this fiction that lies at the basis of morality: when we say "a subject acts," we are presuming that, behind every deed, there is a doer; behind every action or activity, there is an actor, and it is on the basis of this fiction that the moral judgments of good and evil enter into the world. When the lambs say, "birds of prey are evil," they are presuming that "the bird of prey is able to *not* manifest its force, that it can hold back from its effects and separate itself from what it can do" (Deleuze 1983: 123), like the lightning that decides not to flash; and they can therefore condemn their action as evil, and hold the birds of prey "responsible" for it. At the same time, what is deemed to be "good" is the reactive position of the lambs. The lambs say: "Those birds of prey are evil, because they 'choose' to perform the activity that is their own (carrying off little lambs), they do not hold back; whereas we lambs could go carry off birds of prey if we wanted to, yet we choose not to, and therefore we are good." It is assumed here that one and the same force is effectively held back in the virtuous lamb and given free rein in the evil bird of prey. But one can easily see the sleight of hand at work here: The birds of prey are judged to be evil because they perform the activity that is their own, whereas the lambs judged themselves to be good because they do not perform the activity that they . . . do not have – as if their "reactive" position "were a voluntary achievement, willed, chosen, a deed, a meritorious act" (Nietzsche 1992b: 482, Essay I, §13).

In the remainder of the *Genealogy*, Nietzsche famously shows that, even though the positing of the subject is a fiction, activity is nonetheless, as it were, made ashamed of itself, and turns back against itself. As Nietzsche writes, "All instincts that do not discharge themselves outwardly *turn inward* . . . [which is] the origin of the bad conscience" (Nietzsche 1992b: 520, Essay 2, §16; see Deleuze 1983: 128ff). The term "fault" no longer refers to others ("it's your fault that I suffer!") but to myself ("it's my fault that I suffer, I am guilty of my own actions"). And what Nietzsche calls the ascetic ideal, finally, marks the triumph of reactive forces over activity in which life is "judged" by transcendent values superior to life.

Now in *Anti-Oedipus*, Deleuze and Guattari, it seems to me, take up this Nietzschean schema, *mutatis mutandis*. What they call "desire" is nothing other than the state of the impulses and drives. "Drives," they write in *Anti-Oedipus*, "are simply the desiring-machines themselves" (Deleuze and Guattari 1983: 35). Moreover, like Nietzsche, Deleuze and Guattari insist that the drives never exist in a free and unbound state, nor are they ever merely individual; they are always arranged and assembled by the social formation in which we find ourselves, and one of the aims of *Anti-Oedipus* is to construct a typology of social formations – primitive territorial societies, States, capitalism, and, later, in *A Thousand Plateaus*, nomadic war machines – each of which organizes and assembles the drives and impulses in different ways. Behind this claim, there lies an attempt to resolve an old debate that concerned the relationship between Marx and Freud. Like Nietzsche, both Marx and Freud each insisted, in their own way, that our conscious thought is determined by forces and drives that go far beyond consciousness, forces that are, as we say, "unconscious" (though we are far too used to this word; it might be better to formulate a new one). Put crudely, in Marx, our thought is determined by our class ("class consciousness"); in Freud, we are determined by our unconscious desires (stemming, usually, from familial conflicts). The nature of the relationship between these two forms of the unconscious – the "political economy" of Marx and the "libidinal" economy of Freud – was a problem that numerous thinkers tried to deal with in the twentieth-century (Marcuse, Brown, Reich, and others). For a long time, the relation between the two was usually formulated in terms of the mechanism of "introjection" and "projection": as an individual, I introject the interests of my class, my culture, my social milieu, which eventually come to determine my consciousness (my "false" consciousness); at the same time, the political economy was seen as a projection of the individual desires of the population that produced it. Deleuze and Guattari famously reject these mechanisms in *Anti-Oedipus*: they argue that political economy (Marx), on the one hand, and libidinal economy (Freud), on the other, are in fact *one and the same thing*. "The only means of bypassing the sterile parallelism where we flounder between Freud and Marx," Deleuze and Guattari write, is "by discovering . . . *how the affects or drives form part of the infrastructure itself*" (Deleuze and Guattari 1983: 63). This is an extraordinary claim:

your very drives and impulses, even the unconscious ones, which seem to be what is most individual about you, are themselves economic, they are already part of what Marx called the infrastructure.

With these Nietzschean reflections in hand, I want to turn to my second text of an immanent ethics, which comes from Leibniz's great book, *New Essays Concerning Human Understanding*.[10] Although the names of Nietzsche and Leibniz are not usually linked together by philosophers, the relation between the two thinkers is not an accidental one. In *The Gay Science*, Nietzsche praised Leibniz's critique of consciousness and his differential conception of the unconscious, the profundity of which he says, "has not been exhausted to this day" (Nietzsche 1974: 305, §357). In the *New Essays*, Leibniz asks, in effect: What would it mean to act "freely," as we like to say, given this theory of the drives? Leibniz asks us to consider a simple example: suppose I am hesitating between staying at home and writing this paper, or going out to a tavern to have a drink with some friends. How do I go about making a decision between these two options? The error would be to objectify the options, as if "staying in" or "going out" were objects that could be weighed in a balance, and as if deliberation were an act of judgment in which "I" – my self, my ego, my intellect – attempt to assess the direction towards which the balance is leaning, "all things being equal." But in fact these two options are not isolatable "objects" but rather two drives, or as Leibniz calls them, "motives" or "inclinations" of the soul. The strength of Leibniz's analysis in the *New Essays* is to show that drives or motives are not simple things, but rather complex "orientations" or "tendencies," each of which integrates within themselves a host of what he liked to call "minute perceptions." My inclination to go to the tavern, for instance, includes not only the minute perception of the effect of the alcohol, or the taste and temperature of the drink, but also the clinking of glasses in the bar, the smoke in the air, the conversation with friends, the temporary lifting of one's solitude, and so on. The same is true of the inclination to stay at home and work, which includes the minute perceptions of the rustling of paper, the noise of my fingers tapping at the computer, the quality of the silence of the room when I stop tapping, the comfort (or frustration) that I find in my work. Both inclinations are formed within an unconscious complex of auditive, gustative, olfactory, and visual perceptions, an entire *perceptio-inclinatory ensemble*. For just as we have unconscious perceptions, we likewise are constituted by what Leibniz called "insensible inclinations" or "disquietudes" of which we are not aware, that pull us simultaneously in a multitude of directions (Leibniz 1981: 165, 188). Not only are all of us constituted by a multitude of unconscious drives, each drive is itself multiple, an infinite complex of minute perceptions and inclinations. It is these drives and motives that constitute the very tissue of the soul, constantly folding it in all directions. This is what Locke termed the "uneasiness" of the soul, its state of constant disquiet and disequilibrium, and Leibniz, its dark background, the *fuscum subnigrum*.

What then is the act of deliberation? At the moment when I am torn between staying home and going out for a drink, the tissue of my soul is in a state of disequilibrium – oscillating between two complex perceptive poles (the perceptive pole of the tavern and the perceptive pole of the study), each of which is itself swarming with an infinity of minute perceptions and inclinations. Here, the movement of the soul, as Leibniz says, more properly resembles a pendulum rather than a balance – and often a rather wildly swinging pendulum at that (Leibniz 1981: 166). The question of decision is: On which side will I "fold" my soul? With which minute inclinations and perceptions will I make a "decisive" fold? Arriving at a decision is a matter of "integrating" (to use a mathematical term) the minute perceptions and inclinations in a "distinguished" perception or a "remarkable" inclination.

The error of the usual schema of judgment is that, in objectifying my two options – staying home or going out – as if they were weights in a balance, it presumes that they remain the same in front of me, and that the deliberating self likewise remains the same, simply assessing the two options in terms of some sort of decision procedure (whether in terms of my interest, or a calculus of probabilities, or an assessment of potential consequences). But this falsifies the nature of deliberation: if neither the options nor the self ever change, how could I *ever* arrive at a decision? The truth of the matter is that, during the entire time the deliberation is going on, the self is constantly changing, and consequently is modifying the two feelings that are agitating it. What Leibniz (and Bergson, for that matter) calls a "free" act will be an act that effectuates the amplitude of my soul at a certain moment, the moment the act is undertaken. It is an act that integrates the small perceptions and small inclinations into a remarkable inclination, which then becomes an inclination of the soul. But this integration requires time: there is a psychic integration and a psychic time of integration. Thus, at 10:15 p.m. I have a vague urge to go to the tavern. Why do I not go? Because at that moment, it remains in the state of a minute inclination, a small perception, a swarm. The motivation is there, but if I still remain at home, working, I do not know the amplitude of my soul. Indeed, most of the time my actions do *not* correspond to the amplitude of my soul. "There is no reason," says Deleuze, to subject all the actions we undertake to the criterion: Is it free or not? Freedom is only for certain acts. There are all sorts of acts that do not have to be confronted with the problems of freedom. They are done solely, one could say, to calm our disquietude: all our habitual and machinal acts. We will speak of freedom only when we pose the question of an act capable or not of filling the amplitude of the soul at a given moment. (Deleuze 1987)

At 10:30 p.m., I finally "decide" that I'm going to go out drinking. Is that because the drive to go out has won out over the drive to stay home working? Even that simplifies the operation, since what came into play may have been other motives that remain largely unknown to us, such as (these are all examples given by Nietzsche in *Daybreak*): "the way we habitually expend our energy"; "or our indolence, which prefers to do what is easiest"; "or an excitation of our imagination brought about at the decisive moment by some immediate, very trivial event"; or "quite incalculable physical influences"; or "some emotion or other [that] happens quite by chance to leap forth" (Nietzsche 1982: 129, §129). As Bergson puts it, in terms very similar to Leibniz's:

> all the time that the deliberation is going on, the self is changing and is con-
> sequently modifying the [often unknown] feelings that agitate it. A dynamic
> series of states is thus formed which permeate and strengthen one another,
> and which will lead by a natural evolution to a free act. . . . In reality there
> are not two tendencies, or even two directions, but a self which lives and
> develops by means of its very hesitations, until the free action drops from it
> like an over-ripe fruit. (Bergson 1913: 171, 176)

As Leibniz puts it, to say that we are "free" means that we are "inclined without being necessitated." A free act is simply an act that expresses the whole of the soul at a given moment of duration – that is, an act that fills the amplitude of the soul at a given moment.

Parenthetically, one might contrast this theory of decision with the one proposed by Derrida in his well-known essay "Force of Law" (Derrida 2002). Both Derrida and Deleuze insist that decision presupposes an Idea, almost in the Kantian sense. For Derrida, however, these Ideas – for instance, the Idea of justice, which would guide our juridical decisions – are, as he says, "infinitely transcendent," and hence the very condition of possibility of their effectuation is their impossibility. For Deleuze, such Ideas are purely immanent: the Idea is nothing other than the problematic multiplicity of these drives and minute inclinations, which constitutes the condition of any decision. In this sense, one might say that Deleuze "replaces the power of judgment with the force of decision" (Deleuze 1997: 49).

The Theory of Desire

With these two analyses in hand – Nietzsche's theory of the drives (as a way of approaching the nature of modes of existence) and Leibniz's theory of "freedom" (if we can still use this word) in relation to the theory of the drives – we can now turn to the question of desire, and the problem of how desire can desire its own repression. (What Deleuze ultimately means by the term "desire," of course, is different from the usual usage: it does not refer to my conscious desires – to get rich, to get a job, and so on – but rather to the state of the unconscious drives.) There are a number of consequences that follow from these analyses, which I would like to discuss briefly.

1. First, there is a school of economics that sees humans as rational agents who always act in such a way as to maximize their own interests (what is sometimes called "rational choice theory"). Deleuze's distinction between desire and interest seeks to put that claim in its proper context. Someone may have an interest, say, in becoming an academic, so he or she applies to the university, takes courses, writes a thesis, attends conferences, goes on the job market in hopes of securing a job, finding an academic position. You may indeed have an interest in all that, which you can pursue in a highly rational manner. But that interest exists as a possibility only within the context of a particular social formation, our capitalist formation. If you are capable of pursuing that interest in a concerted and rational manner, it is first of all because your desire – your drives and impulses – are themselves invested in the social formation that makes that interest possible. Your drives have been constructed, assembled, and arranged in such a manner that your desire is positively invested in the system that allows you to have this particular interest. This is why Deleuze can say that desire as such is always positive. Normally, we tend to think of desire in terms of lack: if we desire something, it is because we lack it. But Deleuze reconfigures the concept of desire: what we desire, what we invest our desire in, is a social formation, and in this sense desire is always *positive*. Lack appears only at the level of interest, because the social formation – the infrastructure – in which we have already invested our *desire* has in turn produced that lack. The result of this analysis is that we can now determine the proper *object* of a purely immanent ethics, which is neither my conscious will, nor my conscious decisions, but neither is it my pre-conscious interests (say, my class interest, in the Marxist sense). The true object of an immanent ethics is the drives, and thus it entails, as both Spinoza and Nietzsche know, an entire theory of *affectivity* at the basis of any theory of ethics.

2. The second consequence follows from the first. The primacy of the question of desire over both interest and will is the reason Deleuze says that the fundamental problem of political philosophy is one that was formulated most clearly by Spinoza: "Why do people fight for their servitude as stubbornly as though it were their salvation?" (Deleuze and Guattari 1983: 29). In other words, why do we have such a stake in investing in a social system that constantly represses us, thwarts our interests, and introduces lack into our lives? In the end, the answer is simple: it is because your desire – that is, your drives and affects – are not your own, so to speak. They are, if I can put it this way, part of the capitalist infrastructure; they are not simply your own individual mental or psychic reality (Deleuze and Guattari 1983: 30). Nothing makes this more obvious that the effects of marketing, which are directed entirely at the manipulation of the drives and affects: at the drug store, I almost automatically reach for one brand of toothpaste rather than another, since I have a fervent *interest* in having my teeth cavity-free and whiter than white, and my breath fresher than fresh – but this is because my desire is already invested in the social formation that creates that interest, and that creates the sense of lack I feel if my teeth aren't whiter than white, or my breath fresher than fresh.

3. Third, the difference between interest and desire could be said to parallel the difference between the rational and the irrational. "Once interests have been defined within the confines of a society, the rational is the way in which people pursue those interests and attempt to realize them" (Deleuze 2004: 262–3) – the interest for a job, or cavity-free teeth. "But underneath that," Deleuze insists, "you find desires, investments of desire that are not to be confused with investments of interest, and on which interests depend for their determination and very distribution: an enormous flow, all kinds of libidinal-unconscious flows that constitute the delirium of this society" (Deleuze 2004: 263). As Deleuze will say:

> Reason is always a region carved out of the irrational – it is not shel-
> tered from the irrational at all, but traversed by it and only defined by a
> particular kind of relationship among irrational factors. Underneath all
> reason lies delirium and drift. Everything about capitalism is rational,
> except capital ... A stock market is a perfectly rational mechanism, you
> can understand it, learn how it works; capitalists know how to use it;
> and yet what a delirium, it's mad ... It's just like theology: everything
> about it is quite rational – *if* you accept sin, the immaculate conception,
> and the incarnation, which are themselves irrational elements. (Deleuze
> 2004: 262)

4. Fourth, how does Deleuze conceptualize this movement of desire? Interestingly, *Anti-Oedipus* can be read as an explicit attempt to rework the fundamental theses of Kant's *Critique of Practical Reason*. Kant presents the second critique as a theory of desire, and he defines desire, somewhat surprisingly, in *causal* terms: desire is "a faculty which by means of its representations is the *cause* of the actuality of the objects of those representations." In its lower form, the products of desire are fantasies and superstitions; but in its higher form (the will), the products of desire are acts of *freedom* under the moral law – actions which are, however, irreducible to mechanistic causality. Deleuze takes up Kant's model of desire, but modifies it in two fundamental ways. First, if desire is productive or causal, then its product is itself *real* (and not illusory or noumenal): the entire socio-political field, Deleuze argues, must be seen as the historically determined product of desire. Second, to maintain this claim, Deleuze formulates an entirely new theory of "Ideas." In Kant, the postulates of practical reason are found in the transcendent Ideas of God, World, and the Soul, which are themselves derived from the types of judgment of relation (categorical, hypothetical, disjunctive). In response, Deleuze, in the first chapters of *Anti-Oedipus*, formulates a purely immanent theory of Ideas, in which desire is constituted by a set of constituting passive syntheses (connective, disjunctive, conjunctive).

Now, I might, in passing (developing this point would take us too far afield) note that Deleuze formulates his theory of desire in *Anti-Oedipus* partly in relation to Lacan, but by taking Lacan's thought in a direction that most Lacanians would never go, and indeed would insist that one *cannot* go there. *Anti-Oedipus*, as its subtitle ("Capitalism and Schizophrenia") indicates, takes psychosis as its model for the unconscious. Lacan himself had said that the unconscious appears in its purest form in psychosis, but that in effect the unconscious remains inaccessible in psychotics, precisely because psychotics refuse symbolization. Thus, the dimension of the Real can only appear as a kind of negative moment in Lacan, as a kind of "gap" or "rupture" in the field of immanence (thereby introducing into the "gap" an element of transcendence). Deleuze, in this respect, effectively inverts Lacan, and presents *Anti-Oedipus* in its entirely as a theory of the Real that is described in all its positivity – that is, as a sub-representative field defined by differential partial objects or intensities that enter into indirect syntheses; pure positive multiplicities where everything is possible (transverse connections, polyvocal conjunctions, included disjunctions); signs of desire that compose a signifying chain, but which are themselves non-signifying, and so on (Deleuze and Guattari 1983: 309). It is an analysis of *delirium*, showing that – following the principles we have just outlined – the delirium that lies at the heart of the self (*schizophrenia*) is one and the same thing as the delirium that exists at the heart of our society (and appears most clearly in *capitalism* – a monetary mass that "exists" nowhere, and is controlled by no one, and is literally delirious in its operations). But talking about capitalism and schizophrenia is simply another way of saying that our drives are social through and through, that they are part of the infrastructure.

5. Fifth and finally, this is one way of suggesting that the concept of freedom – which plays such a decisive role in Kant's philosophy – also assumes a prominent place in Deleuze's own philosophy of desire, albeit in a new form – namely, as the question of the conditions for the production of the *new*. As Deleuze frequently says, following thinkers like Salomon Maimon, what needed to happen in post-Kantian philosophy was a substitution of a viewpoint of *internal genesis* for the Kantian viewpoint of *external condition*. But "doing this," Deleuze would explain, "means returning to Leibniz, but on bases other than Leibniz's. All the elements to create a genesis such as the post-Kantians demand it, all the elements are virtually in Leibniz" (Deleuze 1980). This is what one finds in Deleuze's post-Kantian (Nietzschean) reading of Leibniz: the idea that the "I think" of consciousness bathes in an unconscious, an unconscious of drives, motives, and inclinations, which contain the differentials of what appears in consciousness, and which would therefore perform the genesis of the conditioned as a function of the condition. In this sense, Deleuze's ethical philosophy might at first sight appear to be the exact opposite of Kant's ethical theory, with the latter's appeal to the transcendence of the Moral Law. Yet Kant himself insisted on a principle of immanence throughout his philosophy, even if he betrayed it in his books on practical philosophy. This is perhaps why, in Deleuze, the *content* of an immanent ethics is taken from Nietzsche and Spinoza, but its immanent *form* winds up being taken primarily from Kant. In this sense, one could say that Deleuze's work, with regard to practical and political philosophy, is in the end at once an *inversion* as well as a *completion* of Kant's critical philosophy.

References

Bergson, H. (1913), *Time and Free Will: An Essay on the Immediate Data of Consciousness*, trans. F. L. Pogson, Mineola: Dover Publications.

Deleuze, G. (1980), Seminar of May 20, 1980, on Leibniz, available at www.web-deleuze.com

Deleuze, G. (1983), *Nietzsche and Philosophy*, trans. H. Tomlinson, New York: Columbia University Press.

Deleuze, G. (1987), Seminar of February 24, 1987, "The Tavern," on Leibniz and Freedom, available at www.webdeleuze.com

Deleuze, G. (1988a), *Foucault*, trans. S. Hand, Minneapolis: University of Minnesota Press.

Deleuze, G. (1988b), *Spinoza: Practical Philosophy*, trans. Robert Hurley, San Francisco: City Lights Books.

Deleuze, G. (1992), *Expressionism in Philosophy: Spinoza*, trans. M. Joughin, New York: Zone Books.

Deleuze, G. (1994), *Difference and Repetition*, trans. P. Patton, New York: Columbia University Press.

Deleuze, G. (1995), *Negotiations, 1972–1990*, trans. M. Joughin, New York: Columbia University Press.

Deleuze, G. (1997), *Essays Critical and Clinical*, trans. D. W. Smith and M. A. Greco, Minneapolis: University of Minnesota Press.

Deleuze, G. (2001), "Nietzsche," in *Pure Immanence: Essays on a Life*, trans. A. Boyman, New York: Zone Books.

Deleuze, G. (2004), *Desert Islands and Other Texts*, trans. M. Taormina, New York: Semiotext(e).

Deleuze, G. and F. Guattari (1983), *Anti-Oedipus: Capitalism and Schizophrenia*, trans. R. Hurley, M. Seem, and H. R. Lane, Minneapolis: University of Minnesota Press.

Deleuze, G. and F. Guattari (1994), *What is Philosophy?*, trans. H. Tomlinson and C. Burchell, New York: Columbia University Press.

Derrida, J. (2002), "Force of Law: The 'Mystical Foundation of Authority'," in *Acts of Religion*, ed. G. Anidjar, New York and London: Routledge.

Foucault, M. (1977), "Preface" to G. Deleuze and F. Guattari, *Anti-Oedipus: Capitalism and Schizophrenia*, trans. R. Hurley, M. Seem, and H. R. Lane, New York: Viking.

Heidegger, M. (1982), *Nietzsche*, vol. 4, *Nihilism*, trans. F. A. Capuzzi, ed. D. F. Krell, San Francisco: Harper & Row.

Leibniz, G. W. (1956), *The Leibniz–Clarke Correspondence*, ed. H. G. Alexander, Manchester: Manchester University Press.

Leibniz, G. W. (1981), *New Essays on Human Understanding*, trans. P. Remnant and J. Bennett, Cambridge: Cambridge University Press.

MacIntyre, A. (1984), *After Virtue: A Study in Moral Theory*, 2nd edn, Notre Dame: University of Notre Dame Press.

Nietzsche, F. (1967), *The Will to Power*, trans. W. Kaufman, New York: Random House.

Nietzsche, F. (1974), *The Gay Science*, trans. W. Kaufman, New York: Vintage Books.

Nietzsche, F. (1982), *Daybreak: Thoughts About the Prejudices of Morality*, trans. R. Hollingdale, Cambridge: Cambridge University Press.

Nietzsche, F. (1992a), *Beyond Good and Evil*, trans. W. Kaufman, in *Basic Writings*, New York: Modern Library.

Nietzsche, F. (1992b), *On the Genealogy of Morals*, trans. W. Kaufman, in *Basic Writings*, New York: Modern Library.

Parkes, G. (1994), *Composing the Soul: Reaches of Nietzsche's Psychology*, Chicago and London: University of Chicago Press.

Spinoza, B. (2002), *Complete Works*, trans. Samuel Shirley, Indianapolis and Cambridge: Hackett Publishing Company.

Notes

1. See Heidegger 1982: 76–7, section 12, "Nietzsche's 'Moral' Interpretation of Metaphysics": "By 'morality,' Nietzsche usually understands a system of evaluations in which a transcendent world is posited as an idealized standard of measure."

2. On the distinction between ethics and morality, see Deleuze 1995: 100–1, 113–14. *Règles facultatives* is a term Deleuze adopts from the sociolinguist William Labov to designate "functions of internal variation and no longer constants"; see Deleuze 1988a: 146–7, note 18.

3. See Deleuze 1995: 135: "Everything tended toward the great Spinoza-Nietzsche identity." Deleuze devoted a full-length monograph and a shorter introductory volume to both of these thinkers. For Nietzsche, see Deleuze 1983 and 2001; for Spinoza, see Deleuze 1988b and 1992.

4. At best, the Spinozistic and Nietzschean critiques were accepted as negative moments, exemplary instances of what must be fought against and rejected in the ethico-moral domain. Alasdair MacIntyre, for his part, summarized the contemporary ethical options in the chapter title: *"Aristotle or Nietzsche"*: "The defensibility of the Nietzschean position turns *in the end* on the answer to the question: was it right in the first place to reject Aristotle?" (MacIntyre 1984: 117).

5. For discussion of these points, see Deleuze 1988b, 22–3 and Deleuze 1992: 269.

6. On the notion of "dramatization," see Deleuze 1983: 75–9.

7. See Deleuze and Guattari 1994: 74: "There is not the slightest reason for thinking that modes of existence need transcendent values by which they could be compared, selected, and judged relative to one another. There are only immanent criteria. A possibility of life is evaluated through itself in the movements it lays out and the intensities it creates on a plane of immanence: what is not laid out or created is rejected. A mode of existence is good or bad, noble or vulgar, complete or empty, independently of Good or Evil or any transcendent value: there are never any criteria other than the tenor of existence, the intensification of life."

8. For instance, in a famous text, which in some respects parallels Nietzsche's analyses in *On the Genealogy of Morals*, Spinoza showed how the notion of the Law arose among the Hebrews from a misunderstanding of affective relations. When God forbade Adam to eat the fruit of the Garden of Eden, he did so because he knew it would affect Adam's body like a poison, decomposing its constitutive relation. But Adam, unable to perceive these affective relations, mistook the prohibition for a *commandment*, the effect of decomposition as a *punishment*, and the word of God as a *Law*. See Spinoza, Letter 19, to Blijenbergh, in Spinoza 2002: 357–61. On the important question, "Can there be inherently evil modes of existence?" see Deleuze's article, "The Letters on Evil (Correspondence with Blyenbergh)," in Deleuze 1988b: 30–43.

9. Parkes' book in its entirety is a profound analysis of Nietzsche's theory of the drives.

10. See Leibniz 1981, Chapters 20 and 21; and Leibniz 1956: 58–60, Leibniz's Fifth Paper, §§14–17.

Chapter 8

"Existing Not as a Subject But as a Work of Art": The Task of Ethics or Aesthetics?

Kenneth Surin

> It's to do with abolishing ways of existing or, as Nietzsche put it, inventing new possibilities of life. Existing not as a subject but as a work of art – and this last phase presents thought as artistry. (Deleuze 1995a: 95)

Deleuze endorsed repeatedly the well-known conviction of Michel Foucault and of Nietzsche that life had to be lived as a work of art. This raises the question whether the terms under which a life is led properly belong to ethics (this of course being the traditional or consensual position taken when it comes to answering the question "how should I lead my life?"). But to suggest that life be led as a work of art implies, palpably, that it is aesthetics, and not ethics, which superintends the question "how should I lead my life?" At one level the answer to this question can only be altogether commonplace and quite worn-out – of course the answer given depends on how "ethics" and "aesthetics" are defined! But at another level it certainly isn't trivial. If Deleuze had an ethics, then what kind of ethics is it, and is it an ethics with a depth and scope capable of superintending the question "how should I lead my life"? Or would this task be left to an aesthetics, and, if so, what kind of aesthetics did Deleuze have? Or are ethics and aesthetics related in such a way in Deleuze's thought that it is *both* ethics and aesthetics which oversee the terms of the question "how should I lead my life"? And if that is the case, then how does Deleuze conceive of the relation between ethics and aesthetics, and how do they function conjointly when dealing with the question of leading one's life as a work of art?

Deleuze, while making a clear distinction between "ethics" and "morality," never in my view made really precise the difference between "ethics" and "aesthetics" when it came to defining the notion of a "style of life" (*un style de vie*) or "life as a work of art" (*la vie comme oeuvre d'art*).[1] The nearest he came to it was in an interview with Foucault's biographer Didier Eribon which dealt with Deleuze's book on Foucault, where it emerges during the course of the interview that while "ethics" has to do with "a set of optional rules that assess what we do, what we say, in relation to the ways of existing involved," aesthetics by contrast has to do with "a style of life, not anything at all personal, but inventing a possibility of life, a way of existing." In a word, ethics centers on *assessing* a way of existing, while aesthetics focuses on *inventing* a way of existing (Deleuze 1995a: 100). But this proposal begs as many questions as it is likely to answer, since the weight of Deleuze's distinction now hinges on the relationship between assessment and invention when it comes to specifying the terms under which a life is led. We need therefore to begin by finding an adequate and principled basis for establishing the demarcation between "ethics" and "aesthetics," otherwise there will be no good grounds for maintaining the distinction between "assessing a way of life" and "inventing a way of life" in the way that Deleuze seems to make it. Someone with contrarian inclinations could come along and insist that ethics alone is capable of sustaining both assessment and invention, while another potential contrarian might maintain that it is aesthetics instead which can do this on its own without any need for recourse to ethics. Consequently, the follower of Deleuze who insists that, contrary to the suggestions of these two contrarians, the assessment of a life lies with ethics, and the invention of a life with aesthetics, has then to show *ab initio* that there is a fundamental distinction to be made between ethics and aesthetics, the essential nature of which requires that assessment and invention be assigned to the realms of ethics and aesthetics respectively. There has, in other words, to be something intrinsic to ethics and aesthetics which warrants the assigning of the assessment of the terms by which a life is led to ethics, and the invention of a life to aesthetics, in the way proposed by Deleuze.

While the distinction between ethics and aesthetics goes all the way back to the pre-Socratics, it was Kant who first made a rigorous division between these two domains with his vitally important critical redaction of a previous form of philosophic reflection based on the so-called medieval transcendentals of truth (knowledge), beauty (aesthetics), and goodness (ethics). Both Foucault and Deleuze, in our view, adhere to, but also advance and significantly modify, the important separation embodied in Kant's second and third Critiques between ethics and aesthetics respectively (and also between these theoretical domains and that of knowledge or epistemology, the latter being of course the focus of Kant's first Critique). But first we need to ask the question of the sense in which Deleuze could have been said to have an ethics. Deleuze was one of the truly great philosophical followers of Nietzsche, and the latter's relentless undermining of any philosophical basis from which a putative project of assessment or evaluation can be undertaken raises the question of whether, for Nietzsche and his epigoni (including Deleuze), ethics can exist as anything more significant than a mere *façon de parler*.

Those who propose that Deleuze (and of course Guattari) had an ethics include Foucault, who in his famous preface to *Anti-Oedipus* declared that "*Anti-Oedipus* (may its authors forgive me) is a book of ethics, the first book of ethics to be written in France in quite a long time (perhaps that explains why its success was not limited to a particular 'readership': being anti-oedipal has become a life style, a way of thinking and living)" (Foucault 1983: xiii). In this volume, Daniel W. Smith has argued that Deleuze (and Guattari) are the exponents of an "immanent ethics," one which has two primary features:

> It focuses on the differences between modes of existence, in terms of their immanent capabilities or power (active versus reactive, in Nietzsche; active versus passive, in Spinoza), and it poses, as one of its fundamental problems, the urge towards transcendence that effectively "perverts" desire, to the point where we can actually desire our own repression, a separation from our own capacities and powers. (See above, p. 126)

My aim here is not to take issue with Smith (or indeed Foucault). Smith, who has been a consistently superior interpreter and translator of Deleuze, shows us what there is in Deleuze's thinking that warrants the characterization of appropriate aspects of it as an "immanent ethics." Smith succeeds in this demonstration – that is, he shows convincingly how Deleuze adheres to the positions of Spinoza and Nietzsche on the passions, as well as maintaining that an ethics which eschews immanence invariably sunders us from our powers and capacities.[2]

Deleuze was, of course, a sympathetic and innovative reader of Foucault, and the primary aim of this essay is to show how Foucault's delineation of an "aesthetics of existence" or a "stylistics of being" is fundamentally in accord with the Deleuzian point of view, and to draw some conclusions from this for understanding Deleuze (and Guattari). Along the way it will be necessary to deal with the Kantian diremption between aesthetics and ethics, expressed by Kant in terms of his baroque theory of the faculties, a theory which happens to be dispensable in its entirety when viewed from a Deleuzian point of view, as we shall shortly see. Also to be discussed is the plausibility or otherwise of Foucault's characterization of an "aesthetics of existence" or "stylistics of being," and, by extension, the compatibility or otherwise of this "aesthetics" or "stylistics" with those propositions of Deleuze which deal with the passions, their enabling conditions, and the assemblages within which they are positioned.

The Kantian partitioning between ethics and aesthetics is judged to be problematic, and inherently so, by Deleuze in his commentary on Kant, since this distinction was required by Kant to address problems posed at quite another level by his multipart philosophical architectonic. For Kant, the fundamental difference between truth (i.e. theoretical judgment or knowledge) and goodness (i.e. practical judgment or ethics) is that while both define an "interest of reason," the former nonetheless defines a "speculative reason" while the latter is associated with a "practical reason." Truth and goodness are quite different with regard to their respective faculties, even though both serve a "legislative" function when it comes to their respective deployments of reason (Deleuze 1984: 47). By contrast, the faculty of feeling (the domain of aesthetics) is not legislative – it has no objects over which it legislates. To quote Deleuze:

> Kant therefore refuses to use the word "autonomy" for the faculty of feeling in its higher form: powerless to legislate over objects, judgment can be only *autonomous*, that is, it legislates over itself. . . . The faculty of feeling has no *domain* (neither phenomena nor things in themselves); it does not express the conditions to which a kind of objects (*sic*) must be subject, but solely the subjective conditions for the exercise of the faculties. (Deleuze 1984: 48)

Deleuze goes on to say:

> in the *Critique of Judgment* [which deals with the faculty of feeling] the imagination does not take on a legislative function on its own account. But it frees itself, so that all the faculties together enter into a free accord. Thus the first two Critiques set out a relationship between the faculties which is determined by one of them; the last Critique uncovers a deeper free and indeterminate accord of the faculties as the condition of the possibility of every determinate relationship. (Deleuze 1984: 68)

In other words, the *Critique of Judgment*, whose focal point is the aesthetic realm, is used by Kant to resolve the problem, necessarily unique and internal to his recondite system, of the relation of the three faculties to each other. Kant, according to Deleuze and numerous other commentators, wanted to extricate purpose from any theological determination and, correlatively, to provide theology itself with an ultimate human ground. Theological principles could therefore only be postulated in the mode of an "as if," since any putatively fuller theological conceptions were sequestered in the noumenal realm unattainable to human beings. The task of the third Critique was to realize this goal by showing that the accord of the faculties is not subject to a more profound or over-arching meta-accord (classically provided by a theologically sustained "transcendental of transcendentals" which for Kant had necessarily to be lodged in the noumenal domain) than the one provided by the "common sense" (*sensus communis*) of aesthetic taste, i.e. "*human practical activity*" (Deleuze 1984: 69).

For all the occasional amusement that Nietzsche enjoyed at Kant's expense, the revolutionary turn to perspectivalism associated with Nietzsche was in truth made possible, philosophically, by Kant's seemingly much less radical "detranscendentalization" of the aesthetic (and also of the complementary metaphysical bases of truth/knowledge and goodness/ethics). After Kant, the classical notions of truth, goodness, and beauty were severed decisively from any such infinitizing meta-accords, these being banished by Kant to the noumenal realm beyond the reach of knowledge as opposed to the exigencies of mere postulation, the latter being of course the only option now open to the schemas of theology. Freed from the tutelage of any such infinitizing meta-accords, truth, goodness, and beauty could finally be opened up to the kind of strictly immanentist genealogy proposed by Nietzsche and subsequently extended by Foucault and taken up by Deleuze. As a consequence, ethics and aesthetics could be served by entirely separate though sometimes overlapping presuppositional frameworks, each constituted by their own specific accords, or by some alternative though not necessarily "superior" accord, capable of subsuming one or the other, or even both. It now became possible, in principle, to subsume ethics under aesthetics. There are at least two roads to this subsumption of the ethical by the aesthetic, and both are compatible with a Deleuzian philosophical perspective. One route is provided by Nietzsche (as interpreted by Deleuze himself in several texts); the other derives from Foucault's depiction of the Greek and Roman "care of self" (though of course Foucault's genealogy of this "care of self" was inspired in large part by Nietzsche's conception of life as a ceaseless dynamism or *energeia*, and by the latter's identification of life with the imperative invention of new styles of existence).

Deleuze's estimation of Foucault's indebtedness to Nietzsche on the question of our positioning with regard to power is worth quoting at length:

[Are] we condemned to conversing with Power, irrespective of whether we're wielding it or being subjected to it? [Foucault] confronts the question in one of his most violent texts, one of the funniest too, on "infamous men." And it takes him time to come up with an answer. Crossing the line of force, going beyond power, involves as it were bending force, making it impinge on itself rather than on other forces: a "fold," in Foucault's terms. Force playing on itself. It's a question of "doubling" the play of forces. Of a self-relation that allows us to resist, to elude power, to turn life or death against power. This, according to Foucault, is something the Greeks invented. It's no longer a matter of determinate forms, as with knowledge, or of constraining rules, as with power: it's a matter of optional rules that make existence a work of art, rules at once ethical and aesthetic that constitute ways of existing or styles of life (including even suicide). It's what Nietzsche discovered as the will to power operating artistically, inventing new "possibilities of life." One should, for all sorts of reasons, avoid all talk of a return to the subject, because these processes of subjectification vary enormously from one period to another and operate through very disparate rules. (Deleuze 1995a: 98)

"Rules at once ethical and aesthetic" is the phrase used by Deleuze in this passage, and yet we know from his previous formulations that this can't really be so: according to these other Deleuzian formulations, "constraining" rules have to do with morality, rules of "assessment" with ethics, whilst "enabling" rules belong to the aesthetic sphere. Given this compartmentalization, how can the same rule be both ethical and aesthetic? Or is Deleuze, rather, proposing that rules drawn from both the ethical and the aesthetic domains are required if new "possibilities of life" are to be invented (these "new possibilities" being of course a requisite for making one's life a work of art)? The latter option is certainly the much more plausible alternative, in which case there remains the business of sorting out the respective parts played by ethical and aesthetic rules when it comes to outlining the sense in which for Deleuze we are capable of "existing not as a subject but as a work of art." Further helpful elaboration where this issue is concerned is provided in the same interview that Deleuze had with Didier Eribon:

Subjectification isn't even anything to do with a "person": it's a specific or collective individuation relating to an event (a time of day, a river, a wind, a life . . .). It's a mode of intensity, not a personal subject. It's a specific dimension without which we can't go beyond knowledge or resist power. Foucault goes on to analyze Greek and Christian ways of existing, how they enter into forms of knowledge, how they make compromises with power. Foucault, true to his method, isn't basically interested in returning to the Greeks, but in us today: what are our ways of existing, our possibilities of life or our processes of subjectification; are there ways for us to constitute ourselves as a "self," and (as Nietzsche would put it) sufficiently "artistic" ways, beyond knowledge and power? And are we up to it, because in a way it's a matter of life and death? (Deleuze 1995a: 98–9)

For Deleuze, as with the later Foucault, it is therefore a question of finding possibilities of life which "go beyond knowledge" and enable a "resistance to power" – that is, finding ways to constitute life in a "sufficiently artistic way." The emphasis in this declaration is clearly on the aesthetic, since if anything for Foucault and Deleuze the power of invention resides in the "creative" aesthetic and not the "evaluative" ethical. This is not to suggest that the ethical is superfluous. Quite obviously, a way of life has to be scrutinized, and scrutinized rigorously, as a condition of shaping one's life as a work of art, which means that ethics (i.e. the set of practices and precepts which makes this scrutiny or evaluation possible) is indispensable for this process of aesthetic life-shaping. But there is another angle to this story which needs to be taken into account.

Deleuze, in his intellectual portrait of Foucault, makes an important distinction between "subject-type individuations" and "event-type individuations." Only the former require a subject. The latter, by contrast, are subject-less, the implication being that only individuations requiring a subject can be assessed from an ethical point of view. To quote Deleuze:

> there are also event-type individuations where there's no subject: a wind, an atmosphere, a time of day, a battle ... One can't assume that a life, or a work of art, is individuated as a subject; quite the reverse. Take Foucault himself: you weren't aware of him as a person exactly. Even in trivial situations, say when he came into a room, it was more like a changed atmosphere, a sort of event, an electric or magnetic field or something. That didn't in the least rule out warmth or make you feel uncomfortable, but it wasn't like a person. It was a set of intensities. (Deleuze 1995b: 115)

The "Foucault" just portrayed by Deleuze is subject-less ("you weren't aware of him as a person exactly"), and, as an amalgam of intensities and nothing more, when individuated as the event that is "Foucault," is surely quite beyond assessment in terms of the ethical.

Deleuze, in the same text on Foucault, provides yet another basis for conceptualizing the respective contributions of the ethical and the aesthetic to the processes involved in shaping one's life. It lies in the interesting distinction that Foucault made between love and passion in a conversation with the German film director Werner Schroeter (Foucault 1994). Deleuze says of Foucault's distinction:

The distinction is nothing to do with constancy or inconstancy. Nor is it one between homosexuality and heterosexuality, though that's discussed in the text. It's a distinction between two kinds of individuation: one, love, through persons, and the other through intensity, as though passion dissolved persons not into something undifferentiated but into a field of various persisting and mutually interdependent intensities ("a constantly shifting state, but not tending toward any given point, with strong phases and weak phases, phases when it becomes incandescent and everything wavers for an unstable moment we cling to for obscure reasons, perhaps through inertia; it seeks, ultimately, to persist and to disappear . . . being oneself no longer makes any sense . . ."). Love's a state of, and a relation between, persons, subjects. But passion is a subpersonal event that may last as long as a lifetime ("I've been living for eighteen years in a state of passion about someone, for someone"), a field of intensities that individuates independently of any subject. Tristan and Isolde, that may be love. But someone, referring to this Foucault text, said to me: Catherine and Heathcliff, in *Wuthering Heights*, is passion, pure passion, not love. A fearsome kinship of souls, in fact, something not altogether human (who is he? A wolf . . .). It's very difficult to express, to convey – a new distinction between affective states. (Deleuze 1995b: 116)

That is to say, individuation through love is susceptible in principle to being evaluated in ethical terms, whereas passion, as a field of uncontrollably oscillating intensities, can only be assessed aesthetically. This alignment – love-ethics/passion-aesthetics – can be expanded further, since it is obvious that for Deleuze (and Foucault) the fundamental operative register for ethics is an evaluative scheme shaped by desiderata based on prudence, whereas the accompanying active principle for aesthetics is transgression (that is, love-ethics [prudence]/passion-aesthetics [transgression]).[3] The complication arising at this point is that while transgression involves, *per definiens*, the violation of a prohibition, and hence is to this extent incompatible with the requirements of morality, it is not obvious that transgression is in all cases incompatible with the requirements of *prudentia* (i.e., ethics, as defined by Deleuze, if we permit the accompanying slightly Aristotelian gloss). For some transgressions, or what appear initially to be transgressions, *can* be prudential: assassinating a ruler in the very early stages of what is seemingly an emerging reign of tyranny, for example.

The affinity between Catherine and Heathcliff is passional, and in its climactic scenes ravishingly so, hence it is certainly not guided by any of the requirements of *prudentia*, and Heathcliff's consistently sadistic behavior towards those around him (albeit driven and intensified by the shattering realization of Catherine's ultimate unattainability) is impossible to characterize as moral or even ethical by any standards reasonably to be associated with the term "ethical," let alone "moral." Deleuze is right – the passional event that is "Heathcliff and Catherine" is profoundly constitutive of an aesthetics or stylistics of existence and hence is "para-ethical." "Heathcliff and Catherine" as an event partook of an art of life in the manner of some of the Greek and Roman personages who fascinated Foucault towards the end of his life, and the reader of *Wuthering Heights* knows that there is no schema of evaluation (the requisite hallmark of ethics) within which the event of "Heathcliff and Catherine" can be contained in order to make it explicable and seemingly rational. (As the third-rate literary critic would say, that is the "beauty" of the story, and for once this untalented critic may be right.)

But what of Tristan and Isolde, whose affinity for each other according to Deleuze is in the register of love, and "courtly" love at that, and thus can presumably be subsumed under something like an ethics (with its forms of evaluation based on something approximating to *prudentia*?).[4] Courtly love (*amour courtois*) permitted the expression of passion, but any such passion had to be disciplined or chastened by the requirements of chivalry or nobility, and above all tempered by the ideals of refinement ("courtliness") expected of a member of a royal court (Schultz 2006). It is simply impossible to view the vulpine Heathcliff (to recall Deleuze's invocation of this particular becoming-wolf) as an exemplar of *amour courtois*. At the same time, the essential ingredient of *amour courtois* – namely, courtly refinement – makes it an ideal that only a few can pursue and attain. In this respect *amour courtois* has an undeniable kinship with Stoic ethics. Foucault characterizes Stoic ethics in the following terms:

> [This is] the reason, I think, that the principal aim, the principal target of this kind was an aesthetic one. First, this kind of ethics was only a problem of personal choice. Second, it was reserved for a few people in the population; it was not a question of giving a pattern of behavior for everybody. It was a personal choice for a small elite. The reason for making this choice was the will to live a beautiful life, and to leave to others memories of a beautiful existence. I don't think that we can say that this kind of ethics was an attempt to normalize the population. (Foucault 1997a: 254)

The "art of life" embodied in Stoic ethics according to Foucault (and *amour courtois* according to us) required the cultivation of a *tekhne tou biou* in which establishing a scrupulous control over the self was central to its attainment.[5] To quote Foucault on this cultivation of self required in Greek ethics:

The Greeks problematized their freedom, and the freedom of the individual, as an ethical problem. But ethical in the sense in which the Greeks understood it: *ethos* was a way of being and of behavior. It was a mode of being for the subject, along with a certain way of acting, a way visible to others. A person's *ethos* was evident in his clothing, appearance, gait, in the calm with which he responded to every event, and so on. For the Greeks, this was the concrete form of freedom; this was the way they problematized their freedom. A man possessed of a splendid *ethos* who could be admired and put forward as an example, was someone who practiced freedom in a certain way ... [E]xtensive work by the self on the self is required for this practice of freedom to take shape in an *ethos* that is good, beautiful, honorable, estimable, memorable, and exemplary. (Foucault 1997b: 286)

It is hard to deny that in this account of the *ethos* of the exemplary Greek male of antiquity, a certain cultivation of style, a turning of one's life into a work of art, becomes pivotal – giving visible form in one's personal bearing to the qualities listed by Foucault ("good, beautiful, honorable, estimable, memorable, and exemplary") are very much the defining feature of this Greek *ethos* (and in our submission, the *ethos* of the medieval *amour courtois*).[6] But is this *ethos* of nobility and chivalry, which bears all the marks of the ethical, justifiably to be regarded as "aesthetic" in its key dimensions?

Clearly "style" *per se* is not the issue here. The consummately excellent Greek male of antiquity is obviously the practitioner of a certain kind of stylistics of existence, and yet the core of this stylistics in the Greek case is a steady and concerted disciplining of the passions. Where does this leave the Deleuzian notion of an individuation based on intensities (the ostensible province of aesthetics, understood in terms of Heathcliff and Deleuze's own encounters with Foucault) as opposed to individuations hinging on a subject or person (the seeming domain of ethics with its emphasis on a regulation of intensities)?

This issue is ultimately irresolvable. Deleuze's distinction between these two kinds of individuation is probably best regarded as a proposal with a heuristic intent. The Kantian separation between ethics and aesthetics is untenable, designed as it was to resolve a problematic specific to the internally disjointed philosophical system of the sage of Königsberg, and the evident inability of Deleuze (and Foucault) to separate the ethical from the aesthetic, except on an ad hoc basis, should consign this demarcation to desuetude. This collapse of the distinction between the ethical and the aesthetic should pave the way for a conceptual possibility that is more Deleuzian than any attempt to differentiate between the ethical and the aesthetic within the seeming residues of the Kantian system. The primary issue here, to pursue this possible Deleuzian insight, admittedly one inspired by Spinoza and Deleuze, is the balance of forces between those that are active and those that are reactive, and how these configurations of forces enable life.

In his last published essay Deleuze provided a lapidary formulation of what is at stake here:

> We will say of pure immanence that it is A LIFE, and nothing else. It is not immanence to life, but the immanent that is in nothing is itself a life. A life is the immanence of immanence, absolute immanence: it is complete power, complete bliss. It is to the degree that he goes beyond the aporias of the subject and the object that Johann Fichte, in his last philosophy, presents the transcendental field as a life, no longer dependent on a Being or submitted to an Act – it is an absolute immediate consciousness whose very activity no longer refers to a being but is ceaselessly posed in a life. (Deleuze 2001: 27)

The "old" demarcation between ethics and aesthetics rested on the "old" philosophy which traded on the distinction between Being and Act. In his last philosophical statement Deleuze therefore pointed to a way of moving beyond both these distinctions – life, with its associated philosophic *a prioris*, for him supplants the distinction between ethics (the correlative of Being) and aesthetics (the correlative of Act). Only in this way can life be lived as a work of art, that is, something at once powerful and blissful.

References

Deleuze, G. (1984), *Kant's Critical Philosophy: The Doctrine of the Faculties*, trans. H. Tomlinson and B. Habberjam, Minneapolis: University of Minnesota Press.
Deleuze, G. (1995a), "Life as a Work of Art," in *Negotiations: 1972–1990*, trans. M. Joughin, New York: Columbia University Press, 94–101.
Deleuze, G. (1995b), "A Portrait of Foucault," in *Negotiations: 1972–1990*, trans. M. Joughin, New York: Columbia University Press, 102–18.
Deleuze, G. (2001), "Immanence: a Life," in *Pure Immanence: Essays on a Life*, trans. A. Boyman, New York: Zone Books, 25–33.
Foucault, M. (1983), "Preface," to G. Deleuze and F. Guattari, *Anti-Oedipus: Capitalism and Schizophrenia*, trans. R. Hurley, M. Seem, and H. R. Lane, Minneapolis: University of Minnesota Press.
Foucault, M. (1994), "Conversation avec Werner Schroeter," in D. Defert and F. Ewald (eds.), *Michel Foucault: Dits et écrits 1954–1984*, vol. IV, Paris: Gallimard.
Foucault, M. (1997a), "On the Genealogy of Ethics: An Overview of Work in Progress," in P. Rabinow (ed.), *The Essential Works of Michel Foucault 1954–1984, vol. I (Ethics)*, trans. R. Hurley, et al., New York: The New Press, 253–80.
Foucault, M. (1997b), "The Ethics of the Concern for Self as a Practice of Freedom," in P. Rabinow (ed.), *The Essential Works of Michel Foucault 1954–1984, vol. I (Ethics)*, trans. R. Hurley, et al., New York: The New Press, 281–301.

Schultz, J. A. (2006), *Courtly Love, the Love of Courtliness, and the History of Sexuality*, Chicago: University of Chicago Press.

Notes

1. When it comes to distinguishing "ethics" (*l'éthique*) from "morality" (*la morale*) Deleuze said the following: "The difference is that morality presents us with a set of constraining rules . . . ones that judge actions and intentions by judging them in relation to transcendent values (this is good, that's bad . . .); ethics is a set of optional rules that assess what we do, what we say, in relation to the ways of existing involved" (Deleuze 1995a: 100).

2. Disputing the viability of this "immanent ethics" is of course a quite separate undertaking, which may or may not interest the interpreter of Deleuze. It does not interest Smith, nor does it this author. Smith's assessment of these two features of Deleuzian thought will be retained in this essay as a springboard for our ensuing discussion.

3. Two words of caution are needed here. First, in today's English "prudence" has strong overtones of wariness and circumspection. By contrast, Aristotelian Φρονησι (*phronesis*), the basis for the medieval virtue of *prudentia*, had the connotations of adroitness, judiciousness, and forethought – connotations which may be lacking in the modern English definition. Deleuze's definition of ethics as "a set of optional rules that assess what we do, what we say, in relation to the ways of existing involved," is certainly compatible with the suggestion that these rules of assessment are guided by *prudentia*. Otherwise the person evaluating his or her life would in effect be saying that such important qualities as adroitness, judiciousness, and forethought – i.e. the defining features of *prudentia* – are somehow merely accidental features of a life led ethically. Second, Dan Smith has pointed out to me several passages where Deleuze explicitly distances himself from the notion of transgression (with its parasitical relation to the figure of the Law). A breach of the law is a violation of the code, whereas Deleuzian (and Foucauldian) transgression is more like a *scrambling* of the code. Much more needs to be said about transgression, and I'm grateful to Smith for alerting me to the issues posed here.

4. There are of course many versions of the story of Tristan and Isolde, some so different from each other that it could make just as much sense, given the appropriate rendition of the story, to view their bond as a doomed passion, less turbulent than Catherine and Heathcliff's certainly, but a passion nonetheless. Hence in Wagner's operatic rendition the love of Tristan and Isolde is fated from the outset to have a ruinous outcome. It would be futile for us to intervene in this debate; our purpose here is served by recognizing, if only for the sake of argument, the contrast between Tristan and Isolde and Catherine and Heathcliff that Deleuze wishes to make.

5. On this *tekhne tou biou* see Foucault 1997a: 258.

6. The two *ethoi* do part ways on the matter of sexual relations between men and women. For the Greeks, the noble *ethos* was impossible to achieve in dealings between men and woman. In the *ethos* associated with the medieval *amour courtois*, by contrast, courtly chivalry was something that only a man could display towards his "fair lady."

Chapter 9

Deleuze, Ethics, Ethology, and Art

Anthony Uhlmann

Ethics is that aspect of philosophy concerned with how to live. The Greek understanding of the word "*ethikos*," involves "the state of being," that which is manifest in the soul or mind. "Ethics" is etymologically linked to "ethology" through the Greek word root, "*ethos*." The original meaning of "*ethos*" is "accustomed place," or "habitat," and by analogy it was quickly associated with "custom, habit." It evolved however to be understood as the "character," "disposition," or core values of individuals or groups. Ethology, then, links ethos and "logos" (which might mean reason or expression); that is, it links disposition and understanding, in naming the scientific study of the behavior of animals within their natural habitats. A secondary meaning is the study of the formation of human ethos. Linking ethics and ethology, then, underlines how forming an understanding of one's disposition within one's habitat enables the proper living of one's life. The word "art," is often associated with human relations to nature (often through ideas of the "representation" or "imitation" of nature, but also, importantly, with regard to "creation" understood to correspond analogically with natural creation). As such it is an understanding both of nature, and of dispositions within nature. Deleuze shows us not only how life is linked with nature, as ethics involves ethology, but how life and nature express dispositions as understandings, and how such processes of expression involve art, and its necessity. To put this another way: Deleuze shows us how art is necessarily concerned with the same fundamental question which concerns ethics and ethology: living.

In *What is Philosophy?* Deleuze and Guattari muse on that time of life when a philosopher feels compelled to reflect upon the question of the nature of her or his practice. The desire for such reflection, they argue, comes with age. It involves self-reflection, something that concerns one's disposition, and one's place in the world. As such it is properly an ethical process. The idea of reflection, however, is also fundamental to both thought itself and to artistic practice, or the practice of creation. In considering the nature of philosophy, then, Deleuze and Guattari turn, through logical necessity, to the nature of thought and the thought of nature: that is, they also consider science, and art. As I will argue in this chapter, this interrelation is at the heart of their understanding of natural being, and links up with the minor traditions of thinking that they trace and extend in their own work. Yet the connection between art and how we should live also occurs in the dominant tradition of thought: rather than ethics, however, this tradition links artistic practice to morals, and the "moral" (or the lesson, or specified meaning). There are a number of distinctions, then, which involve not so much binary oppositions as differences of perspective, and these are crucial to an understanding of the interrelations Deleuze and Deleuze and Guattari develop between art, ethics, and ethology. These distinctions assert an ethics over a morality; thought over (human) consciousness; creation over mimesis.

In *Difference and Repetition*, Deleuze describes a negative image of thought, a dogmatic image which, rather than opening up potentials for thought, closes them down. It does this, in part, by standing as a shared assumption: the idea that all reasonable people will think in the same way. This habit of mind involves a logic of imitative identities: in art, it involves the idea that art imitates nature; in moral philosophy the idea that morality involves imitating set modes of behavior; in philosophy that there is one true thought that each will follow. In *Proust and Signs*, *Nietzsche and Philosophy*, and *A Thousand Plateaus*, on the other hand, we are shown a new image of thought which challenges our idea of what it means to think and opens up possibilities for thinking. This line of argument is consistent with ideas that Deleuze and Deleuze and Guattari develop elsewhere: art does not imitate, it creates; ethics involves living in accordance with one's nature, rather than imitating rules of behavior; philosophy involves engaging with that power of thought which opens up possibilities which are coming into being, rather than describing forms or categories that seek to fix meaning or being.

How, then, do these general ideas offer a more precise understanding of the nature of artistic practice and its relation to ethics and ethology? The traditional reading that links art to morality connects it with moral purpose. For example, in *The Defence of Poesy*, Sir Philip Sidney (1544–86), in trying to explain or justify the value of artistic practice for a skeptical audience, turns to an already longstanding tradition that affirms the importance of art as something which is able to both "teach" and "delight." So art is that which can teach moral lessons, while entertaining us: a spoonful of sugar that helps the medicine go down. While Sidney is a true artist, the pragmatic definition he adopts from tradition, which had held since classical times and still holds, has been counter-productive to arguments which seek to establish, on some firm footing, the value of artistic practice. The object "art" is split into two parts: a) "art" is entertainment, and b) "art" is the worthy vehicle for necessary, if unpalatable, moral and social lessons. That is, art is imagined as being captive to other things: the interests of those who wish to satisfy the expectations of a particular audience; those whose interests lie in the effective transmission of a particular socio-political or moral message. So too, both of these categories impose human consciousness on nature; both affirm moral structures; both function through formal imitation (with audiences clearly recognizing either generic codes or established practices of social understanding). This is apparent in archetypes of moral art, such as Aesop's *Fables*, where entertaining stories involving the personification of nature lead us to a moral lesson. The split is apparent in the two tiers of contemporary Hollywood film: on the one hand so much pure entertainment; on the other hand "important" films dealing with significant issues (big oil, global warming, Iraq, and so on). Such work may well be art, but the assumption that this is all that art might be narrows considerably the potentials for creation which art might effect, and the real effects it might have on our understanding of our conditions of being. As I stated above: it is not so much an opposition that is involved in the matters under consideration here as a question of perspectives. While there is nothing reprehensible about working within modes of representation that affirm mimesis, it is equally true that these are not the only modes possible.

The shift in perspective Deleuze effects allows for the emergence of other traditions, other forms of expression that might open out into new creative modes. This allows us to see how literature has a purpose which is ethical rather than moral; that rather than teaching us, it provides an instrument with which we can reflect upon our own lives. He cites Proust who states that the work is a magnifying glass that can be turned by readers upon their own souls so that they might read and interpret its workings (Deleuze 2000: 145). Rather than personifying nature (animals given human consciousness) to convey moral lessons, art can relate to the understandings of nature (in which animals and even molecules are understood as expressing thought). In considering the question of art, ethics, and ethology, then, Deleuze repeats three gestures: he looks to the kind of ethics developed by Spinoza, which he characterizes as an ethics developed around ethology; he returns to the idea of the animal in its habitat as a reflection of ethology; and he considers the nature of art via this ethological understanding. In each case the three terms – ethics, ethology, and art – are linked through the idea of *affect*.

Spinoza, Ethology, and Ethics

In "On the Difference between The *Ethics* and a Morality" Deleuze argues that Morality was founded upon the traditional principle that consciousness (or the mind) must master the passions (or the body) (Deleuze 1988: 18).[1] Spinozist ethics is not a matter of referring to a moral code first, which specifies an action as Good or Evil, and then acting on that advice; rather, it is a matter of seeking to be joined with that object which agrees with your nature and avoiding that object which disagrees with your nature (Deleuze 1988: 20–1).

In the Garden of Eden God tells Adam, "Thou shalt not eat of the fruit . . ." and Adam interprets this as a moral precept, a prohibition: he must not eat the apple because the apple has been judged to be Evil by God. Deleuze, however, suggests that these words refer to "a fruit that, as such, will poison Adam if he eats it." That is, the fruit will not agree with Adam's nature and so he should avoid it, but "because Adam is ignorant of causes, he thinks that God morally forbids him something, whereas God only reveals the natural consequence of ingesting the fruit." There is no Good or Evil, but there is good and bad. When a body that agrees with one's nature is joined with one it increases one's power and this is good. The analogue Deleuze uses for this is food. When a body that does not agree with one's nature – the analogue for this being poison – is joined with one, this decreases one's power and is bad. "Hence good and bad have a primary, objective meaning, but one that is relative and partial: that which agrees with our nature or does not agree with it" (Deleuze 1988: 22, see also 30–43).

As we have seen, ethology is that which links an animal's behavior to its relationships within its habitat. Spinoza's understanding of ethics in effect does much the same. In "Spinoza and Us," Deleuze states, "studies . . . which define bodies, animals, or humans by the affects they are capable of founded what is today called *ethology*." He explains that every thing in Nature selects those other things in the world that correspond to it; those things which affect it, or which it affects, "what moves or is moved by it" (Deleuze 1988: 125). The ethical question related to any animal then becomes: what affects this animal and what does not affect it? For Deleuze, Spinoza is a philosopher of ethology, because he develops an ethics which functions through an idea of good and bad, in terms of what is good for you and what is bad for you in what affects you and what you affect, rather than a moral system based on rules which designate specific things as "good" and "evil." This process of affecting and being affected in Spinoza, turns around an idea of interrelatedness. I have touched above on how Spinoza moves away from consciousness as that which seeks to master the physical world. Deleuze emphasizes this point in "On the Difference between The *Ethics* and a Morality" underlining how Spinoza devalues consciousness in favor of thought (Deleuze 1988: 17–25). Spinoza is very clear himself about this idea and the implications of it. Everything is laid open to the laws of causation, the laws of nature, and this includes the human mind and what it thinks, and the human body and what it feels:

> Most of those who have written about the Affects, and men's way of living, seem to treat, not of natural things, which follow the common laws of nature, but of things which are outside nature. Indeed they seem to conceive man in nature as a dominion within a dominion . . . [Yet] nature is always the same, and its virtue and power of acting are always one and the same, i.e., the laws and rules of nature . . . The Affects, therefore, of hate, anger, envy, etc., considered in themselves, follow from the very same necessity and force of nature as the other singular things. (Spinoza, *Ethics*, III, Preface, 491–2)

An affect, then, might be understood to be an expression, a modal expression, which, rather than coming from an inside and moving out, is both caused by what is external and becomes involved with the nature of the person through whom it is expressed (not as something which is simply "internal" to that person, but which, in effect, allows that person to perceive their self).[2] We can see this more clearly if we turn again to the *Ethics*, Part II, Proposition 16, where Spinoza explains how the affections we experience, the idea of being affected by something else (i.e., of coming into contact with something else), involves both the nature of our body and the body we touch. That is, the knowledge we have of anything else (the knowledge of the first kind, from the senses for example) is really, and first and foremost, a knowledge of ourselves and how we have been affected: it does not give us a clear idea of the thing we perceive. Yet there is necessarily another way of seeing this: insofar as we do understand ourselves we can only do so through the contact we make with other bodies. Our very thought, then, is determined from the outside: that is, it is inter-involved with our habitat.

Deleuze thus turns immediately to Spinoza in defining how ethics and ethology might be linked. This is not, however, his only strategy. He also moves back from ethology, or an understanding of animal behavior, to ethics, while in the process linking both to art. This is a complex maneuver, which involves viewing Spinoza's *Ethics* from a different angle, and relating these ideas to others drawn from Henri Bergson's *Creative Evolution*. Something of the nature of this approach is revealed if we look to the two main plateaus in *A Thousand Plateaus* that connect art, the animal (ethology), and ethics: "1730: Becoming-Intense, Becoming-Animal, Becoming-Imperceptible . . .," and "1837: Of the Refrain." In the former, Deleuze and Guattari offer a number of "memories" in counterpoint, among which are "Memories of a Bergsonian" and "Memories of a Spinozist, I and II." If we develop a reading of important passages from Bergson and Spinoza through the lens of Deleuze and Guattari and Deleuze, we are able to understand still more fully how art, ethology, and ethics might be linked.

We have touched upon how Deleuze and Guattari turn to the image of the animal to explain these processes of ethological interrelation which might be understood to be ethical. They also, however, turn to art, for three reasons: first, these ethological interrelations are *expressed as affects*, and for Deleuze and Guattari, art itself involves the expression of affects and percepts. Second, art allows for transversal processes through which relations might be made between objects that are only apparently incompatible (and that are in fact connected): that is, art imagines, or creates, the possibility of becoming something other; of becoming-animal, for example. As such art enables us to be moved by a feeling of understanding of this other, and our place in a larger environment. Art, then, not only shows us how *one* is affected (thereby expressing an ethics that might pertain to our own lives), it can also show the interrelated processes of affection that comprise habitats. Third, following on from this, art is capable of building passages which both construct or create territories and build networks of interrelations between territories: that is, art can create the consistency necessary to understand interrelations that are real but difficult to conceive. Art, in effect, expresses an ethology which is coextensive with ethics.

Art and Animals

The connections between art, ethics, and ethology are *consistent*, then. In helping us to see this consistency Deleuze and Guattari return to images of animals taken from ethology, on the one hand, and create a theory of expression capable of encompassing the consistency they perceive between art, ethology, and ethics on the other. As we have seen, Spinoza allows one way of doing this, yet when one reads the *Ethics* separately from Deleuze and Guattari's readings, Spinoza seems an odd choice for developing the connection between ethics and animals, as he has little to directly say about this issue. As we will see, however, he can logically be read to understand the universe as a whole as a composite animal.

Bergson, by contrast, does turn directly to animal behavior in developing his own interrelation between instinct (intuition) and logical thought. In doing this he draws us towards a concept that has become quite unfashionable, but which, if conceived in his terms, allows us to understand how affect might permeate an environment and link participants within this environment transversally. The word he uses is "sympathy."

In *Elizabeth Costello*, J. M. Coetzee has the eponymous character state that there is a faculty – sympathy – which "allows us to share at times the being of another," and she goes on to claim that literature has the capacity to develop this faculty to an extremely high level: "If I can think my way into the existence of a being who has never existed, then I can think my way into the existence of a bat or a chimpanzee or an oyster, any being with whom I share the substrate of life" (Coetzee 2004: 79, 80). Many other voices are raised to disagree with Elizabeth's views, on this and other questions, and we are given no direction, from a narrator, for example, which might affirm whether or not we are supposed to believe what she says, or what those who disagree with her say. We are asked to think, rather than told what to think.

Elizabeth Costello, an Australian novelist who has been invited to give a talk on "The Lives of Animals" in an American University, takes issue with and enters into dialogue with the philosopher Thomas Nagel, who argues that it is not possible for us to understand what it is to be a bat, because our minds are inadequate to the task (Coetzee 2004: 76). She disagrees, arguing that we can enter into relation with the bat, share, in a sense, something of its existence, through the faculty of sympathy:

> The heart is the seat of a faculty, *sympathy*, that allows us to share at times the being of another. Sympathy has everything to do with the subject and little to do with the object, the "another," as we see at once when we think of the object not as a bat ("Can I share the being of a bat?") but as another

human being. . . . there is no limit to the extent to which we can think ourselves into the being of another. There are no bounds to the sympathetic imagination. (Coetzee 2004: 79–80)

Bergson and Sympathy

In *Creative Evolution* Bergson considers three means through which life has developed its capacities to interact within the world, both responding to and creating the environment of which it forms a part: torpor, instinct, and intelligence. Torpor largely concerns Bergson's understanding of plant life. Of most interest to us for the moment is the interaction between instinct and intelligence. These terms are not held in opposition: rather, they are complementary, and can and do coexist: yet instinct is most highly developed in certain parts of the animal kingdom. Indeed, it is, for Bergson, the dominant means through which animals, from the simplest to the most complex, interact within their environment. It is only more highly developed animals which make use of "intelligence," and the animal which makes most use of intelligence is the human. For Bergson all life must answer the question of how it can act on the material world. For animals, he argues, nature has developed two responses (though these are interconnected); two ways in which tools might be used to have an effect on the environment. Both of these might be understood to involve some kind of "thought," but they are different in nature. Both involve a response to the world. A useful way of understanding them is through the example of the use of tools.

Instinct involves an organism using those tools which are a part of its body to effect a task: a butterfly uses its proboscis, for example, to suck nectar from flowers. It has, for Bergson, been organized, or, if you prefer, it has evolved, in order to perform this task among other tasks. It makes use of instinct in performing the task. Instinct, then, is a kind of organized thought. Intelligence, on the other hand, is that capacity which allows certain animals to find or invent tools within their environment with which they might act on that environment. If instinct is thought which has already been organized and is coextensive with the organism it inhabits and comprises, then intelligence is organizing thought: thought which allows for the development of instruments which will serve to effect the environment in a certain way (Bergson 1998: 139–42).

Bergson then goes on to discuss his understanding of consciousness and unconsciousness. He claims there are two kinds of unconsciousness: one in which consciousness is absent, and one in which it is present but nullified. A stone falling has an absence of consciousness. On the other hand, he argues, we can become unconscious when our actions correspond with our idea of them: that is, when we perform perfectly mechanical or habitual actions. When this happens we are not conscious of what we are doing: we become the act of doing itself and this nullifies any thoughts we might have about the action itself. This kind of action is linked with instinct. Consciousness comes into play when we have to solve a problem, or begin to reflect upon an action. This kind of consciousness might be called "self-consciousness." In any case, it is tied up with Bergson's understanding of intelligence (Bergson 1998: 143–4). There is another way of looking at the difference. Instinct involves acting on things: seeing the world in terms of those actual particular things upon which we might act. Intelligence, on the other hand, concerns itself with the abstract forms we use to organize our understanding of things in a general way.

Intelligence then is knowledge of form, whereas instinct is a knowledge of matter. When one starts to think in terms of knowledge and knowing our place in the world, however, there is a paradox for Bergson: *"There are things that intelligence alone is able to seek, but which, by itself, it will never find. These things instinct alone could find; but it will never seek them"* (Bergson 1998: 151, original emphasis). This is because instinct excels in fitting itself to reality: reality for Bergson is movement (Bergson 1998: 155). Intelligence, on the other hand, works by fixing things in place, rendering them artificially static, or abstracting them from movement. That is, intelligence conceives of the living as if it were lifeless (Bergson 1998: 165). Intelligence alone, then, is incapable of fully comprehending reality. Instinct fully comprehends the movement of reality, but it simply acts, it does not reflect. For Bergson, then, *"The intellect is characterised by a natural inability to comprehend life"* (Bergson 1998: 165, original emphasis).

How is it then, that we feel that we can comprehend life, at least intuitively, at least instinctively? This is because we, like those organisms which act through instinct, have sympathy with the world, with our environment. Bergson compares life to a musical theme: there is an original theme which has been played into an immense variety of variations in life on earth. How can we grasp the original theme? "As for the original theme, it is everywhere and nowhere. It is in vain that we try and express it in terms of any idea: it must have been, originally, *felt* rather than *thought*" (Bergson 1998: 172).

The link between music, ethology, and ethics is developed to an extraordinary degree by Deleuze and Guattari in "1837: Of the

Refrain." This connection to Bergson allows us to understand how music moves both out from the individual, which is seeking to establish its territory or place in the world, and from the world to the individual, allowing passage from the self to indefinite sets of transversal interrelations.[3]

Bergson compares this felt understanding with instinct, using as an example the paralyzing instinct of certain wasps. He draws on the work of the entomologist Fabre in describing how the Scolia Wasp attacks the larva of the rose-beetle: it "stings it in one point only, but in this point the motor ganglia are concentrated, and those ganglia alone: the stinging of other ganglia might cause death and putrefaction, which it must avoid" (Bergson 1998: 172). So the Scolia Wasp stings its correspondent, the rose-beetle larva, in the only place which will cause it to be paralyzed but still living, something it needs so that its own young might hatch and feed on the paralyzed beetle larva.

How are we to understand this level of precision? Bergson argues that we get into trouble because we try to express this knowledge in terms of intelligence. We can't conclude that the Scolia learns where to sting its prey, in the same way as the entomologist has learnt the make up of the body of the beetle larva (Bergson 1998: 173). Bergson then concludes that:

> there is no need for such a view if we suppose a *sympathy* (in the etymological sense of the word)[4] between the Ammophila [wasp] and its victim, which teaches it from within, so to say, concerning the vulnerability of the caterpillar. This feeling of vulnerability might owe nothing to outward perception, but result from the mere presence together of the Ammophila and the caterpillar, considered no longer as two organisms, but as two activities. It would express, in concrete form, the *relation* of the one to the other. (Bergson 1998: 174)

A few pages on, Bergson concludes that the concrete explanation of the "original theme" is no longer scientific or purely concerned with intelligence: rather, "it must be sought . . . not in the direction of intelligence, but in that of 'sympathy'" (Bergson 1998: 176). This kind of thinking is then explicitly linked not only with a philosophical project, which Bergson calls metaphysics, but with certain artistic practices:

> intelligence and instinct are turned in opposite directions, the former towards inert matter, the latter towards life . . . But it is to the very inwardness of life that *intuition* leads us – by intuition I mean instinct that has become disinterested, self-conscious, capable of reflecting upon its object and of enlarging it indefinitely. (Bergson 1998: 176)

He continues:

> That an effort of this kind is not impossible, is proved by the existence in man of an aesthetic faculty along with normal perception. Our eye perceives the features of the living being, merely as assembled, not as mutually organized. The intention of life, the simple movement that runs through the lines, that binds them together and gives them significance, escapes it. This intention is just what the artist tries to regain, in placing himself back within the object by a kind of sympathy, in breaking down, by an effort of intuition, the barrier that space puts up between him and his model. (Bergson 1998: 177)

The powerful connection, sympathy, which Coetzee appeals to through Elizabeth Costello, involves a natural affinity between ourselves and our environment, an environment understood as being comprised of those relations themselves.

Deleuze and Guattari turn to ethology and the work of Jacob von Uexküll to underline this process. Just as Bergson uses the example of the wasp, Deleuze and Guattari in *A Thousand Plateaus*, and Deleuze in "Spinoza and Us," use that of the tick which is defined by the affects of which it is capable. To shift from the language of Deleuze and Guattari back to that of Bergson allows us to develop a syncretic interpretation of Deleuze and Guattari's crucial concept of "affect"; one that involves a correspondence between immediate understanding (that is, instinct, or intuition) and ethical action and a *felt* relationship to one's world (sympathy).

Haecceity: "Thisness," an Ethology of the Here and Now

Our understanding of the process which connects the being to Being, the natured nature of the mode to the one Substance of naturing nature, can further be enhanced by attending to other ideas from Spinoza to which Deleuze and Guattari directly allude in "1730: Becoming-Intense, Becoming-Animal, Becoming-Imperceptible . . . ." This is the line of reasoning that allows us to unpack the concept of "haecceity," which is at the heart of Deleuze and Guattari's and Deleuze's notion of the link between ethics and ethology. *The Compact Oxford English Dictionary* defines "haecceity"[5] with reference to the Scholastic Philosopher Duns Scotus as "the quality implied in the use of *this*, as *this man*; 'thisness'; 'hereness and nowness'; that quality or mode of being in virtue of which a thing is or becomes a definite individual; individuality." Deleuze and Guattari qualify this definition, suggesting that haecceity "is sometimes written 'ecceity,' deriving the word from *ecce*, 'here is.' This is an error, since Duns Scotus created the word and the concept from *haec*, 'this thing.' But it is a fruitful error because it suggests a mode of individuation that is distinct from that of a thing or a subject" (Deleuze and Guattari 1987: 540–1). The term is intimately connected with the concept of the univocity of Being which they have adapted from Spinoza (Deleuze and Guattari 1987: 254). Deleuze and Guattari make these points in indicating that Spinoza displays an interest in animals by reasoning that all Being is, at one level (that of natured nature or modes), a composite body: a single, infinite animal. So haecceity provides a means of determining an individuation which, *at the same time*, maps a differentiation *and* a unity of being. "At most," Deleuze and Guattari suggest, "we may distinguish assemblage haecceities . . . and interassemblage haecceities . . . But the two are strictly inseparable" (Deleuze and Guattari 1987: 262–3).

The whole of Spinoza's *Ethics* is built upon this logic of relations understood not simply as involving the relations of self within self, but the relationships of all things (see Spinoza, *Ethics*, II, Lemmas 1–7, 458–62; II, Prop. 40, 478; and IV, Prop. 39, 568), and this in turn reminds us of Bergson's "sympathy." To offer a rough summary: all interrelations, for Spinoza, necessarily involve relationships of love and hate. In effect, relationships of love draw bodies together into larger bodies (a process which increases one's power as the greater the body the more powerful the body). There is a logic of accumulation through relationship: a husband and wife, for example, might be understood as forming one, more powerful, body as they enter into relationship through marriage. So too, a nation might be understood as comprising a single body (see Spinoza, *Ethics*, II, Lemma 7, 462). As I have mentioned, Deleuze and Guattari emphasize that this logic might be extended to infinity, so that everything that exists might be thought to comprise one single body or animal. On the other hand, relationships of hatred sunder bodies, drawing them apart from one another and decreasing their power. There are two aspects of this intellectual system, then, which I feel are of particular importance to a reading of artistic practice. First, the conception of essence Spinoza develops and the manner in which he relates this to the soul. Rather than drawing us towards what has been a dominant understanding of being, this takes us the second aspect, one which allows us to recognize the interrelatedness at the core of any "individual" essence; or, if you prefer, a different conception of individuality, linking art, ethics, and ethology in the manner of Deleuze and Guattari's haecceity.

Spinoza's Essence, Ethology, and Ethics

It is worth working through some of Spinoza's understandings of the processes involved in achieving one's essence in order to fully understand the implications of this point for our reading of Deleuze and Guattari. In Part II, Proposition 7 of the *Ethics*, Spinoza identifies our essence with our "conatus" or striving to continue to exist: "*The striving by which each thing strives to persevere in its being is nothing but the actual essence of the thing.*" He develops this idea more fully in the Scholium to Proposition 9 that follows:

> When this striving is related only to the Mind, it is called Will; but when it is related to the Mind and Body together, it is called Appetite. This Appetite, therefore, is nothing but the very essence of man . . . desire can be defined as appetite together with consciousness of the appetite. (Spinoza, *Ethics*, II, Prop. 9, 500)

Essence, therefore, is now linked to Spinoza's concept of "desire" (as that which leads to one's continuing to exist). Spinoza goes still further in developing this chain of states of being (essence = conatus = power = will = appetite = desire) to include "virtue":

> By virtue and power I understand the same thing, i.e. (by Part 3, Prop 7), virtue, insofar as it is related to man, is the very essence, *or* nature, of man, insofar as he has the power of bringing about certain things, which can be understood through the laws of nature alone. (Spinoza, *Ethics*, IV, Definition 8, 547)

Desire is, for Spinoza, "man's very essence, *or* nature" (Spinoza, *Ethics*, III, Definitions of the Affects I, 531). Yet some of the things which affect us (even many of those which we seem to want), affect us in a negative way. When we are affected in a negative way our power decreases and therefore (as power = essence = one's nature) we become less perfect; that is, we move away from our true nature (see Deleuze 1988: 23).

Spinoza sets out the manner in which we can move from greater to lesser power and vice versa in Part III, the "Origin and Nature of the Affects." Midway through this Part he sets out a series of "Definitions of the Affects." When we move to greater power, we move closer to perfection: that is, we move closer to our true nature. We experience this positive change as an emotion – Joy: "Joy is a man's passage from a lesser to a greater perfection" (Spinoza, *Ethics*, III, Definitions of the Affects II, 531). When we become less powerful, that is, when we move away from our true nature (allowing other powers to take over or efface our essence), we become less perfect, and we experience this negative change as an emotion – Sadness: "Sadness is man's passage from a greater to a lesser perfection" (Spinoza, *Ethics*, III, Definitions of the Affects III, 531). Spinoza then links these primary emotions to a logic of relations (or relationships). "Love is a Joy, accompanied by the idea of an external cause" (Spinoza, *Ethics*, III, Definitions of the Affects VI, 533). Opposed to this, "Hate is a Sadness, accompanied by the idea of an external cause" (Spinoza, *Ethics*, III, Definitions of the Affects VII, 533). There are, broadly speaking then, two kinds of affect: on the one hand there are *active* affects which increase our power and our perfection by drawing us more closely to our nature; on the other hand there are *passive* affects which decrease our power and our perfection and move us away from our nature. To put this another way, when your perfection increases the greater part of you corresponds to your true nature, whereas when your perfection decreases the greater part of you corresponds to something else which does not agree with your nature.

Spinoza adds another link to our chain of essence by linking it to understanding, "because the Mind's essence, i.e., power, consists only in thought." Insofar as we adequately understand (our own nature, or anything else) we increase our power. Insofar as we are unable to understand our power decreases: "Affects which are contrary to our nature, i.e., ... which are evil, are evil insofar as they prevent the Mind from understanding" (Spinoza, *Ethics*, V, Prop. 9, Dem., 601). As the power of the body consists in action, one assumes that true action involves acting in accordance with one's nature, to increase one's power, to realize one's essence (though in Part V Spinoza does not treat this question). To recapitulate the identified terms: essence = conatus = power = will = appetite = desire = understanding = acting in accordance with one's nature.

Of the Refrain

In "1837: Of the Refrain" Deleuze and Guattari trace two movements in images chosen to introduce their conception of the interaction between art, ethics, and ethology. They begin with the image of the child singing, which moves out from the child's fear to his interaction with the world. Fear makes the child sing to calm himself; he then builds a milieu about himself with his song, until he is sufficiently at home that he might develop links, through his song, from the small circle of his milieu to the great circle of the world. The song is itself an "ethos" or an abode: it is a milieu created by the child in relation to the world in order to live with and within that world (Deleuze and Guattari 1987: 311–12). A "space" becomes a "milieu" when the world is translated from space or physical matter to the matter of expression: the song itself is a signature whose meaning is the marking of a milieu (Deleuze and Guattari 1987: 315). The creation of a milieu is linked to expression, not aggression: rather than fighting with rivals over a shared space, it creates a particular milieu in which one might live (Deleuze and Guattari 1987: 316). This marks the conditions of possibility for art, but it is not yet art. Art emerges when the signature is transformed into style, through the variation of motifs and counterpoints which no longer merely offer a placard "I am," but generate affects which can in turn make others feel. That is, it involves moving from asserting the self to creating an expression of the world into which others might enter. In life the world is composed of the actual interrelations of actual bodies and actual thought and we gauge its meaning by sensing the resonance of multiple points of relation. Art presents those relations that resonate in life, even though the terms of the actual relations (the bodies and minds) are absent: "The relation to joy and sadness, the sun, danger, perfection, is given in the motif and counterpoint, even if the term of each of these relations is not given" (Deleuze and Guattari 1987: 319). The artist, then, can generate sympathy by creating inter- and intra-relational resonance.

The first image Deleuze and Guattari develop, then, concerns the self faced by the world, who expresses milieus which pass into greater milieus. Yet while these circles involve interaction with the world a further process, which involves the exchange between selves, between and among their milieus, emerges; a process of passage which creates the very territories through which one passes. "The territory itself is a place of passage." It is the territory which allows "assemblages" to form: "The territory is the first assemblage, the first thing to constitute an assemblage" (Deleuze and Guattari 1987: 323). While the self moves out from the milieu it moves among territories passing from one to another: the assemblage is this passage from one to another. What is the role of art in this process? In short it is crucial to it: crucial to the realization and understanding of worlds and habitats (which have to be imagined to be either realized or understood). Art imagines and expresses dispositions. Deleuze and Guattari offer four classifications of refrains: first there are refrains that create and mark territories; second there are refrains that mark relations (such as love); third there are refrains that mark shifts between assemblages involving the movement between territories; and finally there are refrains "that collect or gather forces, either at the heart of the territory, or in order to go outside it ... They cease to be terrestrial, becoming cosmic" (Deleuze and Guattari: 1987: 327). If the first set of images – the singing child – relate to the self confronting the world, then the second set of images – the territory, the assemblage, the passage, the cosmos – involve the manner in which matters of expression move through worlds confronting life and forming both worlds and individuals. Art, like ethics and ethology, emerges in the process of interrelation. Interrelation, however, and the worlds formed through it, must be *created*, and this process of creation occurs through expression. That is, the logic of sensation that comprises art is already present in nature and both work to generate an understanding while forming dispositions.

References

Bergson, H. (1998), *Creative Evolution*, trans. A. Mitchell, London: Dover.

Coetzee, J. M. (2004), *Elizabeth Costello*, London: Vintage.

Deleuze, G. (1983), *Nietzsche and Philosophy*, trans. H. Tomlinson, New York: Columbia University Press.

Deleuze, G. (1988), *Spinoza: Practical Philosophy*, trans. R. Hurley, San Francisco: City Lights.

Deleuze, G. (1990), *Expressionism in Philosophy: Spinoza*, trans. M. Joughin, New York: Zone.

Deleuze, G. (1994), *Difference and Repetition*, trans. P. Patton, New York: Columbia University Press.

Deleuze, G. (2000), *Proust and Signs*, trans. R. Howard, Minneapolis: University of Minnesota Press.

Deleuze, G. and F. Guattari (1987), *A Thousand Plateaus*, trans. B. Massumi, Minneapolis: University of Minnesota Press.

Deleuze, G. and F. Guattari (1994), *What is Philosophy?*, trans. H. Tomlinson and G. Burchell, New York: Columbia University Press.

Dictionnaire Historique de la langue Française (1992), Sous le direction de Alain Rey, Paris: Dictionnares le Robert.

Sidney, Sir Philip (2006), "The Defence of Poesy," in S. Greeblatt et al. (eds.), *The Norton Anthology to English Literature*, vol. 1, 8th edn, New York: Norton.

Spinoza, Benedictus de (1985), *The Collected Works of Spinoza*, vol. 1, trans. E. Curley, Princeton: Princeton University Press.

Uhlmann, A. (1999), *Beckett and Poststructuralism*, Cambridge: Cambridge University Press.

Uhlmann, A. (2009), "Expression and Affect in Kleist, Beckett and Deleuze," in L. Cull (ed.), *Deleuze and Performance*, Edinburgh: Edinburgh University Press.

Notes

1. I discuss these ideas in relation to Samuel Beckett's *Malone Dies* in Uhlmann 1999.
2. I discuss the concept of "expression" that Deleuze develops through his reading of Spinoza and Leibniz in *Expressionism in Philosophy: Spinoza* in Uhlmann 2009.

3. Among other terms, Deleuze and Guattari use the concept of the "Dividual" to account for this interaction among and between (intra- and inter-) that occurs in "group individuation" (Deleuze and Guattari 1987: 341).

4. The etymological definition of "sympathy" from Le Robert, *Dictionnaire Historique de la Langue Française* is as follows: "from latin *sympathia 'accord, affinité naturelle'* [agreement, natural affinity] taken in turn from the Greek *sumpatheia 'participation à la souffrance d'autrui'* [participating in the suffering of another], *'communauté de sentiments ou d'impressions'* [community of sensations or impressions], and in the language of Epicurus and the Stoics *'rapports de certaines choses entre elles, affinities'* [the relation of certain things between themselves, affinities]."

5. I touch on these ideas in regard to Samuel Beckett's *Malone Dies* in Uhlmann 1999.

Chapter 10

Never Too Late? On the Implications of Deleuze's Work on Death for a Deleuzian Moral Philosophy

James Williams

Quicksand

So you lie on the rushed mattress of torn branches; terrified as you feel the same wet mass suck at your dampening clothes. And you reach out. The human beast claws at your hand, nails scraping down the inner flesh of your forearm, leaving minute traces of living matter, its rigid fingers a premonition of the tar pit skeleton they are to become. Then it's gone. An individual life, with all its singular values and loving relations, connected to yours for a desperate and too brief time, incomparable and never to return, putrefying in the airless swamp.

Too Late

What could have been done differently? What should be learned? How can we salvage a general moral consolation from the particular disaster, when perhaps even the shared label of "particular" is already a betrayal of the singular events? Is there any consolation to be drawn from the end, from the choking, terrified, doomed struggle of the beast, perhaps some other rebirth, a memorial, a celebration of survival and a remembrance of sacrifice? More wisely, and against the corrosion of guilt and what ifs, of necessary communal self-deception, how can we work together against any repetition? *They let it happen again . . .*

The moral problem under consideration here is not in any given prescription. "Keep away from the sands." It is not even in any more abstract law. "Always act to preserve a fellow beast's life; right up to the very limit of yours." It knows almost nothing of calculations and recipes. "The needs of the many outweigh the needs of the few . . ." It shies away from the lofty versions of such work on scales, either (and rightly) calibrated according to lower thresholds, or set within hybrid systems of measurement and assessment. "We must eradicate poverty first." "What we need is a non-monetary, non-capital based account of value." "Calculation is on the rules, not on any specific circumstance." The problem is in a prior valuation about life, about who and what is worth saving and why. This valuation and its many obscure links to desires, thoughts and emotions explains the despair when it is too late, the guilt at having failed and the resolution to be ready next time, better next time. A valued life has been lost. We have to know and feel for something worth saving, before debating about how to save and when. We also have to be aware of the need for preservation, of the finiteness and singularity of what is to be saved. What then to make of a philosophy of life and death, *of life in and through death*? What happens when late is never too late, because part of life is never extinguished, because death is not an end. What happens when life is affirmed in death, despite its consumption of living creatures? Do we then find reasons not to act, or to temper our acts, because absolute lateness never comes, because any resolution of "never again" resonates as nonsense in a world where nothing is ever the same again, where it is always too late and still too early in every passing instant and atom, and hence never too late *for this life here*?

So the cruel demagogue stares at the fading rings and bubbles on the surface of the pool and tells us that in some sense the beast is not dead. In our grief and remorse we cling to those words and commit the double violence of trading away the living for some illusion of an afterlife for those who have passed, while betraying the dead in divining a living image in a terminal event. We project the phantasm of a life after death into the future and turn away from new living beings, erasing the truth of "too late" in favor of the consolation of "still here, still time."[1]

What is the secret move here – the move eluding the implausibility of an afterlife against the present fact of another being's bodily death? It is to render life and death double. "Each event is deathlike; double, and impersonal in its double" (Deleuze 1969: 178). But this is more than a simple doubling; it is dual in a complex manner. First, death becomes ubiquitous: every live event, every birth and novelty, is also a little death and an inching step towards a final death of the whole: the reddening of an autumn leaf; the poisoning of Socrates; the cracking of a deep intercontinental fault; the crushing of bodies between two tiers of a concrete flyway, destroyed as the slipping fault shakes the top geological layers; the breaking of a shell as a chick emerges; the slaughter of another battery animal; your birth; your death; slow ageing or sudden disappearance. Something has to pass because something else becomes.

Second, death is split into a personal death, the death of an actual identified body given a social identity, and an impersonal death, dying as
universal event. A personal death is an end. It is a final destruction and
passing away. Impersonal death is a living on through participation in a
cycle of dying. Everything dies and because everything dies we live on in
the dying and living of others. Our death reverberates in later deaths; it
survives in them. It is a very old argument passing from despair at what
appears to be total loss, to a twofold redemption in some form of shared
eternity, perhaps in a soul eternally reincarnated, allied to an injunction
to rise up to the demands of this eternity in the actual death. The more
"noble" the life facing death, the better it participates in the eternal side
of death:

> Transmutation operates at the mobile and precise point where all events
> collect thus in one: the point where death turns against death, where dying
> is like the destitution of death, where the impersonality of the to die not
> only marks the moment where I become lost outside of myself, but also
> the moment where death is lost in itself; it is the figure taken by the most
> singular life to substitute itself for me. (Deleuze 1969: 179)

Philosophical alchemy, where death is made to consume itself and turn
into a new kind of life: transmutation is a passage from one of death's
doubles, the actual end of an individual thing, to the other, to the
eternal, "to die," a unique event all other deaths participate, "collect,"
or become lost in. In transmutation the person, defined in terms of personal identity and the self, effectively dies, but in dying it also lives on in
a communal struggle against death.[2]
   The collection of marks defining us as this selfsame person disappear
in death, this torn clawing nail and its record of DNA, growth and
disease will rot, never to return, but the singular events of each death
and the ways in which we confront them, the suppressed howl of fear,
comforts extended through a gentle parting, remain as potentials to be
expressed anew in future deaths, just as they were enacted in earlier
ones. There is a new howl and a new comforting each time, yet each
expresses a shared lineage in universal comfort and fear and thereby
connects to past and future. After our vocal chords disintegrate, the
expressed in the tone of our voices can reappear in novel events and
beings; no longer my voice, but an inflection of calm or panic repeated
in other voices. But does this argument mistakenly invert what can and
cannot survive, since, as Barthes argues, tone and inflection lead us to
the "grain of the voice": "The 'grain' is the body in the singing voice, in
the writing hand, in the limb executing a movement"? (Barthes 1982:

243). This body dies and the grain therefore passes too. The answer to this objection turns on the abstract and impersonal nature of that which is repeated. We do not repeat the grain of a voice but the many potential inflections and affects the grain expresses. We move away from Barthes' singular jouissance to a universal form of expression through singular events (Barthes 1982: 244). The actual events are indeed unrepeatable, but the universal ideas are the condition for any repetition and continuity given the unrepeatable nature of any actual instant or bounded event.

This is why Deleuze adopts Blanchot's phrase "One dies" in its difference from but also presence in "I die."[3] The self becomes lost in death as its distinguishing marks fade and disappear, but in this erasure all deaths connect, because now they all express the "one dies" free of their recognizable personal differences.[4] It is of little importance how long a death takes in historical time, for the point depends on assigning a duration to the death itself and, in this dying time, in any stretch towards it, in all the little deaths preparing for it, there is a gradual erasure of the individual and a drift into the shared "One dies": "How greatly does this *one* differ from the one of everyday banality. It's the *one* of impersonal and pre-individual singularities, the *one* of the pure event where *it* dies as much as *it* rains" (Deleuze 1969: 178). An expressive howl and caring gesture, floating free of the particular person emitting them, become such singularities and thereby rejoin a shared "one dies."[5] It is also an ancient argument that states that this second eternal death is unique – the one and only. Though it is neither one in the countable sense, nor one as whole and finished; but unique and unlike any other, alone, as the connection of the eternal doubles of all passing particulars and ever-changing with every singular death participating in it. Here, unique means singular and incomparable. It also means inclusive, not of everything, as in a complete collection, but rather in touch with all actual events, expressed through them, transformed with them, yet also independent of them, that is, neither identified with the totality of all actual events, nor completely determined by them. This shared "one dies" is therefore unique, yet open and ever changing. Finally, unique means unlimited by anything external to it, as a boundary or an essential identifying condition; unique, then, in the sense of Spinoza's substance.[6] The unique event resonates and changes as each personal life is extinguished. It resonates back and forward in time "at infinite speed" (because not beholden to any given actual speed). As unique and eternal, it is impassive and impervious to my personal death (as to any end, for in this account identified animals, grasses, and rocks are persons too). Yet, as the transformer in which we not only participate but also communicate with all other deaths – past and future – it becomes and alters each time it is expressed anew.[7] So a particular death emits something to all other deaths through this impassive transformer.[8] Therein resides the nobility or baseness of each death. The more it clings to its personal individuality the less well it resonates, for then it struggles against its communication with all others through the impersonal medium.[9] So when a death is inflicted on others, above all in war, or when a death is resented as a private loss, then participation in the impersonal and shared "one dies" is diminished. The more particular deaths are sacrificed to reasons of war and to the particular interests of warmongers, the more life is betrayed for the illusion of final deaths, of deaths inflicted for the living. According to Deleuze, these reasons and interests are always drawn from resentment:

> Nonetheless, there is much ignominy in saying that war is the concern of all; that's not true, since it is of no concern to those making use of it or in its service, creatures of resentment. There is just as much ignominy in saying that each one of us has his war, his particular wound; that's not true either for those who worry at their wounds, also creatures of bitterness and resentment. (Deleuze 1969: 179)

Resentment is the vehicle for personal identity since it demands an identification of the object of resentment, the thing we resent, as well as the subject of resentment: our identity as defined against the object. When war becomes a means or a task, we use it both to destroy that object and cement our presence as warrior subjects, for instance, in the two faces of propaganda, one aimed outwards at a reviled enemy identity, the other turned inwards on to a cherished superiority.[10] Death as inflicted on the other persons in war, as their eradication, is then also an attempt to evade or ignore the eternal side of death, where honor lies in resisting death as the final elimination of identities. Equally, though, when war wounds become a means for self-identification and self-pity, then resentment overcomes us and we become involved in a struggle against what remains of life.

For Deleuze, war concerns us all because it is private *and* collective. From the perspective of the collective, war must always be immoral, since part of the collective brings down death on another part. As private it must always be immoral, since the deaths inflicted in war are always a collective matter:

> The splendor of the *one* is of the event or the fourth person. That's why there are not private events and collective ones; no more than there is the individual and the universal, particularities and generalities. Everything is

singular and thereby collective and private at the same time, particular and general, neither individual nor universal. (Deleuze 1969: 178)

Deleuze's use of "splendor" here, in the sense of honor and glory, emphasizes a moral imperative in relation to the impersonal that resonates with his use of ignominy in relation to those who use war. When war is waged and experienced resentfully the collective and impersonal nature of death in war is missed, we care about our dead and not theirs, about our particular wounds, rather than the fact that these wounds are replicated as singular and universal signs of war. We only begin to wage war against war when we absorb the truth that it is a collective scandal, a division of the common, in its inflicting of personal death and wounds.[11] The guidance to wage war against war through the splendor of the one is then a moral guideline emerging from Deleuze's work on the dual nature of death and his emphasis on the primary nature of the "one dies." Its twin moral affect can be found in shame, a moral affect that runs throughout his work.[12]

This moral position is reinforced a few lines further on in *The Logic of Sense* where Deleuze pursues the Nietzschean theme of creatures of *ressentiment* through the contrasting model of the "free man." Here, freedom should be understood as freedom from resentment and freedom to seize events as destiny, by acting to express the universal and impersonal side of the event:

> It is only true of the free man [that he has a particular war and wound], because he grasps the event itself, and because he does not let it take place without putting its counter-effectualisation into operation as an actor. Only the free man can therefore understand all violence in one violence, all deadly events in one Event, leaving no place for the accidental and denouncing or rendering destitute the power of resentment in the individual as well as oppression in society. (Deleuze 1969: 179)

The free man is an actor playing a part; that is, taking events that are occurring and selecting within them in such a way as to play them differently.[13] This is what is meant by "counter-actualization" or "counter-effectualization," where counter does not imply opposition to, but rather selection within through an actualization, a creating of something actual and new. The moral principle of this selection is again drawn from the virtual, impersonal, and impermeable "one dies," mirrored in the unique "one Event." An act of counter-actualization must attempt to express the sides of death and violence that concern all actual moments of violence and death, for instance in the way any violence is a form of oppression and any death is countered by living acts of love and kindness. The one "Event" Deleuze invokes here is then the complex multiplicity of relations between the impersonal "to die," "to oppress," "to resist," "to love," "to shame" . . . all of which must be counter-actualized through a war against war and a resistance to death that is not born by or of resentment.

The struggle to wage war against war, and to bring death to death, therefore rests on the ideas of the double death and "one dies." Particular deaths are transformed through their participation in the multiple minor deaths and attendant creative novelties accompanying their duration. In place of a final passing away of personal identity, we have myriad impersonal continuities. Yet this is only under a difficult condition, since this continuity cannot simply be a representation of the death of given identities multiplied at smaller scales. There would then be a vicious regress in Deleuze's position, where on closer inspection we would find the difficulty we hoped to solve but at greater magnifi-cation: the multiple ongoing lives are subject to the same obliterating endpoints. This regression is not Deleuze's point at all. Instead, what matters is the relation between deaths and not the deaths themselves. Any continuity is in those relations and in none of the actual deaths. Each death changes those ongoing and continuous relations, but also, each death is shaped by its relations to all others. These relations must be of a different order than final deaths and destructions of identified things. There is an afterlife in new and different lives but not through physical remnants, in a genetic code passed on to descendants, in the exchange of blood through a tiny wound, or in fertile ashes and bursting seeds scattered among burned-out stumps. Instead, it must pass through something expressed in physical lives and wounds, in sensations, affects and acts, but not reducible to them. Deleuze explains this in *Difference and Repetition* in a paragraph that sets up a connection between death as negativity in the Freudian death drive and death as productive and life creating in Eros or love.[14] Actual death is death as "negation" and "opposition" (Deleuze 1968a: 148). That is not all it is, though, since death is something that comes from the outside and introduces some-thing new into the dying thing, in the dying duration. That's why death takes the form of a problem, as something unknown and unknowable, rendered through the questions "Where?" and "How?" whose source is "that (non) being that every affirmation is fed from" (Deleuze 1968a: 148). This non-being isn't nothingness or a void. It is a positive reality, but one taking a different form than being or than identified existents.

Deleuze explains this formal difference in relation to time in the second chapter of *Difference and Repetition*. Actual death takes place in relation to the present, in a struggle in the present against a limit that "makes everything pass" (Deleuze 1968a: 148). Impersonal death, or virtual death, the "one dies," eludes the present and the past.[15] Instead, it is always "to come" and as such has no relation to the dying self, but is rather "the source of a ceaseless multiple adventure in a persisting question" (Deleuze 1968a: 148). This split in times is reproduced in *The Logic of Sense* in the descriptions of the times of Chronos and Aion, where the former corresponds to the present that concentrates past and future and makes them pass, and the latter is a time where everything either has been or is to come, but is never present (Deleuze 1969: 190–4). A good way of understanding Deleuze's points here is to focus on the important terms of problem and question, both of which play central roles in *Difference and Repetition* and *The Logic of Sense*. A problem is a network of questions that express a situation incapable of solutions but operative as a driver for action to change that situation in creative and novel ways. Thus, as much as reflection on the when and where of an actual death can induce paralysis and despair when considered in relation to the identity that must pass away with its past and future, there is also a desire to affirm life by eluding this death since it is never finally given in terms of when and where it will happen. Death is our destiny, but it can be counter-actualized, not in the sense of negated or fled, but changed in its "When?," "Where?" and "How?"[16] The questions describe a productive problem in relation to death and the death drive because until actual death arrives, the questions have no fixed answer and therefore open up the possibility of novel acts in relation to death, underwritten by "non-being" as a condition for the openness of the problem.[17] This allows us to understand the difficult phrase cited earlier. The time of the problem is always "to come" because it is characterized by a lack of definite answers and an open field of potential connections and relations between past and future – independent of the certainty of the present.[18] This leads to an "adventure" because the way to express this potential is to alter present situations in relation to this open potential: it is a creative venture into what is necessarily unknown as actual identity. This adventure is "ceaseless" because the potential is not extinguished when a particular actual death arrives. It remains for others as expressed by earlier lives and deaths. It is "multiple" not only due to the multiplicity of questions making up the problem of death, but also because of the multiplicity of relations reserved as a potential for different actual lives. Mirroring this ceaselessness and multiplicity, questions persist because each time they are answered in a particular death as "here" "like this" and "now," they remain as the same questions but calling for different answers in relation to different adventures for future lives. The present passes, but the future is always to come.

Deleuze's study of the relation of two related yet formally distinct deaths in *Difference and Repetition* implies that any life has two different relations to death: one in relation to an actual passing present and the other in relation to a potential future that never arrives. It also implies that any life is itself double: a succession of actual events of passing away and a projection into an impersonal potential future, putting it in touch with all other lives, past and future. This, though, invites the objection that in choosing to die at a particular place and time and in a particular way we bring the two deaths together. In a rather shocking development the perfect counter-actualization would seem to be suicide. In response to this thought and directly after having spoken about the two aspects of death, Deleuze considers whether suicide draws both together to the point of making their distinction false. He denies this conclusion by arguing that even in suicide, the first personal death, the deliberate return to inanimate matter in "a process of entropy" (Deleuze 1968a: 149), there is something that comes from the outside, beyond the past life that selects its ending. The attempt might fail. Even if it succeeds, unforeseen elements enter the life, perhaps a passer-by attempting to dissuade, or a witness, a moment of doubt, an unforeseen flicker of the body, or even too much speed or an unplanned violence or peace. These are novel elements;[19] novel in the sense of outside the past history supposedly destined to end in a certain way: "Despite all appearances, that death always comes from the outside, at the very moment when it constitutes the most personal possibility, and always comes from the past, at the very moment when it is most present" (Deleuze 1968a: 149).

There is therefore a life-affirming reading of Deleuze's work on death and of his division of death into an actual passing death, associated with the person, and a death that participates in the future, associated with the impersonal and a reserve of potential affects. This potential and the openness of problems have been referred to in recent work on Deleuze, morality and politics by John Protevi:

> This means that problems are fluid and complex: our moves change the conditions for future moves, often in ways we cannot predict. The interactivity of moves and problems means that no one solution exhausts a problematic field; thus, we cannot bracket pragmatics or the study of concrete action and its relation to the conditions of future action. (Protevi 2009: 190)

The interactivity of moves and problems corresponds to counter-actualization in this study. It forms the basis, according to Protevi, for a pragmatics that is scientifically aware, morally pluralistic, flexible and affirmative (in the sense of innovating and hopeful). Yet, in relation to the critique driving my reading of Deleuze on death, there seems to be a contradiction between the openness and unpredictability of future moves and the conditions for future action. This is because those conditions themselves rest on Deleuze's work on time and on death which imply that it is never too late in relation to a certain form of eternity. There is a danger, then, that the entire pragmatics could be determined by this conception of the eternal, for instance, through a tight characterization of what we can legitimately invest our hopes in. This comes out strongly in the apparently strict imposition of the distinction between the personal and impersonal in relation to eternity, a distinction that is one of the most consistent in Deleuze's long series of works from *Proust and Signs* and *Difference and Repetition*, through *The Logic of Sense* and *A Thousand Plateaus* (as becoming-imperceptible) and on to "Immanence: a Life . . .".

It is not that Protevi's interpretation of Deleuze and of moral problems departs from the one given here. On the contrary, his work on the role of the virtual body politic is consistent with the role of the virtual in relation to the extension of life beyond death: "Thus, as much as any natural environment (much more so, in fact) the social field is virtual, and moral perception is the resolution of a dynamic field of potentials for practical action" (Protevi 2009: 190). When analyzing the Terri Schiavo case, turning on questions of when to end a life for a patient and loved one in a persistent vegetative state, Protevi turns to affects associated with depersonalized singular situations (where the person is instead determined by general social norms and defined properties). According to him, these affects are those that should guide moral decisions and decisions about the imposition or not of social norms. This leads to a sensitive pragmatism where rights become flexible in relation to singular situations and affects, as opposed to a general or universal blanket imposition on the basis of common sense or universal identities: "One of the ways to the new right we search for must be through such love, the sacrificial love that Terri Schiavo had for her loved ones – for her husband and for her parents and for her siblings – a love that, obscenely, we glimpse in the media spectacle to which they were subjected" (Protevi 2009: 139).

One of the most important developments in recent work on Deleuze, moral philosophy and politics has been in the construction of a new political pragmatism and case-based jurisprudence around his philosophy. This approach, defended by Paul Patton, Brian Massumi and William Connolly,[20] among others, takes the Deleuzian critique of norms and legal identities then adds a pragmatic, case-by-case and affect-led form of moral and political action. The concern here is whether the reasons behind this turn to singularities and to affects imply a constraint on action in the form of a turn away from actual urgency and towards disembodied potentials due to the participation in a novel form of philosophical eternity as defined in Deleuze's work on death. It could be objected, however, that this restraint is not a strongly visible feature in the work of Patton, Massumi, Connolly, or Protevi. Each of them gives specific cases for action and advocates paths for direct progressive philosophical involvement in them. Yet the role of the eternal is nonetheless discernible in their pragmatism, their optimism with respect to a case-by-case approach, to a valuation of singularities, and their confidence in a plurality of affects allied to a pluralistic politics. Each of these general characteristics depends on a sense of life as ongoing, multiple, flexible, and resilient. Each of them, then, has an inbuilt resistance to death as final and as a carrier of urgencies negating the reserves of time, creativity, and living energy necessary for the new pragmatism. We can see this in the political and moral motivation Protevi finds in love beyond sacrifice in his moving reading of the Schiavo case. It seems that the price of a resistance to reactionary nihilism is a latent dependence on an eternal affective renewal which can itself be traced back to Deleuze's dualist account of death.

My worry is that this pluralistic optimism rests on a philosophy of death that remains unacknowledged in its full ramifications. I do not want to prejudge what follows from this elision, but instead to draw attention to Deleuze's work on death and to its implications with respect to time and action, to final lateness and restorative eternity. Underlying Deleuzian moral and political action there is a version of eternity dependent on his encounter with Blanchot and on his interpretation of Nietzsche's eternal return. In this eternity, we find a necessary role for death and its duality, where the same always passes and dies, and where pure difference is the only potential remaining for future repetition and reincarnation:

> Only the third repetition returns. At the price of Zarathustra's own resemblance and identity: Zarathustra must lose them, and the resemblance of the self and identity of the I must perish, Zarathustra must die . . . Because "one" repeats eternally, but "one" now designates the world of impersonal individualities and preindividual singularities. (Deleuze 1968a: 382)[21]

When constructing a Deleuzian moral philosophy, it will be important to keep in mind the negative aspects of this strong relation drawn between Deleuze's critique of identity, his division of death into two, and his demonstrations that it is only death as impersonal that secures a projection into the future. A case-based and open pragmatism is a good candidate for building sensitive moral guidelines, but it will be important to remember that, at least in relation to death, it is neither as open nor as singular as one might think.

References

Agamben, G. (2000), *Potentialities: Collected Essays in Philosophy*, Stanford: Stanford University Press.
Barthes, R. (1982), *L'Obvie et l'obtus: essais critiques III*, Paris: Seuil.
Baugh, B. (2005), "Death," in A. Parr (ed.), *The Deleuze Dictionary*, Edinburgh: Edinburgh University Press
Bogue, R. (2009), "Sigmund Freud," in G. Jones and J. Roffe (eds.), *Deleuze's Philosophical Lineage*, Edinburgh: Edinburgh University Press, 219–36.
Borges, J. L. (1964a), "The Immortal," in *Labyrinths*, Harmondsworth: Penguin, 135–49.
Borges, J. L. (1964b), "The Garden of Forking Paths," in *Labyrinths*, Harmondsworth: Penguin, 44–54.
Brassier, R. (2006), "The Pure and Empty Form of Death: Deleuze and Heidegger," Actual and Virtual, April 2006, http://www.eri.mmu.ac.uk/deleuze/journal-april06_2.php (accessed December 3, 2009)
Brassier, R. (2007), *Nihil Unbound*, Basingstoke: Palgrave Macmillan.
Colebrook, C. (2006), *Deleuze: a Guide for the Perplexed*, London: Continuum.
Connolly, W. (2005), *Pluralism*, Durham: Duke University Press.
Critchley, S. (1997), *Very Little . . . Almost Nothing*, London: Routledge.
Deleuze, G. (1962), *Nietzsche et la philosophie*, Paris: Presses Universitaires de France.
Deleuze, G. (1968a), *Différence et repetition*, Paris: Presses Universitaires de France.
Deleuze, G. (1968b), *Spinoza et le probléme de l'expression*, Paris: Minuit.
Deleuze, G. (1969), *Logique du sens*, Paris: Minuit.
Deleuze, G. (1981a), *Spinoza: philosophie practique*, Paris: Minuit.
Deleuze, G. (1981b), *Francis Bacon: logique de la sensation*, Paris: Éditions de la difference.
Deleuze, G. (1993), *Critique et Clinique*, Paris: Minuit.
Deleuze, G. (2003), *Deux régimes de fous*, Paris: Minuit.
Deleuze, G. and Guattari, F. (1980), *Mille Plateaux*, Paris: Minuit.
Derrida, J. (1995), "Il me faudra errer tout seul," *Libération*, November 7, available at http://www.liberation.fr/culture/0101158943-il-me-faudra-errer-tout-seul (accessed December 3, 2009)
Hallward, P. (2006), *Out of this World: Deleuze and the Philosophy of Creation*, London: Verso.
Levinas, E. (1969), *Totality and Infinity*, trans. A. Lingis, Dordrecht: Kluwer.
Malpas, J. (1998), "Death and the Unity of a Life," in Malpas and Solomon 1998: 120–34.
Malpas, J. and Solomon, R. (eds.) (1998), *Death and Philosophy*, London: Routledge.
Massumi, B. (2002), *Parables for the Virtual: Movement, Affect, Sensation*, Durham: Duke University Press.

de Montaigne, M. (1953), *Essais de Michel Montaigne*, Paris: Gallimard, Bibliothèque de la Pléiade

Montebello, P. (2008), *Deleuze*, Paris: Vrin.

Pascal, B. (1977), *Pensées I*, Paris: Gallimard.

Parkes, G. (1998), "Death and Detachment," in Malpas and Solomon 1998: 83–97.

Patton, P. (2000), *Deleuze and the Political*, London: Routledge.

Protevi, J. (2009), *Political Affect: Connecting the Social and the Somatic*, Minneapolis: University of Minnesota Press.

Schérer, R. (1998a), "L'impersonnel," *Rue Descartes*, "Gilles Deleuze: immanence et vie," 20, 69–76.

Schérer, R. (1998b), "*Homo tantum*, l'impersonnel: une politique," in E. Alliez (ed.), *Gilles Deleuze: une vie philosophique*, Le Plessis-Robinson: Institut Synthélabo.

Schopenhauer, A. (1969), *The World as Will and Representation*, vol. 1, New York: Dover.

Smith, D. W. (2005), "The Concept of the Simulacrum: Deleuze and the Overturning of Platonism," *Continental Philosophy Review* 38:1–2, 89–123.

Solomon, R. (1998), "Death Fetishism, Morbid Solipsism," in Malpas and Solomon 1998: 152–76

Spinoza, Benedict de (2005), *Ethics*, trans. E. Curley, Harmondsworth: Penguin.

Stivale, C. (2008), *Gilles Deleuze's ABCs: The Folds of Friendship*, Baltimore: Johns Hopkins University Press.

Williams, B. (1973), "The Makropulos Case: Reflections on the Tedium of Immortality," in *Problems of the Self*, Cambridge University Press, 82–100.

Williams, J. (2008), "How to be Bicameral: Reading William Connolly's Pluralism with Whitehead and Deleuze," *British Journal of Politics and International Relations* 10:2, 140–55.

Notes

1. There is a resonance in these considerations with Plato's presentation of an afterlife, for instance in the *Phaedo*. This is not the direct focus of this chapter, but it can be pursued through Deleuze's overturning of Platonism and their related yet different treatments of death. For an important introduction to this idea of overturning see Smith 2005.

2. Deleuze's understanding on the dual nature of death should not be confused with what Robert Solomon calls the denial of death: "Then, of course, the denial of death can also take the form that death is not really death, that life goes on, in some more or less self-identical medium" (Solomon 1998: 159). Deleuze's point is that actual death really is death for personal identity, but that in this death we participate in something eternal that cannot be understood in terms of personal identity.

3. For an introduction to death in Deleuze, approached more from his work with Félix Guattari, see Baugh 2005. Jacques Derrida, in his short text written in the aftermath of Deleuze's death, draws attention to the important role played by the event of death in Deleuze's thought: "Deleuze, the thinker, is above all the thinker of the event and always of this event" (Derrida 1995). That "this event" is death is made clear when Derrida turns to Deleuze's work on Joë Bousquet's "taste for death." For a beautiful discussion of the double nature of death in Blanchot, see Critchley 1997: 65–72.

4. Jeff Malpas recognizes the necessity of this loss of identity in the infinity of relations in his critique of Sartre's position on death: "Given an endless span of time, the possibilities that an individual life might accomplish are themselves endless.

In that case it seems that the Sartrean claim that death, as the ending of a span of life, bears no relation to finitude would seem to be simply false" (Malpas 1998: 131). This may well be an effective critique of Sartre, but Deleuze's account offers a counter were the same critique to be extended to his work on the death of a finite actual person. For Deleuze, the endless relations implied by the "one dies" do indeed contrast with a finite individual identity, but the key point is that individual identity is a limiting expression and transformation of these relations, rather than a straightforward mapping on to them.

5. For an extended example and study of this concept of death and dying, see Deleuze's comments on Dickens' character Riderhood, from *Our Mutual Friend*, in "Immanence: a Life . . ." (in Deleuze 2003); see also Giorgio Agamben's analysis of the Deleuze essay, especially in relation to the unique-ness and immanence of Deleuze's conception of transcendental life in relation to death (Agamben 2000). Agamben's definition of bare life in relation to Deleuze has been responded to from a Deleuzian point of view in Protevi 2009: 122–5. Another literary treatment of death in relation to eternity and a shared afterlife can be found in Deleuze's discussion of Melville's "Bartleby," where Deleuze studies the effect of death on a "paternal function," on those who resist its destruction of the subject and person and who are set in turmoil when they encounter a death free of such resistance: "The paternal function is lost in favor of more obscure ambiguous forces" (Deleuze 1993: 99). For a treatment through painting rather than literature, see Deleuze's work on the scream in Bacon as "cosmic dissipation" (Deleuze 1981b: 23–6).

6. Deleuze discusses death in relation to Spinoza in *Spinoza and the Problem of Expression*. This reference is important because it shows the consistency between his work on Spinoza and the dual nature of death in *Difference and Repetition* and *The Logic of Sense*. Deleuze raises the criticism that, if life is to be defined as a power to be affected through the body, then in death it seems that this power is greatly diminished, thereby contradicting Spinoza's claims for immortality in book V of his *Ethics*. Deleuze then responds to this criticism by referring to three kinds of affection, of which the third kind, those associated with the third kind of knowledge and with action rather than passion, remain after we die as our essence in God. We cannot exercise these through the body after our death, yet they remain as a power to be affected. So the highest affects, those associated with knowledge and beatitude, are our immortality: "after death, the active affections explicated [through our intensive part] absolutely fill our power to be affected; what remains of us is absolutely effectuated" (Deleuze 1968b: 298). Note that Deleuze picks up these points again also in relation to death in his definition of power in Spinoza in *Spinoza: Practical Philosophy* (Deleuze 1981a: 134–43). Note also that, although Deleuze does not discuss Spinoza on death and immortality through the concept of counter-actualization, we can think of counter-actualization through Deleuze's study of the way of salvation in relation to expression in *Spinoza and the Problem of Expression*: "Hence, after death, our essence will have all the affections it is capable of; and all of these will be of the third kind. Thus is the difficult way of salvation" (Deleuze 1968b: 298).

7. Deleuze studies this alteration of the eternal mainly through two references: Nietzsche's eternal return (to be discussed later in this essay) and Borges' short stories such as "The Garden of Forking Paths." Jeff Malpas also draws on Borges' stories of eternity when responding to Bernard Williams' account of the Makropulos case in "The Makropulos Case: Reflections on the Tedium of Immortality" (Williams 1973). Malpas' reading of Borges' "The Immortal" and Williams' reading of the Makropulos affair differ greatly from Deleuze's interpretation of Borges because they do not take account of the potential of

differing cycles of immortality and different levels or types of time: "The immortals described in one of Borges's stories are indeed creatures in whose infinitely extended lives everything is possible and consequently nothing is significant" (Malpas 1998: 131). Deleuze's point is different and consists in the claim that the infinity is fully real only in relation to play or a throw of the dice made by an actual individual under the condition that the throw connect in a novel and singular manner to all other throws through that infinity. Each play therefore affirms the whole of chance – infinity – but by inventing a new rule – singular significance: "The system of the future . . . should be called a divine game, because there is no pre-existing rule, because the child-player can only win – since the whole of chance is affirmed once and for all times" (Deleuze 1968a: 152). Note that very similar points to these are made in *The Logic of Sense* in the series on the ideal game, also with a reference to Borges (Deleuze 1969: 78–82).

8. It is important to contrast this account of impersonal connection with *all* deaths and selective connections through religious affinity and selection, for instance in Pascal: "But the example of the deaths of martyrs touches us because they are our limbs . . . There's nothing of that in the example of the pagans. We have no links to them" (Pascal 1977: 224).

9. It is helpful to contrast Deleuze's view on immortality, with regard to how we ought to behave in relation to death, with Jeff Malpas' remarks, based on a reading of Heidegger, whereby immortality and a focus on it leads to an inauthentic relation to death: "To be a creature that has a life, to be a creature that has a world, to be a creature that has a sense of value and significance, is also to be a creature that has a grasp of the possibility of its own ending" (Malpas 1998: 134). Deleuze's moral position combines this facing up to mortality with a sense of continuation and a set of moral principles associated with it. For further discussion on Deleuze and Heidegger and death see Brassier 2006 and Brassier 2007: 178–201. These important readings of Deleuze's work on death develop a crucial connection to Heidegger that has been left in the background here.

10. Deleuze studies Nietzsche's concept of *ressentiment* at length in *Nietzsche and Philosophy*. It is a significant reference for the discussion of resentment and war because it allows us to understand that resentment is not in the inflicting of suffering, which can be an affirmative act, but rather in the use made of that suffering which negates any affirmation in the first act (Deleuze 1962: 149). This then avoids the contradiction in Deleuze's principle of waging war against war; the war against war has no other use or purpose than eliminating war.

11. There is an apparent mismatch between the work on war in *The Logic of Sense* and the plateau "Treatise of Nomadology: The Nomadic War Machine" in *A Thousand Plateaus*, since the injunction to wage war against war appears to apply against the positive use of the term of nomadic war machine. It is outside the scope of this work to seek a full account of the relation between the earlier work and the later one with Guattari; however, one direction of enquiry could be that the war machine is a form of war against war that only sets war down as a means when it is co-opted by the state: "It is at the same time that the state apparatus *appropriates* the war machine, subordinates it to 'political' *goals*, and gives it war as direct *object*" (Deleuze and Guattari 1980: 524).

12. See Deleuze's discussion of shame in relation to T. E. Lawrence and the shame of battles (Deleuze 1993: 151), and shame in relation to the massacre of Palestinians at Sabra and Chatila in "Grandeur of Yasser Arafat" (Deleuze 2003: 221).

13. There is a connection to Montaigne's essay on philosophy and death here, since Montaigne too connects freedom not only to meditation on death as something to be affirmed but also, as such, through the uncertainty of when it will

strike: "It is uncertain as when death will strike, so let's wait for it everywhere. Premeditation of death is premeditation of liberty. Who has learned to die, has unlearned how to serve. Knowing how to die frees us from all subjection and constraint" (de Montaigne 1953: 110–11).

14. For a detailed discussion of time and death in Deleuze in relation to the Freudian death drive, see Bogue 2009: 223–7. For a discussion of how this work on the death drive reappears in later work, notably in *Anti-Oedipus*, see Montebello 2008: 178–82.

15. René Schérer has analyzed Deleuze's work on the impersonal in two elegant essays (Schérer 1998a; 1998b). The latter essay also makes the point about the importance of freedom in relation to death and adds a helpful connection to thought as phantasm in *The Logic of Sense* (Schérer 1998b: 28).

16. For an opposite view to my reading of the role of counter-actualization in relation to death see Peter Hallward's *Out of this World: Deleuze and the Philosophy of Creation*: "Counter-actualization does not require the death of the self alone. It also requires the sacrifice of that most precious sacred cow of contemporary philosophy – the other" (Hallward 2006: 92). The rhetoric in this passage operates a shift from Deleuze's argument that counter-actualization works through actual selves as they move towards death and in order to connect to others, to the impression that Deleuze simply "requires" the death of the self and of others in order to move to another pure plane. In his reading of Blanchot's role in Deleuze's thought as mediated by Foucault, Charles Stivale offers a different understanding of the relation of death and impersonal life, the "a life ..." from Deleuze's "Immanence: a Life ...." Stivale speaks of death as the obverse of life in relations of folds and friendship, thereby demonstrating that Hallward's "requirements" set a break in Deleuze's system when in fact there is continuity in "folds" of life and death (Stivale 2008: 133). A similar point is made by Claire Colebrook when explaining the relation between life, death, and desire in *Anti-Oedipus*: "the desire which is both life (as multiple degrees of difference) and death as zero intensity ..." (Colebrook 2006: 3).

17. For a moral and political reading of Deleuze and Guattari that takes their understanding of the fundamental nature of problems as a basis for action, see Protevi 2009: 190.

18. There are very interesting parallels here with Levinas' study of death in *Totality and Infinity*: "Death threatens me from beyond" (Levinas 1969: 234). Where Deleuze and Levinas part is on the latter's characterization of that beyond in terms of the Other: "like the alienation of my will by the Other" (Levinas 1969: 234).

19. It is worthwhile contrasting Deleuze's arguments against the capacity of suicide to bring together the two sides of death with Schopenhauer's arguments against suicide as the capacity to deny the will. For Deleuze something always comes from the outside in death, even in suicide. In a similar vein, Schopenhauer claims that the individual death fails to deny life as willing: "The suicide denies merely the individual, not the species" (Schopenhauer 1969: 399). Deleuze also discusses suicide in relation to the two sides of death and Blanchot in *The Logic of Sense* (Deleuze 1969: 182–3). Note also that Deleuze's own suicide cannot be interpreted as a contradictory attempt to draw the two sides of death together, something that he calls an illusion, following Blanchot. Instead, an end-of-life suicide, in the sense of one carried out when death is close and life coming to an end, fits Deleuze's account of times when the body has arrived at the end of its power to the point where life becomes unbearable. The suicide is then not an attempt to bring the two sides of death together, but rather a response to an unbearable condition.

20. See Patton 2000: 109–31, Massumi 2002: 243–50, and Connolly 2005 (see Williams 2008 for a commentary on the Deleuzian elements in Connolly's work on pluralism)
21. I thank Dan Smith for drawing my attention to Deleuze's remarks on Zarathustra's death.

Chapter 11

Ethics between Particularity and Universality

Audronė Žukauskaitė

Deleuze and Badiou as Contemporaries

Deleuze and Badiou are exceptional figures in the field of contemporary philosophy. They both created influential patterns of thinking which encompass not only philosophy, but also art, science, politics, and ethics. Both Deleuze and Badiou struggle with such concepts as singularity, the multiple/multiplicity, the Real, and the event. But the meanings they assign to these concepts are absolutely different: for Badiou even the idea of the multiple is grounded in the metaphysics of the One; Deleuze, by contrast, replaces the very idea of the One with the idea of multiplicity. The same antagonism between Deleuze and Badiou can be discerned in the ethical-political field: Badiou claims that the way out of the deadlock of neoliberal democracy is a militant universalism; Deleuze, by contrast, suggests that the proper ethical-political approach is that of becoming-minoritarian. In other words, even though they operate with similar philosophical vocabulary and reflect similar ethical-political themes, Deleuze and Badiou are on different sides of contemporary philosophical debates. As Éric Alliez points out:

> Deleuze and Badiou constitute the extreme polarities, not only of the contemporary domain of French philosophy, but perhaps of the real of thought as such – to the extent that thought, in accordance with the plurality of all its modalities, has no other choice today than to counter the pseudo-democracy of Empire with a materialist necessity that can no longer be elaborated except in terms of singularities and multiplicities. These are notions that our two philosophers entrust with absolutely antagonistic missions, renegotiating the theoretical and practical sense of the very idea of materialism. (Alliez 2006: 151–2)

It is interesting to note that Badiou himself tends to represent this extreme polarity as an almost ideal sameness. In his *Deleuze: The*

Clamor of Being Badiou describes his relationship with Deleuze as "a conflictual friendship that, in a certain sense, had never taken place" and thinks that they both "constituted, without ever having decided to do so (on the contrary!), a sort of paradoxical tandem" (Badiou 2000: 6, 4). Badiou claims that he was positioning his endeavor "vis-à-vis Deleuze and no one else." He points out that in contemporary philosophy there are two paradigms that govern the manner in which the multiple is thought: the "vital" paradigm of open multiplicities (related to Bergson) and the mathematical paradigm of sets. Badiou asserts that Deleuze is the contemporary thinker of the first paradigm, and that he strives to harbor the second (Badiou 2000: 3–4). At the same time he admits that the controversy about the notion of the multiple/multiplicity clearly separates their positions:

> Moreover, the notion of "multiplicity" was to be at the centre of our epistolary controversy of 1992–94, with him maintaining that I confuse "multiple" and "number," whereas I maintained that it is inconsistent to uphold, in the manner of the Stoics, the virtual Totality or what Deleuze named "chaosmos," because, with regard to sets, there can be neither a universal set, nor All, nor One. (Badiou 2000: 4)

Badiou acknowledges that Deleuze works in a different paradigm, insofar as "he carries out a decisive critique of representation, substitutes the logic of sense for the search for truth, and combats transcendent idealities in the name of the creative immanence of life: in sum, that he adds his contribution to the ruin of metaphysics" (Badiou 2000: 9). Nevertheless, Badiou reads Deleuze against Deleuze, sticking to rare citations from *Difference and Repetition* and *The Logic of Sense* and ignoring the wider corpus of Deleuzian works, especially those co-written with Guattari. Badiou claims:

> contrary to the commonly accepted image (Deleuze as liberating the anarchic multiple of desires and errant drifts), contrary even to the apparent indications of his work that play on the opposition multiple/multiplicities . . . it is the occurrence of the One – renamed by Deleuze the One-All – that forms the supreme destination of thought and to which thought is accordingly consecrated . . . We can therefore first state that one must carefully identify a metaphysics of the One in the work of Deleuze. (Badiou 2000: 11)

Badiou dedicates his book to finding proof that Deleuzian philosophy is organized around the metaphysics of the One and should be reconsidered in terms of classical philosophy, in other words, as a metaphysics of Being. As Alliez points out, "Badiou in his book erects an image of

Deleuze as a metaphysician of the One, whose essential *monotony – in itself indifferent to differences,* subtracted as it is from the 'inexhaustible variety of the concrete' and from the anarchic confusion of the world – can and must cause us to dismiss the works co-authored with Félix Guattari, beginning with *Anti-Oedipus*" (Alliez 2006: 152).

This "capture" of Deleuzian philosophy was enthusiastically supported by Slavoj Žižek, who suggests that there are two versions of that philosophy: one that of "Deleuze proper" of the early monographs and another that of the "Guattarized" Deleuze (Žižek 2004: 20). Žižek's premise is that "beneath this Deleuze (the popular image of Deleuze based on the reading of the books he coauthored with Guattari), there is another Deleuze." Žižek promises to discern an inner tension between Deleuze and Guattari's *Anti-Oedipus* and Deleuze's *The Logic of Sense,* between "the Deleuze who celebrated the productive multitude of Becoming against the reified order of being and the Deleuze of the sterility of the incorporeal becoming of the Sense-Event" (Žižek 2004: xi). The simple question arising from reading these lines is: why does Žižek want to multiply Deleuze? Why is the conflict or antagonism between metaphysical and post-metaphysical thinking, or between Badiou and Deleuze, replaced by the antagonism between the two images of Deleuze? This multiplication of Deleuzian figures reflects Žižek's perplexity when it comes to situating Deleuze in contemporary ethical-political debates: on the one hand, Žižek suggests that Deleuze serves to provide the theoretical foundation of today's anti-globalist Left and its resistance to capitalism; on the other hand, he claims that there are, effectively, features that justify calling Deleuze the ideologue of late capitalism (Žižek 2004: xi, 183–4). This undecidability can be taken as a sign of a "real" philosophical question: what consequences do Deleuzian ideas have in the arena of capitalist neoliberal democracy? Why are these ideas so unacceptable for Badiou and Žižek? Why do we need this difference between "Deleuze proper," an elitist author, indifferent towards ethics and politics, and a "politicized" Deleuze compromised by Guattari? Žižek suggests that, for Deleuze, Guattari presented an alibi, an escape from his previous position (Žižek 2004: 21). Reversing that question, we can ask: why does Badiou need Deleuze as an alibi, why does he rewrite Deleuzian philosophy in metaphysical terms? Isn't it the symptom of a fear of raising ethical questions without having a stable metaphysical foundation?

Deleuze (with Guattari) on Minor Politics

To answer these questions we have to distance ourselves from Badiou's appropriation of Deleuze. There is no need to fantasize about two different images of Deleuze, because there is a clear conceptual continuity between Deleuze's earlier monographs and his works co-authored with Guattari. For example, the Deleuzian distinction of differentiation/differenciation is echoed in his later notion of multiplicity. On the other hand, the notion of multiplicity is very closely related to the ideas of "the minor" and "becoming-minoritarian." Nicholas Thoburn, in his book *Deleuze, Marx and Politics*, summarizes the concepts of "minor literature," "the minor," and "becoming-minoritarian" under the heading of "minor politics." "Minor politics" is a very precise description of Deleuze and Guattari's strategies, not only because they promote minorities but also because they never claim to establish a "major" or politically specific program definable in terms of neoliberal democracy. This is the reproach Badiou has made against Deleuze: Badiou argues that, in generalizing politics everywhere, Deleuze's system lacks a specifically political register of thought (see Thoburn 2003: 5). However, not being specifically political, Deleuze and Guattari's philosophy is saturated with ethical ideas. Ethics in the Levinasian sense concerns the relationship between the subject and the other which cannot be regulated by the principles of knowledge; it is intrinsically unpredictable and anarchic. Levinasian ethics is structured around the difference of the other, which, as Levinas insists, is irreducible: it cannot be reduced to social expectations or become the theme of general knowledge. In this sense we can say that "minor politics" operates like "minor ethics," conceptualizing the position of those who are different, subjected to violence and injustice, and are oppressed in "cramped spaces."

"Minor ethics" is firstly articulated in Deleuze and Guattari's *Kafka: Toward a Minor Literature* through the notion of minor literature. Here Deleuze and Guattari claim that minor literature, regardless of its authorship, is the people's concern and that it is expressed only in the collective assemblages of enunciation:

> The three characteristics of minor literature are the deterritorialization of language, the connection of the individual to a political immediacy, and the collective assemblage of enunciation. We might as well say that minor no longer designates specific literatures but the revolutionary conditions for every literature within the heart of what is called great (or established) literature. (Deleuze and Guattari 2006: 18)

The deterritorialization of language here implies the minor use or practice of major language. For example, Deleuze and Guattari refer to Kafka, a Prague Jew, writing in German. This example reveals that minor literature refers not to the language of some particular minority but to the "minor treatment" of a language:

> How many people today live in a language that is not their own? . . . This is the problem of immigrants . . . the problem of minorities, the problem of minor literature, but also the problem for all of us: how to tear a minor literature away from its own language, allowing it to challenge the language and making it follow a sober revolutionary path? How to become a nomad and an immigrant and a gypsy in relation to one's own language? (Deleuze and Guattari 2006: 19)

The "minor treatment" of language relates to such phenomena as popular or proletarian literature, which gives expression to "the people to come."

The connection between the "minor treatment" of language and the "people to come" is more clearly discussed in Deleuze's *Cinema 2: The Time-Image*. Here Deleuze describes the "minor treatment" of cinematographic language specific to so-called third-world or minority filmmakers: "Sometimes the minority filmmaker finds himself in the impasse described by Kafka: the impossibility of not 'writing', the impossibility of writing in the dominant language, the impossibility of writing differently" (Deleuze 2005: 209). Nevertheless, the writer or filmmaker has to go through all this to extract from the given language the elements of a people who are missing: this is the task not only of minor literature or minor cinema (modern political cinema) but also of minor politics in general:

> This acknowledgement of a people who are missing is not a renunciation of political cinema, but on the contrary the new basis on which it is founded, in the third world and for minorities. Art, and especially cinematographic art, must take part in this task: not that of addressing a people, which is presupposed already there, but of contributing to the invention of a people. (Deleuze 2005: 209)

Deleuze never specifies who these "missing people" are: they are becoming, inventing themselves but never form a homogeneous unity. Although Deleuze points out that the invention of the people is the task of modern political cinema, "a people" is not a political term, it does not refer to a specific class, race, or minority group. As Philippe Mengue indicates, "this 'people' is condemned to be *forever* 'to come' . . . it cannot have any historical existence" (Mengue 2008: 229). It is an ethical concept, implying that an artist – a filmmaker or a writer – has to take up not the position of power but the task of expressing the position of those who still lack recognition in the public space. Minor art *is* "minor ethics" in a sense that it creates cinematographic or discursive means of expression for this new collective subjectivity, and creates a new medium for these collective utterances. As far as minor literature and minor cinema have this capacity to transmit political messages and express collective subjectivity, "everything becomes political." As Deleuze and Guattari point out, "its cramped space forces each individual intrigue to connect immediately to politics" (Deleuze and Guattari 2006: 17). Speaking about modern political cinema, Deleuze also asserts that it merges the private affair with social or political immediacy. The conceptual problem here is that "the political" means not the existing social or political group, but the impossibility of forming a group: "a double impossibility, that of forming a group *and* that of not forming a group, 'the impossibility of escaping from the group and the impossibility of being satisfied with it'" (Deleuze 2005: 211). This (im)possibility of forming a social or political group is reflected through the notion of becoming, and, more precisely, through the notion of becoming-minoritarian.

Deleuze and Guattari discuss the concept of becoming-minoritarian in *A Thousand Plateaus* and claim that "all becoming is minoritarian" because "there is no becoming-majoritarian; majority is never becoming" (Deleuze and Guattari 2004: 117). For example, there is no becoming-man, because man is majoritarian par excellence whereas all becoming is minoritarian: "In this sense women, children, but also animals, plants, and molecules, are minoritarian." Deleuze and Guattari stress that it is important not to confuse "minoritarian" as a becoming or process with a "minority," as an aggregate or a state: "Even blacks, as the Black Panthers said, must become-black. Even women must become-woman. Even Jews must become-Jewish" (Deleuze and Guattari 2004: 321). This means that becoming-minoritarian is not a "natural" state or condition but a political affair and "necessitates a labor of power, an active micropolitics" (Deleuze and Guattari 2004: 322). We can say that a deliberate act of becoming-minoritarian can be thought as a line of escape from one's own position as a minority. As Deleuze and Guattari put it, "minorities, of course, are objectively definable states, states of language, ethnicity, or sex with their own ghetto territorialities, but they must also be thought of as seeds, crystals of becoming whose value is to trigger uncontrollable movements and deterritorializations of the mean or majority" (Deleuze and Guattari 2004: 117). In this sense the act of becoming is a revolutionary act, because it enables the repressed to reach an autonomous condition and in this way changes the constellation of power. As Deleuze and Guattari point out:

> continuous variation constitutes the becoming-minoritarian of everybody, as opposed to the majoritarian Fact of Nobody. Becoming-minoritarian as the universal figure of consciousness is called autonomy. It is certainly not by using a minor language as a dialect, by regionalizing or ghettoizing, that one becomes revolutionary; rather, by using a number of minority elements, by connecting, conjugating them, one invents a specific, unforeseen, autonomous becoming. (Deleuze and Guattari 2004: 118)

In what sense is becoming-minoritarian seen as a universal figure? Are Deleuze and Guattari suggesting the revolutionary act of becoming-minoritarian as a universal ethical stance? On the one hand, the figure of becoming-minoritarian continues, although in different terms, the Levinasian and Derridian theme of otherness and the problem of taking the responsibility for the other. On the other hand, there are decisive attempts to interpret the figure of becoming-minoritarian in the political field. For example, Thoburn interprets the act of becoming-minoritarian as a situation where politics emerges:

> The minor, then, is a creativity of minorities: those who find their movements and expressions 'cramped' on all sides such that they cannot in any conventional sense be said to have carved out a delineated social space of their 'own' where they could be called 'a people' . . . It is from their very cramped and complex situations that politics emerges – no longer as a process of facilitating and bolstering identity, or 'becoming-conscious', but as a process of innovation, of experimentation, and of the complication of life, in which forms of community, techniques of practice, ethical demeanours, styles, knowledges, and cultural forms are composed. (Thoburn 2003: 8)

However, is every process of innovation and experimentation necessarily a political act? Can we change social and political reality by introducing new creative practices and patterns of thinking? Of course, a real political act implies innovation and experimentation but not every attempt at innovation and experimentation leads to political changes. In this sense the process of becoming-minoritarian has the pathos of the avant-garde or artistic activism but can hardly be convincing as a political movement.

The specific feature defining becoming-minoritarian and minorities as such is related to the notion of multiplicity. Deleuze and Guattari assert that the difference between minorities and the majority is not a difference in number but a difference between denumerable and non-denumerable units:

> A minority can be numerous or even infinite; so can a majority. What distinguishes them is that in the case of a majority the relation internal to the number constitutes a set that may be finite or infinite, but is always denumerable, whereas the minority is defined as a non-denumerable set, however many elements it may have. What characterizes the non-denumerable is neither the set nor its elements; rather it is the *connection*, the "and" produced between elements, between sets. (Deleuze and Guattari 2004: 519)

The key idea is that the majority is composed of denumerable or quantitative elements, regardless of how many elements it has, while minorities are defined by non-denumerable or qualitative elements, which cannot be counted or integrated into the axiomatic logic of capitalism. Deleuze and Guattari point out that "the axiomatic manipulates only denumerable sets, even infinite ones, whereas the minorities constitute 'fuzzy', non-denumerable, non-axiomizable sets, in short, 'masses,' multiplicities of escape and flux" (Deleuze and Guattari 2004: 519). This distinction recalls Deleuze and Guattari's distinction between divisible or quantitative multiplicities and indivisible or quantitative multiplicities:

> Thus we find in the work of the mathematician and physicist Riemann a distinction between discrete multiplicities and continuous multiplicities . . . Then in Meinong and Russell we find a distinction between multiplicities of magnitude or divisibility, which are extensive, and multiplicities of distance, which are closer to the intensive. And in Bergson there is a distinction between numerical or extended multiplicities and qualitative or durational multiplicities . . . On the one hand, multiplicities that are extensive, divisible, and molar; . . . on the other hand, . . . molecular intensive multiplicities composed of particles that do not divide without changing in nature. (Deleuze and Guattari 2004: 36)

This distinction, quite understandable on the abstract level, gets complicated when we try to define in what way Deleuze and Guattari apply it to the social. As I understand it, Deleuze and Guattari argue that the majority as a denumerable multiplicity is compatible with the axiomatic logic of capitalism, which transforms every heterogeneous element into the flow of homogeneous quantities. This is why the majority is always supported by the state and other structures of power. Minorities, by contrast, function in different ways than those established by a capitalist economy and the state. This is why the state makes efforts to translate minorities into denumerable sets or subsets and to include minorities as elements into the majority. This is the way to reduce the qualitative differences of minorities. Deleuze and Guattari point out that

> The power of the minorities is not measured by their capacity to enter and make themselves felt within the majority system, nor even to reverse the necessary tautological criterion of the majority, but to bring to bear the force of the denumerable sets, even if they are infinite, reversed, or changed, even if they imply new axioms or, beyond that, a new axiomatic. The issue is . . . a calculus or conception of the problems of non-denumerable sets, against the axiomatic of denumerable sets. Such a calculus may have its own compositions, organizations, even centralizations; nevertheless, it proceeds not via the States or the axiomatic process but via a pure becoming of minorities. (Deleuze and Guattari 2004: 520)

Here again Deleuze and Guattari assert that minority is a universal figure or becoming-everybody/everything (*devenir tout le monde*). In the light of the distinction between quantitative and qualitative multiplicities this means that becoming-minoritarian implies the flow of molecular intensive multiplicities composed of particles that do not divide without changing in nature. Becoming-minoritarian thus necessarily implies a moment of change and transformation, not only on the part of so-called minorities but also – and this is the most important thing – on the part of standard or denumerable members of the majority: "Woman: we all have to become that, whether we are male or female. Non-white: we all have to become that, whether we are white, yellow, or black" (Deleuze and Guattari 2004: 520). Deleuze and Guattari believe that being in a state of permanent becoming or transformation the minorities can escape the mortifying grasp of the capitalist axiomatic. However, as Janell Watson wittily asks, are they really serious that we should all become minorities? Watson argues that minorities could initiate a global power shift that would do away with majority privilege by eliminating the very concept of majority, the majority as an axiom (Watson 2008: 200–1; Deleuze and Guattari 2004: 518). But it is precisely this relationship with the capitalist axiomatic that seems the most problematic: on the one hand, Deleuze and Guattari state that the minorities' issue is that "of smashing capitalism, of redefining socialism, of constituting a war machine capable of countering the world war machine by other means"; on the other hand, they explain the emergence of minorities or the non-denumerable sets as an internal tendency akin to capitalism: "At the same time as capitalism is effectuated in the denumerable sets serving as its models, it necessarily constitutes non-denumerable sets that cut across and disrupt those models" (Deleuze and Guattari 2004: 521–2).

In this sense the non-denumerable nature of minorities simultaneously expresses the revolutionary moment of change and the deepest tendency of capitalism.

Badiou: The Foundation of Universalism

Badiou, in his books *Saint Paul: The Foundation of Universalism* and *Ethics: An Essay on the Understanding of Evil*, reflects on similar topics, such as the role and place of so-called particularities or minorities in the era of global capitalism. He interprets the proliferation of different minority groups as a threat to the universal foundation underlying any social or political project. If Deleuze and Guattari interpret the process of becoming-minoritarian as a way of "smashing capitalism," Badiou, by contrast, reads the proliferation of minorities as a final realization of capitalist logic:

> What is the real unifying factor behind this attempt to promote the cultural virtue of oppressed subsets, this invocation of language in order to extol communitarian particularisms (which, besides language, always ultimately refer back to race, religion, or gender)? It is, evidently, monetary abstraction, whose false universality has absolutely no difficulty accommodating the kaleidoscope of communitarianisms. (Badiou 2003: 7)

Badiou makes a direct connection between the social processes of fragmentation into closed identities (racial, religious, national, or sexual minorities), and the process of abstract monetary homogenization. He asserts that capitalist monetary abstraction is capable of reducing every (social) particularity to the homogeneity of number. But it is precisely this connection that should be critically reconsidered. It is not difficult to discern that in connecting particular identities with capitalist monetary flows Badiou conflates two different things: the qualitative nature of social particularities (so-called minorities) and the quantitative nature of commodities and monetary flows. Surprisingly, Badiou interprets particularities *as* commodities and links these two phenomena into a cause-effect relationship:

> Both processes are perfectly intertwined. For each identification (the creation or cobbling together of identity) creates a figure that provides a material for its investment by the market. There is nothing more captive, so far as commercial investment is concerned, nothing more amenable to the invention of new figures of monetary homogeneity, than a community and its territory or territories. The semblance of a non-equivalence is required so that equivalence itself can constitute a process. What inexhaustible

> potential for mercantile investments in this up-surge – taking the form of communities demanding recognition and so-called cultural singularities – of women, homosexuals, the disabled, Arabs! (Badiou 2003: 10)

This quotation raises many questions: first, why would equivalence need the semblance of a non-equivalence? Why would capitalist logic need to disguise itself? Second, can we equate two different things – the particularity of a social group and the homogeneity of monetary flow? Is it not too simplistic to state that the proliferation of minority groups is influenced by the corrupted nature of capitalism? Badiou asserts that "the capitalist logic of the general equivalent and the identitarian and cultural logic of communities or minorities form an articulated whole" (Badiou 2003: 11). It follows that the existence of minorities is justified to the extent that it starts functioning as a target group in market capitalism. Here Badiou adds a long list of commodified social particularities:

> Black homosexuals, disabled Serbs, Catholic pedophiles, moderate Muslims, married priests, ecologist yuppies, the submissive unemployed, prematurely aged youth! Each time, a social image authorizes new products, specialized magazines, improved shopping malls, "free" radio stations, targeted advertising networks, and, finally, heady "public debates" at peak viewing times. Deleuze put it perfectly: capitalist deterritorialization requires a constant reterritorialization. (Badiou 2003: 10)

Here Badiou is trying to suggest that social minorities are responsible for the fact that market capitalism positions certain minorities as a target group. But the most disturbing thing is that Badiou asserts this idea by referring to Deleuze! As Alliez has put it,

> Badiou . . . cannot write these lines without also inviting Deleuze to this wedding between capitalist logic and identitarian logic, a wedding whose stakes are precisely to refuse emancipatory reality to any kind of *becoming-minoritarian* . . . The perfection to which Badiou refers is entirely nominal, and ultimately presents a complete misunderstanding of Deleuze, since the reterritorialisation of capitalism is no longer practiced upon the absolute form of deterritorialisation . . . For Badiou becoming turns out to be purely and simply the occasion for the 'mercantile investments' it gives rise to . . . This ultimately leads Badiou to accept *de facto* the point of view of Capital . . . *The minoritarian is frozen into the identitarian.* (Alliez 2006: 156)

Badiou's aversion to particularities or minorities can be explained in the broader context of his ideas. He opposes the fragmented social reality of late capitalism with an idea of creating a foundation for universalism. To this end, he addresses the figure of Saint Paul, interpreted not in the register of religion or faith but in the context of political action. What interests Badiou is the possibility of a new ethical and political project based not on so-called identitarian singularities but on universalizable singularities, in other words, on singularities which can be subjected to a universal truth procedure. The example of Saint Paul here thus represents the universal character of Christianity: "There is neither Jew nor Greek, there is neither slave nor free, there is neither male nor female" (Badiou 2003: 9). To renounce the differences between social, religious, or gender groups means to establish Christianity's potential universality. This universality requires every social subject to abstract from his or her particularity and become subject to the universal truth. This miraculous transformation is associated with a truth-event, which is represented not only by such examples as Saint Paul's conception of an apostolic subjectivity that exists only through the proclamation of a specific event (the resurrection of Christ) but also by such events as the Jacobin or Bolshevik revolutions (Hallward 2001: x). Badiou takes the event of the Resurrection as the metaphor of an ("fictitious") event which has the power to transform social reality: if a man is resurrected, it follows that there is neither Greek nor Jew, neither male nor female, neither slave nor free man. The same possibility of a miraculous transformation grounds every Communist project – from Lenin to Mao. This is why Badiou interprets Paul as a militant figure and risks comparing Paul with Lenin, saying that Christ for Paul has the same weight as did Marx for Lenin (Badiou 2003: 2). Badiou introduces both Christianity and Communism as a remedy for the fragmented capitalist society. Following Badiou, Žižek defines this position as a politics proper: "Is, then, our task today not exactly homologous to that of Christianity: to undermine the global empire of Capital, but not by asserting particular identities, but through the assertion of a new universality?" (Žižek 2006: 204–5). Here Žižek, as if not aware of the fatal consequences that Leninism had in Central and Eastern Europe, advocates Badiou and conflates Paulinian "love" with Leninist "intolerance." Žižek points out that

> true universalists are not those who preach global tolerance of differences and all-encompassing unity but those who engage in a passionate fight for the assertion of the truth that engages them. Theoretical, religious and political examples abound here: from Saint Paul, whose unconditional Christian universalism . . . made him into a proto-Leninist militant fighting different 'deviations', through Marx, . . . up to Freud, and including many great political figures. (Žižek 2006: 198)

How is this transformation possible? In what ways can the "fictitious" truth-event change social reality? Badiou points out that the truth-event has a totalizing power: "for if it is true that every truth erupts as singular, its singularity is immediately universalizable. Universalizable singularity necessarily breaks with identitarian singularity" (Badiou 2003: 11). In other words, the place of truth should always remain empty and cannot be occupied by any identitarian singularity. If, by contrast, the truth is conflated with some particular identity, for example, with the Nazis' notion of the master race, then the "truth" is compromised into totalitarianism with all its criminal consequences. The place of truth should remain empty and precisely because of this feature it is equally valid "for all." However, this project meets substantial obstacles. First, not every identitarian or minority group prefers to be subjected to the universal truth. Badiou himself notices that particular cultural or social identities potentially remain non-universalizable. Moreover, they remain comprehensible only to someone who belongs to the subset in question: "Only a homosexual can 'understand' what a homosexual is, only an Arab can understand what an Arab is, and so forth. If, as we believe, only truths (thought) allow man to be distinguished from the human animal that underlies him, it is no exaggeration to say that such minoritarian pronouncements are genuinely *barbaric*" (Badiou 2003: 12).

A second theoretical problem to be solved here is that the truth-event always takes place in a certain situation which by definition cannot be universal. Every situation is specific; therefore Badiou has to admit the simple fact that differences exist. He points out:

> although it is true, so far as what the event constitutes is concerned, that there is "neither Greek nor Jew," *the fact is* that there are Greeks and Jews. That every truth procedure collapses differences, infinitely deploying a purely generic multiplicity, does not permit us to lose sight of the fact that, in the situation (call it: the world), *there are differences*. (Badiou 2003: 93)

These differences are found and addressed; finally they have to be reduced to construct universality, which Badiou defines as the genericity (*généricité*) of the true. Badiou asserts that this genericity of truth can be accessed through a certain indifference to differences, and quotes from Paul:

> For though I am free from all men, I have made myself a slave to all, that I might win the more. To the Jews I became as a Jew, in order to win the Jews; to those under the law, I became as one under the law – though not being myself under the law – that I might win those under the law. To those outside the law I became as one outside the law – not being without the law toward God but under the law of Christ – that I might win those outside the law. To the weak I became weak, that I might win the weak, I have become all things to all men. (Cor. I.9.19–22; Badiou 2003: 99)

Badiou himself comments on these lines not as an opportunist text, but as an example of a Communist "mass line," which finds its expression in the "serving of people." In some sense the idea of "becoming all things to all men" echoes Deleuze and Guattari's conception of becoming everyone/everything (*devenir tout le monde*). However this similarity is only nominal because for Deleuze and Guattari becoming everyone/everything is an autonomous process anticipating creative, innovative, and emancipatory movement. Badiou, by contrast, interprets "becoming all things to all men" as the first phase in the process of collapsing differences and deploying genericity. As he points out:

> the moment all, including the solitary militant, are counted according to the universal, it follows that what takes place is the subsumption of the Other by the Same. Paul demonstrates in detail how a universal thought, proceeding on the basis of the worldly proliferation of alterities (the Jew, the Greek, women, men, slaves, free men, and so on), *produces* a Sameness and an Equality (there is no longer either Jew, or Greek, and so on). The production of equality and the casting off, in thought, of differences are the material signs of the universal. (Badiou 2003: 109)

However, it is very difficult to understand, especially for those who don't believe in resurrection, how these differences can be subsumed into the genericity of the One. Badiou explains this moment by saying that no evental One can be the One of particularity; the only possible correlate to the One is the universal. The universal, in its turn, correlates with the two types of subjectivity which are also two types of multiplicity. One of them is the "particularizing multiplicity" and another one "the multiplicity that, exceeding itself, upholds universality. Its being in excess of itself precludes its being represented as a totality" (Badiou 2003: 78). If the first type of multiplicity leads the subject to the cult of particularity and the carnal path of finitude and death, the multiplicity that exceeds itself allows the possibility of overstepping finitude. It is precisely this universalizable multiplicity that can be subsumed within the truth procedure. The subject is activated for the service of truth while the One as truth proceeds in the direction of all. Badiou points out that this transformation takes place in thought, or, more precisely, in faith. But what happens to the other type of particularizing multiplicity? And what happens if the truth of the event does not hold true for all?

Badiou poses the same question in his *Ethics*, which in the original appeared the year after *Saint Paul*. In this book the notion of multiplicity, paradoxically, is defined by the absence of the One:

Let us posit *our* axioms. There is no God. Which also means: the One is not. The multiple "without-one" – every multiple being in its turn nothing other than a multiple of multiples – is the law of being . . . In fact, every situation, inasmuch as it is, is a multiple composed of an infinity of elements, each one of which is itself a multiple. Considered to their simple belonging to a situation (to an infinite multiple), the animals of the species *Homo sapiens* are ordinary multiplicities. (Badiou 2001: 25)

The same argument is repeated in *Being and Event*, where Badiou assumes that if the One is not, then what there is must simply be pure multiplicity, or multiples of multiples. As a consequence of that, Badiou equates ontology with the discourse of pure mathematics. As Hallward points out, "what matters is the conclusion Badiou draws, rather quickly, from his fundamental ontological 'axiom': all situations can be defined as 'infinite multiples,' that is, as sets with an infinite number of elements. And what 'relate' these elements, *qua* elements, are only relations of pure difference (or indifference): x as different from y" (Hallward 2001: xxxvii). That means that any experience is the infinite deployment of infinite differences. As Badiou notes, "there are as many differences, say, between a Chinese peasant and a young Norwegian professional as between myself and anybody at all, including myself" (Badiou 2001: 26). It's clear that the infinite deployment of infinite differences means the reduction of every human experience to quantitative mathematical differences and it is precisely this reduction which enables the comparison of any element with another. As Hallward observes:

Badiou's consequent characterization of all human situations, individual and collective, as *immeasurably* infinite multiplicities . . . dramatically *simplifies* these situations, leaving no space for the acknowledgement of effectively universal structural principles . . . on the one hand, or certain "specifying" attributes . . . on the other. Instead, we are left with "generic human stuff" that is ontologically indistinguishable from pure mathematical multiplicity. (Hallward 2001: xxxii)

This mathematical multiplicity can be easily subsumed within the universal truth procedure but is inevitably abstracted from its qualitative attributes.

Now, having in mind both *Saint Paul* and *Ethics*, we can ask what universality means not only in the political but also in the ethical field. Can we detach the thinking of the ethical from the notion of difference and reconsider ethics in terms of Sameness and Equality? Badiou's insistence that universalism should be militant (for example, Christianity or Communism) leads to the idea that the foundation of universalism necessarily has to be supported by power structures. Doesn't that mean that the choice for universalism is always a forced choice? And don't we recognize in this insistence the experience of totalitarianism? Badiou reflects on this affinity between a militant universalism and totalitarianism at the end of *Saint Paul*: "Against universalism conceived of as production of the Same, it has recently been claimed that the latter found its emblem, if not its culmination, in the death camps, where everyone, having been reduced to a body on the verge of death, was absolutely equal to everyone else" (Badiou 2001: 109). Badiou disposes of this objection by saying that the Nazi regime was based not on universalism but on an absolute difference, that of the master race, which couldn't be projected to everyone, and that caused the "mass production of corpses" of those who were different. Universalism, on the contrary, would mean the identifying of oneself, as well as everyone else, on the basis of the universal. In this sense universalism implies the dissolution or altering, when necessary, of one's own identity. Badiou's frequent references to Leninism or Maoism force me to think about that universalism which places at its center not absolute difference (the German Aryan), but Sameness itself ("the people," a proletarian). These references, for example, recall the lessons of Stalinism and the sad fate of those who didn't fit into the quantitative notion of the proletariat. In this respect Badiou's call for universalism makes for a sharp contrast with Deleuze and Guattari's notion of the "people to come" which presupposes qualitative and autonomous change.

Conclusion: Multiplicity versus the Multiple

Badiou's claim for universalism is also in deep contradiction with Deleuze and Guattari's concept of becoming-minoritarian, regardless of the fact that both Badiou and Deleuze and Guattari are interpreted as being critics of capitalism and neoliberal democracy. As was stated earlier, the process of becoming-minoritarian entails a transformation which enables someone in the position of the oppressed to use this "minor" situation as a starting point for a creative and innovative change. Consequently, the majority does not simply have to accept or acknowledge differences but has to renounce its privileged place and take the position of the minority: we all have to become woman, we all have to become non-white. Deleuze and Guattari's notion of becoming-minoritarian thus presupposes a radical qualitative change from the position of molar majority to molecular becoming-minoritarian. This change differs from that described by Badiou, who treats differences only as quantitative differences which can be easily transformed into Sameness. Although both Badiou and Deleuze and Guattari ground their theories in a notion of multiplicities, the multiplicities they have in mind are completely different. The process of becoming-minoritarian can be compared to qualitative multiplicities, which differ in kind and are continuous and virtual in the sense that their potential is real but not actualized (becoming as the line of flight/escape). The collective multiplicity to which Badiou refers can be compared to numerical or quantitative multiplicity, discontinuous and actual (the differences already exist and have to be transformed into Sameness). For Deleuze and Guattari becoming-minoritarian implies a rhizomatic connection with other multiplicities, forming an assemblage: it is this increase in the dimensions of a multiplicity that necessarily changes in nature as it expands its connections. In this sense rhizomatic multiplicities cannot be subsumed by any notion of the One and they preclude any possibility of power relations. By contrast, Badiou's theory of universality implies the homogeneity of the "generic human stuff" which should be subsumed under the notion of universal truth. Thinking about what consequences Deleuze and Guattari's notion of qualitative multiplicity might have for society we can imagine an utopian "community of those who have nothing in common," as Alphonso Lingis has put it. By contrast, Badiou's plea for universalism, founded in a generalization of quantitative multiplicities, has an uncanny affinity to totalitarianism.

Can we think of these two positions not as contradictory but as complementary? In *What is Philosophy?* Deleuze and Guattari discuss Badiou's notion of multiplicity comparing it to an infinite set:

> It seems to us that the theory of multiplicities does not support the hypothesis of any multiplicity whatever (even mathematics has had enough of set-theoreticism [*ensemblisme*]). There must be at least two multiplicities, two types, from the outset. This is not because dualism is better than unity but because the multiplicity is precisely what happens between the two. (Deleuze and Guattari 1994: 152)

Badiou himself comments on this passage as being "strange, rather than false or incorrect." He points out that the problem of multiplicity in Deleuze is the "impracticable vantage point" that makes it impossible for him to understand what is at stake or what we are dealing with; Deleuze's take on multiplicities is considered as one of the most enigmatic concepts of his philosophy (Badiou 2007: 252). Badiou correctly points out that for Deleuze the main issue is to introduce the notion of qualitative multiplicities:

Now, in my view the construction of this concept is marked (and this indicates its overtly Bergsonian lineage) by a preliminary deconstruction of the concept of *set*. Deleuze's didactic of multiplicities is from beginning to end a polemic against sets, just as the qualitative content of intuition of duration in Bergson is only identifiable on the basis of the discredit that must attach to the purely spatial quantitative value of chronological time. (Badiou 2007: 71)

Badiou relates this contradiction to the different understanding of the set, saying that this concept has changed since the end of the nineteenth century. Badiou asserts that the concept of multiplicities remains inferior – even in its qualitative determinations – to the concept of the multiple that can be extracted from the contemporary history of sets (Badiou 2007: 72). It follows that Badiou's notion of multiplicities is subordinated to the mathematical notion of the multiple, while Deleuze asserts the possibility of qualitative multiplicities. These two different notions of multiplicity underlie two paradigms of contemporary philosophy that provide contradictory theories of the ethical. Deleuze and Guattari's "minor ethics" continues Levinasian thinking, asserting difference, particularity, and change without any recourse to the metaphysics of the One. Badiou also rejects the notion of the One and replaces it with the notions of quantitative differences and sameness. But do we need ethics to conceptualize sameness? It seems that Badiou's militant universalism actually annihilates the very thing it tries to assert, namely, ethics.

References

Alliez, É. (2006), "*Anti-Oedipus*: Thirty Years On (Between Art and Politics)," in M. Fuglsang and B. Meier Sørensen (eds.), *Deleuze and the Social*, Edinburgh: Edinburgh University Press, 151–68.

Badiou, A. (2000), *Deleuze: The Clamor of Being*, trans. L. Burchill, Minneapolis: University of Minnesota Press.

Badiou, A. (2001), *Ethics: An Essay on the Understanding of Evil*, trans. P. Hallward, London: Verso.

Badiou, A. (2003), *Saint Paul: The Foundation of Universalism*, trans. R. Brassier, Stanford: Stanford University Press.

Badiou, A. (2007), "One, Multiple, Multiplicities," in A. Badiou, *Theoretical Writings*, trans. R. Brassier and A. Toscano, New York: Continuum, 68–82.

Deleuze, G. (2005), *Cinema 2: The Time-Image*, trans. H. Tomlinson and R. Galeta, New York: Continuum.

Deleuze, G. and F. Guattari (1994), *What is Philosophy?*, trans. H. Tomlinson and G. Burchell, New York: Continuum.

Deleuze, G. and F. Guattari (2004), *A Thousand Plateaus*, trans. B. Massumi, New York: Continuum.

Deleuze, G. and F. Guattari (2006), *Kafka: Toward a Minor Literature*, trans. D. Polan, Minneapolis: University of Minnesota Press.

Hallward, P. (2001), "Translator's Introduction," in A. Badiou, *Ethics: An Essay on the Understanding of Evil*, trans. P. Hallward, London: Verso, vii–xlvii.

Mengue, P. (2008), "People and Fabulation," in I. Buchanan and N. Thoburn (eds.), *Deleuze and Politics*, Edinburgh: Edinburgh University Press, 218–39.

Thoburn, N. (2003), *Deleuze, Marx and Politics*, London: Routledge.

Watson, J. (2008), "Theorising European Ethnic Politics with Deleuze and Guattari," in I. Buchanan and N. Thoburn (eds.), *Deleuze and Politics*, Edinburgh: Edinburgh University Press, 196–217.

Žižek, S. (2004), *Organs Without Bodies: On Deleuze and Consequences*, London: Routledge.

Žižek, S. (2006), "A Leftist Plea for 'Eurocentrism'," in S. Žižek, *The Universal Exception: Selected Writings*, vol. 2, ed. R. Butler and S. Stephens, New York: Continuum, 183–208.

Notes on Contributors

Jeffrey Bell
Jeffrey Bell is Professor of Philosophy at Southeastern Louisiana University in Hammond, Louisiana. He is the author of *Deleuze's Hume: Philosophy, Culture and the Scottish Enlightenment* (2009), *Philosophy at the Edge of Chaos: Gilles Deleuze and the Philosophy of Difference* (2006), and *The Problem of Difference: Phenomenology and Poststructuralism* (1998).

Levi R. Bryant
Levi R. Bryant is Professor of Philosophy at Collin College in Frisco, Texas. He is the author of *Difference and Givenness: Deleuze's Transcendental Empiricism and the Ontology of Immanence* (2008), *The Democracy of Objects* (forthcoming), and the editor, with Graham Harman and Nick Srnicek, of *The Speculative Turn: Continental Materialisms/Realisms* (2010).

Laura Cull
Laura Cull is Lecturer in Performing Arts at Northumbria University in Newcastle, UK. She is editor of *Deleuze and Performance* (2009), author of a number of articles on Deleuze, and is currently working on a monograph entitled *Theatres of Immanence: Deleuze and the Ethics of Performance*. She is also Chair of the Performance and Philosophy working group within Performance Studies international, and a member of the SpRoUt collective, a UK-based artists' group.

Erinn Cunniff Gilson
Erinn Cunniff Gilson is Assistant Professor of Philosophy at the University of North Florida in Jacksonville, Florida. Her research and teaching focus on feminist philosophy, contemporary European

philosophy, and ethical and social theory. In addition to articles on Deleuze in *Philosophy Today* and *Chiasmi International*, her article "Vulnerability, Ignorance, and Oppression" is forthcoming in *Hypatia*. She is currently working on a manuscript that seeks to elaborate on the nature of vulnerability, the import of how we think about and understand the concept, and its potential as an ethical resource.

Nathan Jun

Nathan Jun is Assistant Professor of Philosophy and Coordinator of the Philosophy Program at Midwestern State University in Wichita Falls, Texas. He is co-editor (with Shane Wahl) of *New Perspectives on Anarchism* (2009) and author of *Anarchism and Political Modernity* (forthcoming).

Eleanor Kaufman

Eleanor Kaufman is Professor of Comparative Literature and French and Francophone Studies at the University of California at Los Angeles. She is co-editor of *Deleuze and Guattari: New Mappings in Politics, Philosophy, and Culture* (1998) and the author of *The Delirium of Praise: Bataille, Blanchot, Deleuze, Foucault, Klossowski* (2001), *At Odds with Badiou: Politics, Dialectics, and Religion from Sartre and Deleuze to Lacan and Agamben* (forthcoming), and *Gilles Deleuze: Dialectic, Structure, and Being* (forthcoming).

Daniel W. Smith

Daniel W. Smith is an Associate Professor in the Department of Philosophy at Purdue University. He is the translator of Gilles Deleuze's *Francis Bacon: The Logic of Sensation* and *Essays Critical and Clinical* (with Michael A. Greco), as well as Pierre Klossowski's *Nietzsche and the Vicious Circle* and Isabelle Stengers' *The Invention of Modern Science*. A collection of his essays on the work of Gilles Deleuze will be published by Edinburgh University Press in 2011.

Kenneth Surin

Kenneth Surin is Professor of Literature and Professor of Religion and Critical Theory at Duke University in the Durham, North Carolina. In his previous career he was a theologian. He is the author of *Theology and the Problem of Evil* (2004) and editor of *Christ, Ethics and Tragedy: Essays in Honour of Donald MacKinnon* (2004) and *The Turnings of Darkness and Light: Essays in Philosophical and Systematic Theology* (2007). His articles have appeared in *SubStance*,

Theory, Culture and Society, Social Text, South Atlantic Quarterly and *Polygraph.*

Anthony Uhlmann

Anthony Uhlmann is Associate Professor in the Writing and Society Research Group at the University of Western Sydney. He is the author of *Thought in Literature: Joyce, Woolf, Nabokov* (2011), *Samuel Beckett and the Philosophical Image* (2006), and *Beckett and Poststructuralism* (1999). He is the editor of the *Journal of Beckett Studies.*

James Williams

James Williams is Professor of European Philosophy at the University of Dundee. He has published widely on recent French philosophy. His most recent books include *Gilles Deleuze's Philosophy of Time: A Critical Introduction and Guide* (forthcoming) and *Gilles Deleuze's Logic of Sense: A Critical Introduction and Guide* (2008).

Audronė Žukauskaitė

Audronė Žukauskaitė is a senior researcher at the Department of Contemporary Philosophy at the Lithuanian Culture Research Institute in Vilnius. She is the author of *Beyond the Signifier Principle: Deconstruction, Psychoanalysis, Critique of Ideology* (2001), and *Anamorphoses: Non-Fundamental Problems of Philosophy* (2005); editor and translator of the volume *Everything You Always Wanted to Know About Žižek But Were Afraid to Ask Lacan* (2005); and the editor of seven volumes on different aspects of contemporary philosophy and culture. She recently co-edited the volume *Interrogating Antigone in Postmodern Philosophy and Criticism* (2010) and completed a draft of a book entitled *Gilles Deleuze and Félix Guattari's Philosophy: The Cultural Consequences.*

Index